Thomas Lowndes Snead

The Fight for Missouri

From the Election of Lincoln to the Death of Lyon

Thomas Lowndes Snead

The Fight for Missouri

From the Election of Lincoln to the Death of Lyon

ISBN/EAN: 9783337372552

Printed in Europe, USA, Canada, Australia, Japan

Cover: Foto ©ninafisch / pixelio.de

More available books at **www.hansebooks.com**

THE FIGHT FOR MISSOURI

FROM THE ELECTION OF LINCOLN
TO THE DEATH OF LYON

BY

THOMAS L. SNEAD

A. D. C. OF THE GOVERNOR; ACTING ADJUTANT-GENERAL OF THE MISSOURI
STATE GUARD; CHIEF OF STAFF OF THE ARMY OF THE WEST
MEMBER OF THE CONFEDERATE CONGRESS

WITH MAPS

NEW YORK
CHARLES SCRIBNER'S SONS
1886

PREFACE.

I HAVE written this book because it was my duty to write it; because, too, I fancy that I know more about the events that are narrated in it, than does any one who will ever take the trouble to write about them; and because I am the only living witness to many facts the remembrance of which ought to be preserved.

That the reader may know whereon I ground these assertions, and that he may, before reading my testimony, be able to decide whether it be worth his attention, I will tell him frankly how I happen to know about these things.

In the elections of 1860—for Governor of Missouri, and for President of the United States—I took an active, though inconspicuous part, chiefly in the political management of the St. Louis *Bulletin*, which was owned and edited by one of my friends, Mr. Longuemare. In its columns and elsewhere I advocated earnestly the election of Breckinridge to the Presidency, and of Claiborne F. Jackson to the Governorship. But when the latter, in obedience to the manifest will of a majority of the Democratic

Party of Missouri whose candidate he was, announced his determination to support Mr. Douglas for the Presidency, we Breckinridge Democrats refused to support him any longer, and nominated a candidate of our own, Hancock Jackson. We did this because we believed that the slave-holding States could not remain in the Union, with either safety or honor unless the North should consent to give them Constitutional guarantees that their rights as coequal States of the Union should be both respected and protected by the Federal Government, and because we thought that this question should be plainly submitted to the North in the then pending Presidential election, and a positive answer demanded. As Mr. Douglas' candidacy, with his policy of equivocation, prevented this question from being put fairly to the North, we opposed him and every body who supported him. Claiborne F. Jackson was, nevertheless, elected Governor, in August, and Missouri, alone of all the States, cast her electoral vote in November for Douglas.

On assuming the office of Governor just after the formal secession of South Carolina, Governor Jackson declared in his Inaugural Address that, in his opinion, it was both the interest and the duty of Missouri to make common cause with the other slave-holding States in the impending conflict. This declaration brought the *Bulletin*, which had meanwhile fallen under my absolute control, to his zealous support. The great interest which I felt in the matter caused me to spend most of the time at Jefferson City, where measures looking to the secession of Missouri, and to arming her militia, and getting the State ready otherwise for the emergency, were pending before the General Assembly; and finally, toward the middle of February, I disposed of the *Bulletin*, and took up my abode at Jefferson City, and remained there as the guest of the Governor till we were all driven thence by Blair and Lyon, in June. During this time I assisted Governor Jackson in conducting his correspondence and in other confidential matters, and upon the enactment of the military law in May was commissioned as one of his *aides-de-camp*. General Price had asked me to accept the position of adjutant-general of the State forces, to the command of which he had just been appointed, but I introduced to him, and got him to appoint instead, Captain Henry Little who had just resigned his commission in the United States Army and was a thousand times better fitted than myself to discharge the duties of the place.

I therefore remained with the Governor; followed him when he left Jefferson City; was with him at Booneville, and Carthage; and went with him to Cowskin Prairie, in the south-western corner of the

State. When, however, on arriving there, he relinquished the command of all the State forces to General Price, and was about to go East, I got his permission to remain with the army, and was the next day assigned to duty by General Price as his chief of ordnance. A few days later Colonel Little left for Richmond in order to secure his commission in the regular army of the Confederate States, and I was then assigned to duty as Acting Adjutant-General of the State Guard. This position I held during all of the eventful campaign, in which were won the Battles of Wilson's Creek, Fort Scott, and Lexington.

During this time—from the election of Lincoln in November 1860, to the death of Lyon at Wilson's Creek on the 10th of August 1861—occurred all the events that I have narrated in this volume; but I remained with General Price till the last year of the war, as adjutant-general and sometimes as chief of staff, of the commands that he held, except that for brief periods I was entrusted with special duties. I left him in the summer of 1864, in order to attend a meeting of the Confederate Congress, of which I was a member, and did not return to the army.

When the war ended General Price took to Mexico the records of the several commands which he had held, and also other important papers relating to the war. On returning to this country he brought these records and papers with him and gave them to me, with the understanding that I would one day write the story of his campaigns. I turned over most of them to the War Department several years ago, and many of them have been, and the rest will be, published in the *Official Records of the War of the Rebellion.*

In preparing the political part of this volume, I have relied chiefly upon the Journals of the General Assembly of Missouri, and of the State Convention, and on the official reports of their debates, and upon contemporaneous publications, particularly the *Missouri Republican;* and upon the original documents published in Peckham's *Life of Lyon*—a book whose glaring faults are more than compensated by the important facts the remembrance whereof it has preserved.

For military details I am indebted above all to the *Official Records*, which the Government is publishing. The zeal, the fairness, the intelligence, the care, and the ability with which they have been collected, compiled, arranged, and edited by Lieutenant-Colonel Robert N. Scott, U. S. A., entitle that gentleman to the gratitude of every one who took an honorable part in the war, and of all who shall ever desire to learn its true history. Valuable as these *Records* are to the student, they need nevertheless the elucidation of those, who, by reason of their personal knowledge of the men, and in other ways, are competent to sift the statements of those witnesses—most of them now silent forever—whose testimony they perpetuate. As it was my fortune to know personally most of the men who took a prominent part in the struggle for Missouri, and something about the character and credibility of every one of them, I feel sure that my little book will for that reason be a useful guide to those who may wish to comprehend that struggle aright.

I have been greatly assisted in my search after the truth by many of the survivors of the war, who have furnished me important documents and valuable reminiscences, all which I have freely used. I would, perhaps, win favor for this volume if I were to mention their names, but higher considerations induce me to be silent. I must, however, express my great obligations to Mr. R. I. Holcombe, author of *An Account of the Battle of Wilson's Creek*, for much valuable information.

I have doubtless made many trifling mistakes and may have made some that are important, but no man ever labored more earnestly to ascertain the truth and to tell it plainly and impartially, than I have done, in preparing to write, and in writing, this account of the fight that was made for Missouri in 1861.

NEW YORK, *January*, 1886.

I. POLITICAL.

THE FIGHT FOR MISSOURI.

CHAPTER I.

THE GOVERNOR.

Election of Lincoln—Meeting of Congress—Buchanan's Message—He Denies the Right of Congress to Prevent Secession by Force, and Urges Concessions to the South—The North Objects—The Crittenden Proposition—Tacit Agreement between the President and South Carolina as to Reinforcing Sumter—South Carolina Secedes—Major Anderson retires to Fort Sumter—South Carolina sends Commissioners to Washington—Failure of Negotiations—Meeting of the General Assembly of Missouri—Message of Governor Stewart—Claiborne F. Jackson—His Inaugural.

THE enactment in 1850 of a Fugitive Slave Law, some of whose provisions were not only inconsistent with the civilization of the age, but required citizens of Massachusetts, New York, and Ohio to do what no self-respecting Virginian could have been forced to do; together with the repeal, in 1854, of the Missouri Compromise, brought about, in 1860, the election of Abraham Lincoln to the Presidency, and the transfer of the Federal Government to a party which was pledged to prevent the extension of slavery beyond the limits of the States in which it was then established by law, and whose ablest and most influential leaders were known to be in favor of using all lawful means to abolish it even within those States.

Thoroughly frightened by this fact, for they firmly believed that their well-being, and indeed their safety, were involved in the continued existence of slavery, all of the Cotton States, except Texas (whose action was hindered by her governor, Gen. Houston), took instant steps to secede from the Union, and to establish a slave-holding Confederacy; and when Congress met on the 3d of December, it had become certain that one, at least, of these States would secede before the end of the year.

President Buchanan, in calling the attention of Congress to this fact, in his annual message, implored it to consider carefully what the Government must do; to consider whether it had the power by force of arms to compel a State to remain within the Union; and whether, if it had the power, it would be expedient to exercise it. For his own part he did not believe that the Constitution delegated any such power to Congress, or to any other department of the Government; but, on the contrary, that to make war against a State was at variance with the whole spirit and intent of the Constitution. "Congress," said he, "possesses many means of preserving the Union by conciliation, but the sword was not placed in its hand to preserve it by force." The best way to preserve it was, in his opinion, to satisfy the just demands of the South by adopting a Constitutional amendment which should not only protect slavery in the States where it was already established, but in all of the Territories, so long as they remained Territories; and which should also compel the Northern States to restore fugitive slaves to their owners. He promised that while Congress was considering this all-important matter he would, to the extent of his ability, defend the public property, and take care that the Federal laws should be enforced, in all the States.

The President's recommendations were referred in both Senate and House to special committees, but it soon became manifest that the North would not give heed to them. Mr. Crittenden, therefore, submitted what became known as the Crittenden Proposition. It differed from the President's chiefly in this, that, while requiring Congress to enforce the rendition of fugitive slaves, and to protect slavery in the States where it then existed, it declared that slavery should never exist north of the Missouri Compromise line, but should be protected in all the territory south of that line (36° 30' north latitude).

As the South claimed that it had the right to demand protection for its slave property in *all* of the common territory of the Union, it felt that it would be yielding a great deal for the sake of peace, and the preservation of the Union, if it consented to accept Mr. Crittenden's proposition. But every Southern State, with the exception of South Carolina, manifested its willingness to accept it. Most Northern Democrats quickly showed their willingness to sustain it, and the President, abandoning his own proposition, urged the country to adopt Mr. Crittenden's.

Many Republicans, too, averse to strife and bloodshed, consented to it, while others, like Horace Greeley, were ready to let the Cotton States go in peace, if they thought that they could do better out of the Union than in it. But the great majority of Republicans were not willing either to concede to the South the right to establish slavery in the Territories, or to let any State secede. They would not abandon, in the hour of victory, the principles for which they had manfully contended through forty years of defeat and disaster; nor would they let those, whom they had just vanquished, destroy the Union in the very hour that it was about to be dedicated, as they believed, to a wider freedom and a higher humanity. They were content to await the fast-coming 4th of March.

Meanwhile the Cotton States were all hastening

towards secession. This brought the President to the consideration of the most important question that had ever been submitted to any President: Whether he should attempt to reinforce the Federal forts in those States which were preparing to secede.

While denying his own right, and the right of Congress, to make war upon a State, he had expressly said in his message that it was his duty and his determination to protect the public property, and to enforce the laws, in all the States. On the other hand, he knew that, if he attempted to reinforce the forts at Charleston, the attempt would be regarded by the South Carolinians as a threat of subjugation, and would be resented by them as an act of war.

Happily the Representatives of South Carolina in Congress came to his assistance by giving him the strongest assurances that South Carolina would neither attack nor molest the forts, until her State Convention had met and decided to withdraw the State from the Union; nor until she had sent commissioners to treat with the Federal Government as to the forts and other matters; *provided* the Government of the United States would not, meanwhile, send any reinforcements to the forts, or change the military status in Charleston harbor.

The President, while accepting these assurances

"as a happy omen that peace might still be preserved, and time be thus gained for reflection," replied that, whilst he could not *promise* not to reinforce the forts, it was his then determination not to reinforce them until they should be actually attacked, or until he had certain evidence that they were about to be attacked.

Upon this tacit understanding both the President and the State continued to act in good faith until after the State had seceded.

General Scott, who had been detained in New York by sickness, came to Washington on the 12th of December, and, being ignorant of the assurances which had been given to the President by the South Carolina representatives, urged him, at an interview on the 15th, to send a reinforcement of 300 men to Major Anderson, at Charleston. The President, knowing that Major Anderson was in no danger of attack, and that an attempt to reinforce him would needlessly "impair the hope of compromise, provoke collision, and disappoint the country," refused to send the reinforcements. General Cass, who had insisted upon the President's compliance with General Scott's advice, thereupon resigned the Secretaryship of State (December 15th). The resignation was rather gladly accepted, and Judge Black became Secretary of State, while Edwin M. Stanton succeeded Black as Attorney-General.

Howell Cobb had already resigned the Secretaryship of the Treasury (December 8th) and returned to Georgia.

On the 20th of December the South Carolina Convention adopted an ordinance of secession, and sent commissioners to Washington to treat with the United States Government as to the forts within her limits, and as to other matters.

These commissioners reached Washington on the 26th of December; but the very next morning—before they had had time to present their credentials to the Secretary of State—they were themselves startled, and the whole country electrified, by the news that, during the preceding night, Major Anderson had secretly dismantled Fort Moultrie, spiked its guns, burnt the gun-carriages, and removed his command to Fort Sumter, which occupied a more tenable, and a more commanding, position in the harbor.

The Secretary of War, Governor Floyd, of Virginia, protested against Major Anderson's conduct in a paper which he read, on the 27th of December, to the President, in presence of the Cabinet. In this paper he insisted that Major Anderson had, by removing his command to Fort Sumter, changed the military status at Charleston, and had thereby violated a solemn pledge of the Government; that there was now but one way to vindicate the honor of the Administration and to prevent civil war; and that was to withdraw the garrison from the harbor of Charleston altogether. He accordingly asked the President to authorize him to make that order at once. The President refused to do this, and on the 29th of December the Secretary of War tendered his resignation, saying that he could no longer hold the office "under his convictions of patriotism, nor with honor; subjected as he was to the violation of solemn pledges and plighted faith." His resignation was instantly accepted, and Postmaster-General Holt was transferred to the War Department.

The South Carolina commissioners had presented their credentials to the President on the 28th. He said at once that he "could only recognize them as private gentlemen, and not as commissioners from a sovereign State," but would communicate to Congress—"the only competent tribunal" to which they could appeal—any proposition which they might have to offer.

To this the commissioners replied that they could not offer any proposition, nor even enter upon the negotiations with which they had been entrusted, until Major Anderson's conduct had been satisfactorily explained, nor until the United States troops had been removed not only from Fort Sumter, but away from the harbor of Charleston. These demands were formally repeated in a written communication which they sent to the President the next day.

While considering the reply which he should make to this communication the President learned that the authorities of South Carolina had, on the day after Major Anderson's removal to Sumter, seized Fort Moultrie, Castle Pinckney, the Custom-House, and the Post-Office, and had raised the Palmetto flag over them all; that every officer of the Customs—collector, naval officer, surveyor, and appraiser—together with the postmaster, had resigned their appointments; and that, on Sunday, the 30th of December, the State had seized the Arsenal of the United States, containing $500,000 worth of munitions of war, and had expelled the United States Government from all its property except Fort Sumter.

Distressed and angered by these facts, the President replied to the South Carolina commissioners that he would not withdraw the Federal troops from Fort Sumter; but would, on the contrary, defend that fort by all the means in his power, against all attacks from whatever quarter they might proceed. This reply was delivered to the commissioners on the 31st of December.

On that day the Senate Committee of Thirteen reported that they could not agree upon any settlement of the questions at issue between the North and the South.

In the midst of the great excitement that was caused by these momentous events, the General Assembly of Missouri met at Jefferson City on the last day of December, 1860.

At the presidential election Lincoln had received in the entire State barely seventeen thousand of the one hundred and sixty-five thousand votes which were cast, and most of these were given to him by the German inhabitants of the State. Fifty-eight thousand eight hundred and one had been given to Douglas; fifty-eight thousand three hundred and seventy-two to Bell, and thirty-one thousand three hundred and seventeen to Breckinridge.

The General Assembly reflected the sentiment of the people as expressed in the presidential election. In the Senate there was only one Republican; in the House there were twelve Republicans, thirty-seven Bell men, and eighty-three Democrats.

The outgoing Governor, Robert M. Stewart, transmitted his message to the two Houses on the 3d of January.

Stewart was a typical Northern Democrat. He believed that the Southern people had the constitutional right to take their slaves into all the Territories and to hold them there, under the protection of the territorial and Federal laws, and that this right ought to be assured to them. Not that he loved slavery, for he did not; but because he loved the Union and revered the Constitution.

Himself a native of New York, though long time a resident of Missouri, he felt none of that humiliation which most Southern men felt in view of the fact that the long political struggle between the North and the South had at last ended in the defeat of the South, and in the triumph of the abolitionized North; none of that blended anger and apprehension, which they felt, in contemplation of the fact that the South was thenceforth to be ruled by a party hostile to their institutions and unfriendly to their people.

The right of secession he not only denied, but he denied it utterly; and believed too that South Carolina was acting with consummate folly in attempting to destroy a Union, which was the source of all her prosperity, and her surest bulwark and defence.

As to Missouri, *she* certainly had no right to secede. For she belonged to the United States by right of purchase—had been bought by the Federal Government, and paid for out of its treasury. Whatever other States might do, it was her plain duty, and her interest, too, to remain within the Union.

His message set forth clearly and strongly his own feelings and opinions at the beginning of the New Year, and it expressed in great measure the sentiments of a majority of the people of Missouri, at that time.

"Missouri occupies a position in regard to these troubles that should make her voice potent in the councils of the nation. With scarcely a disunionist *per se* to be found in her borders, she is still determined to demand, and to maintain, her rights at every hazard. She loves the Union while it is the protector of equal rights, but will despise it as the instrument of wrong. She came into the Union upon a compromise, and is willing to abide by a fair compromise still; not such ephemeral contracts as are enacted by Congress to-day, and repealed to-morrow; but a compromise, assuring all the just rights of the States, and agreed to in solemn Convention of all the parties interested.

"Missouri has a right to speak on this subject, because she has suffered. Bounded on three sides by free territory, her border counties have been the frequent scenes of kidnapping and violence, and this State has probably lost as much, in the last two years, in the abduction of slaves, as all the rest of the Southern States. At this moment several of the western counties are desolated, and almost depopulated, from fear of a bandit horde, who have been committing depredations — arson, theft, and foul murder—upon the adjacent border.

"Missouri has a right, too, to be heard by reason

of her present position and power, as well as from the great calamities which a hasty dissolution of the Union would bring upon her. She has already a larger voting population than any of the slave States, with prospective power and wealth far beyond any of her sister States. . . .

"Indeed, Missouri and the other border Slave States should be the *first* instead of the LAST, to speak on a subject of this kind. They have suffered the evil and the wrong, and they should be the first to demand redress. . . .

"As matters are at present Missouri will stand by her lot, and hold to the Union as long as it is worth an effort to preserve it. So long as there is hope of success she will seek for justice within the Union. She cannot be frightened from her propriety by the past unfriendly legislation of the North, nor be dragooned into secession by the extreme South. If those, who should be our friends and allies, undertake to render our property worthless by a system of prohibitory laws, or by reopening the slave trade in opposition to the moral sense of the civilized world, and at the same time reduce us to the position of an humble sentinel to watch over and protect their interests, receiving all of the blows and none of the benefits, Missouri will hesitate long before sanctioning such an arrangement. She will rather take the high position of armed neutrality. She is able to take care of herself, and will be neither forced nor flattered, driven nor coaxed, into a course of action that must end in her own destruction.

"If South Carolina and other Cotton States persist in secession she will desire to see them go in peace, with the hope that a short experience at separate government, and an honorable readjustment of the Federal compact, will induce them to return to their former position. In the mean time Missouri will hold herself in readiness, at any moment, to defend her soil from pollution and her property from plunder by fanatics and marauders, come from what quarter they may. The people of Missouri will choose this deliberate, conservative course, both on account of the blessings they have derived from the Union, and the untold and unimagined evils that will come with its dissolution.

". . . Whilst I would recommend the adoption of all proper measures and influences to secure the just acknowledgment and protection of our rights, and in the final failure of this, a resort to the last painful remedy of separation; yet, regarding, as I do, the American Confederacy as the source of a thousand blessings, pecuniary, social, and moral, and its destruction as fraught with incalculable loss, suffering, and crime, I would here, in my last public official act as Governor of Missouri, record my solemn protest against unwise and hasty action, and my unalterable devotion to the Union so long as it can be made the protector of equal rights."

In the evening Claiborne F. Jackson took the oath of office as Governor, in the presence of both Houses.

Born in Kentucky, of Virginia parents, he had come to Missouri in his boyhood and found employment in a country store in Howard County. By the time that he was thirty he had acquired a sufficient fortune to retire from business and to devote himself to politics, for which he had a natural aptitude and great fondness. Saline County sent him to the Legislature in 1836. He was one of the delegates from Howard County to the State Convention of 1845, and one of its representatives in the Legislature in 1846. He was a member of the State Senate in 1848-9, and, as Chairman of the Committee on Federal Affairs, reported the Resolutions which bear his name. These resolutions took high Southern ground on the matter of slavery in the territory then just acquired from Mexico, and instructed Colonel Benton and his colleague in the United States Senate to conform their action to the doctrines therein laid down. Benton refused to obey, and appealed from the Legislature to the people of Missouri. In the angry contest which ensued Jackson bore a conspicuous part, and was ever after recognized as one of the ablest leaders of the anti-Benton, or Southern Rights' Democrats.

His election as Governor had devolved upon him the gravest responsibilities. He now assumed the office with becoming modesty, but with an unshakable determination to defend the honor and the interests of Missouri against all assailants whatever.

He was fifty-five years of age; tall, erect, and dignified; a vigorous thinker, and a fluent and forcible speaker, always interesting, and often eloquent; a well-informed man, thoroughly conversant with the politics of Missouri and of the Union; with positive opinions on all public questions, and the courage to express and uphold them; courteous in his bearing towards all men, for he was kind-hearted, and by nature a democrat; and a truthful, honest, and honorable gentleman. He loved the Union, but not with the love with which he loved Missouri, which had been his home for forty years, nor as he loved the South, where he was born, and where his kindred lived.

In his inaugural address to the General Assembly, he said, after rapidly commenting upon the growth of the antislavery party:

" The prominent characteristic of this party . . . is that it is purely sectional in its locality and its principles. The only principle inscribed upon its banner is *Hostility to Slavery;* . . . its object, not merely to confine slavery within its present limits; not merely to exclude it from the Territories, and prevent the formation and admission of any slave-holding States; not merely to abolish it in the District of Columbia, and interdict its passage from one State to another; but to strike down its existence everywhere; to sap its foundation in public sentiment; to annoy and harass, and gradually destroy its vitality, by every means, direct or indirect, physical and moral, which human ingenuity can devise. The triumph of such an organization is not the victory of a political party, but the domination of a Section. It proclaims in significant tones the destruction of that equality among the States which is the vital cement of our Federal Union. It places fifteen of the thirty-three States in the position of humble recipients of the bounty, or sullen submissionists to the power, of a government, which they had no voice in creating, and in whose councils they do not participate.

"It cannot, then, be a matter of surprise to any —victors or vanquished—that these fifteen States, with a pecuniary interest at stake reaching the enormous sum of $3,500,000,000 should be aroused and excited at the advent of such a party to power. . . . Would it not rather be an instance of unprecedented blindness and fatuity, if the people and governments of these fifteen slave-holding States were, under such circumstances, to manifest quiet indifference, and to make no effort to avoid the destruction which awaited them? . . .

"Accordingly, we find the result of the recent Presidential election has already produced its natural effects. From Florida to Missouri a feeling of discontent and alarm has manifested itself, more or less violent, according to the imminence of the danger, and the extent of the interest at stake. The cotton-growing States, having a larger and more vital interest in jeopardy than the Border States, are the first to awaken to a sense of insecurity. The sagacious Southern statesman is fully aware that his section, although necessarily the *last* victim, will be *the greatest sufferer;* that when the outposts yield, the citadel will not long afford safety. With them the alternative is the maintenance of that institution which Great Britain forced upon their ancestors, or the conversion of their homes into desert wastes. With them it is not a mere question of property, but, what is to them dearer than property or life, a question of duty and of honor.

"It has been said to be quite easy to bear the calamities of our neighbors with philosophical equanimity. Let us not illustrate this maxim by criticising the precipitancy of the South. They are not the aggressors. They only ask to be let alone. If some have regarded their action as hasty, has not the occasion been extraordinary? I do not stand here to justify or to condemn the action of South Carolina in withdrawing her allegiance to the Federal Government. She is a gallant State, and will not forfeit that renown which a long list of distinguished dead has conferred on her history. When she unrolls that list—when she points to her Marions and Sumters, and Jaspers and Moultries, and Laurenses and McDonalds, to her Pinckneys, and Rutledges, and Middletons, to her Lowndeses and Chevises, and McDuffies and Hamiltons, to her Haynes and Legares, to her Prestons and her Butlers, and to that pre-eminent statesman who divided the public esteem with Webster and Clay—her sister States, blessed with larger and more fertile territory, may well covet the glory of having given birth to such citizens, and may at least safely leave the honor of the State in the hands of their descendants. If South Carolina has acted hastily, let not her error lead to the more fatal one—an attempt at coercion.

"The destiny of the slave-holding States of this Union is one and the same. . . . The identity, rather than the similarity, of their domestic institutions; their political principles and party usages; their common origin, pursuits, tastes, manners, and customs; their territorial contiguity and commercial relations—all contribute to bind them together in one sisterhood. And Missouri will in my opinion best consult her own interests, and the interests of the whole country, by a timely declaration of her determination to stand by her sister slave-holding States, in whose wrongs she participates, and with whose institutions and people she sympathizes.

"These views are advanced, gentlemen, not upon a belief that all hope of the present Union is lost, but upon a conviction that the time has arrived when a further postponement of their consideration would be unwise and unsafe. The issue of present embarrassments depends entirely upon the sentiments and action of the North. I trust that there is patriotism enough left in our common country to harmonize the conflicting views now in agitation, and to place the Union on a basis consistent with the honor and safety of its constituent members. So far as Missouri is concerned, her citizens have ever been devoted to the Union, and she will remain in it so long as there is any hope that it will maintain the spirit and guarantees of the Constitution.

"But if the Northern States have determined to put the slave-holding States on a footing of inequality, by interdicting them from all share in the Territories acquired by the common blood and treasure of all; if they have resolved to admit no more slave-holding States into the Union; and if they mean to persist in nullifying that provision of the Constitution, which secures to the slave-holder his property when found within the limits of States which do not recognize it, or have abolished it; then *they* have themselves practically abandoned the Union, and will not expect our submission to a government on terms of inequality and subordination.

"We hear it suggested in some quarters that the Union is to be maintained by the sword. Such suggestions, it is to be hoped, have sprung from momentary impulse, and not from cool reflection. The project of maintaining the Federal Government by force may lead to consolidation or despotism, but not to Union. . . . That stands upon the basis of justice and equality, and its existence cannot be prolonged by coercion. . . . The first drop of blood shed in a war of aggression upon a sovereign State will arouse a spirit which must result in the overthrow of our entire Federal system, and which this generation will never see quelled.

"As the ultimate fate of all the slave-holding States is necessarily the same, their determination and action in the present crisis should be the result of a general consultation. To produce united action there must be united counsel; and as the wrong is common to all, the redress for the wrong should be submitted to the consideration and judgment of all. It may not become me, therefore, to suggest what ought to be the *ultimatum* to be insisted upon by the slave-holding States. Candor compels me to say, however, that a mere *Congressional* compromise is not to be thought of. . . . Experience shows that such compromises only lay the foundation for additional agitation. They are but laws, and like all other laws, liable to be repealed; and their duration depends altogether upon the fluctuations of public opinion, operating through the representatives of that opinion at Washington. The object of *Constitutional* guarantees is to protect the rights of minorities, and it is to such guarantees, and not to Legislative compromises, that the South must look for protection and security. . . . If the Northern States are willing to remain with the South under a general government, where domestic slavery is entitled to the protection of that government, instead of being the object of its hostility, they can have no reasonable objection so to declare in terms, and in a form which will leave no ground for cavil or misunderstanding. If they are not content with such an association, it is due to their own character, as well as to the rights of their associate States, that their determination should be made known.

"I am not without hope that an adjustment

alike honorable to both sections may be effected, . . . but in the present unfavorable aspect of public affairs it is our duty to prepare for the worst. We cannot avoid danger by closing our eyes to it. The magnitude of the interests now in jeopardy demands a prompt but deliberate consideration; and in order that the will of the people may be ascertained and effectuated, a State Convention should, in my view, be immediately called. . . . In this way the whole subject will be brought directly before the people at large, who will determine for themselves what is to be the ultimate action of the State. . . .

"In view of the marauding forays which continue to harass our borders, as well as of the general unsettled condition of our political relations, a due regard to our honor and safety requires a thorough organization of our militia."

Both Stewart and Jackson held the North solely responsible for the deplorable condition of the country; both of them maintained that the only way to prevent the dissolution of the Union was for the North to give to the South Constitutional guarantees against the threatened aggressions of the Abolitionists; and both insisted that if the North should refuse to give these guarantees, and the Southern States should thereupon attempt to withdraw from the Union, the Federal Government ought not to undertake to coerce them to remain within it, but should let them go in peace.

Thus far they agreed, and thus far nine-tenths of all the people of Missouri agreed with them.

But when they came to consider what Missouri ought to do, in case the Federal Government should undertake to maintain the Union by force of arms, Governor Stewart, true to his Northern birth and Northern associations, insisted that Missouri must adhere to the Union; while Governor Jackson, true to his Southern birth and sympathy with the South, insisted with equal earnestness that she should stand by her sister slave-holding States, and share their destiny.

But most men—nearly all men—still believed that a compromise would be agreed upon; that secession would be stayed; that even South Carolina would resume her place in the Union; and that Missouri would never be called upon to choose between the North and the South!

CHAPTER II.

THE GENERAL ASSEMBLY.

The President breaks off Negotiations with South Carolina, and Orders Fort Sumter to be Secretly Reinforced—Southern Senators advise their States to Secede—Lieutenant-Governor Reynolds—His Advice to Missouri—The General Assembly takes the First Steps towards Secession—The Cotton States Seize Federal Forts, Arsenals, etc.—The President's Special Message—He Promises to Enforce the Laws Everywhere—The *Star of the West* off Charleston—The First Gun of the War—Mississippi, Florida, and Alabama Secede—The North offers Men and Money to the President—Union Meetings in Northern Cities—The Border Slave-holding States Declare that they will Resist the Invasion of the South—Great Union Meeting in St. Louis—It Denounces Coercion—The General Assembly Calls a Convention; Receives a Commissioner from Mississippi; and Pledges the State to Resist Coercion.

THE President's declaration to the South Carolina commissioners, that he not only would not withdraw the United States troops from Fort Sumter, but would, on the contrary, defend that stronghold to the best of his ability, elicited from the commissioners, on the 2d of January, a reply which was, in the opinion of the President and his Cabinet, "so violent, unfounded, and disrespectful," that he could not receive it. He therefore sent it back to the commissioners, and, the negotiations having been thus angrily terminated, they returned to South Carolina.

This incident left no doubt in the minds of those who were made acquainted with its details, that the President would take prompt measures to repossess those forts which had been seized, and to reinforce and hold those over which the flag of the Union still floated.

He had, in fact, already acted. For while negotiations with South Carolina were still pending—on the very Sunday, indeed, that he prepared the communication in which he announced to the commissioners his purpose to hold Fort Sumter—he had concerted with General Scott and the Secretary of War plans for reinforcing and provisioning Fort Sumter, and had that day ordered them and the Secretary of the Navy to secretly despatch to Sumter a fast-sailing steamer laden with men and supplies for the fort. General Scott insisted at first upon the immediate execution of this order, but finally assented to the President's suggestion that it would not be "gentlemanly and proper" to reinforce the fort till after the negotiations had been terminated. The order was accordingly withheld from execution until the commissioners had left Washington.

Friday, the 4th of January, had been set apart by the President, and by the Governors of most of the

States which had not seceded, as a "Day of National Humiliation, Fasting, and Prayer." In no part of the Union was it more devoutly observed than in Missouri.

Hardly, however, had the people risen from their supplications, when, with the coming of the next day's sun, salvos of artillery, reverberating from the Atlantic to the Pacific, proclaimed the grim approval with which the loyal North regarded Major Anderson's warlike act.

On the same day the *Star of the West*, by order of the President, crept stealthily out of the harbor of New York, bearing men and munitions of war southward towards Sumter.

On the same fateful day the Senators of Georgia, Florida, Alabama, Mississippi, Louisiana, Texas, and Arkansas, satisfied that the Federal Government was making ready to coerce their States by force of arms to remain within the Union, and that the President was even then sending troops to overawe them into submission, met at Washington and solemnly advised their respective States to secede at once and organize a slave-holding Confederacy.

Missouri, awakened from her dreams of peace by the swelling din of the approaching conflict, seemed for a moment about to respond to the wise counsels of her chief magistrate, and to arm herself for inevitable war.

Among those who most urgently besought her people to follow these counsels, was the Lieutenant-Governor of the State, Thomas Caute Reynolds. He was then nearly forty years of age, a man of medium height and compact mould, with regular features, that were at once refined and strong—a rather handsome man. His jet-black hair and beard were always closely cut, and his dark eyes always shaded by gold-rimmed glasses, which served a two-fold purpose. A South Carolinian by birth, he was a Virginian by race, and in full sympathy with the conciliatory disposition of the Virginia people. He was a man of many accomplishments and of graceful manners, for he had been accustomed from childhood to the usages and refinements of good society, and his active intellect had been highly cultivated both at home and abroad. Latin and Greek were almost as familiar to him as his own tongue, and he spoke French and German and Spanish fluently and gracefully. He was well taught in all the learning of the Schools, and an adept in the mysterious ways of diplomacy, for which he had a strong, natural predilection, that had been strengthened by some service as Secretary of Legation and Chargé d'Affaires *ad interim*, near the Court of Madrid. Though he was a good speaker, it was in counsel and in action that he excelled; for his busy intellect delighted to devise schemes, which it pleased his tireless energy to carry out; and the more difficult and the more intricate the pathway to success, the more did it fascinate his diplomatic brain, and the more command his unwearied efforts to thread its mazes and overcome all its difficulties.

He was a man of tried courage, and had borne his part in several "affairs," in one of which he had wounded Gratz Brown. No one ever doubted his integrity, and he had always discharged with scrupulous fidelity the duties of the various public offices which he had held. A somewhat diligent letter-writer, his letters were alike remarkable for their admirable style and chirography, and generally for their substantial good sense. He was wont to number them after the manner of diplomatists, and to keep a careful record of their contents. He sometimes wrote what he had better have left unwritten, but his prudence and reticence, and a passionless judgment, generally controlled his pen, as they always controlled his tongue.

He had sought the nomination for Lieutenant-Governor, because of the actualities and the possibilities of that position in the troublous times, whose rapid approach he clearly foresaw. Preferring Breckinridge to Douglas, he had, nevertheless, like Jackson, prudently—and fortunately, too, for the glory of Missouri—supported the candidacy of the gifted Illinoisan, and had thereby made his own election sure. Chosen Lieutenant-Governor in August, he began at once to prepare himself for the rôle which he proposed to enact. Diligent and painstaking at all times, he was doubly so now; for he comprehended the vastness of the stage on which he was to appear, and the grandeur of the tragedy in which he proposed to play a conspicuous part. When Congress met in December, he hurried to Washington, and put himself in accord with the most thoughtful Southern leaders. Returning to Missouri, he anticipated both the message of Governor Stewart, and the inaugural of Governor Jackson, by publishing, on the day that the Legislature met, a letter in which he expounded his own views, and advised Missouri what course to pursue in the grave crisis that was already at hand.

In this letter he urged the General Assembly to forthwith declare the determination of Missouri to resist all attempts on the part of the Federal Government to coerce any State to remain in the Union against her will, whether such coercion were attempted by the exhibition and use of *force*, or by peaceful efforts to collect the Federal revenues and enforce the Federal laws within her limits after she had seceded; and pointed out very clearly "the transparent sophistry" of drawing a distinction, as President Buchanan had done, between "coercing a State," and "compelling the citizens of a seceded

State to obey the laws of the United States." " In our system," he said, " a State is its people, citizens compose that people, and to use force against citizens acting by State authority is to coerce the State and to wage war against it. To levy tribute, molest commerce, or hold fortresses, are as much acts of war as to bombard a city.'

He also advised the State that to make her determination to oppose coercion effective, she must without delay organize her militia thoroughly, and make other preparations for whatever contingency might happen. While this was being done she ought to call a convention of all the States, to devise, if possible, some final adjustment of all controversies. If she should fail to secure such adjustment before the 4th of March, she "should not permit Mr. Lincoln to exercise any act of government" within her borders.

In appointing the Senate committees, the Lieutenant-Governor, who was *ex-officio* President of the Senate, took good care to so constitute them that they should be favorable to the policy which he had thus proposed.

Bills were immediately introduced (January 5) to provide for calling a State Convention; to arm and equip the militia; and one which was intended to take away from the Republican Mayor of St. Louis the power to call out the Wide-Awakes of that city in the event of political disturbances there. These Wide-Awakes were a semi-military organization, composed almost exclusively of anti-slavery Germans, and it was feared that the Mayor would, if an opportunity occurred, invest them with the panoply of the law, and use them to subdue the Southern sympathizers and to hold the city for Lincoln.

The prompt and almost unanimous favor with which the General Assembly received these measures shows the strength of the feeling which was then forcing Missouri onward towards secession. To the casual observer it seemed to be irresistible, and the Southern Rights people were exultant and even defiant.

Nor was fuel to feed the flames of passion wanting in those early days of 1861. The Governors of all the Gulf States, except Texas, taught by the experience of South Carolina and warned by the President's declaration that he was determined to reinforce and hold all the Southern forts, resolved to forthwith seize and occupy the forts within their several States, without waiting, as South Carolina had unwisely done, for their own formal secession.

The vigilant Governor of Georgia, Joseph E. Brown, with that courage and common sense which have distinguished his whole career, disdaining those forms which are useful in peace but mischievous in war, sent a detachment of State troops under Colonel Alexander R. Lawton to seize and occupy Fort Pulaski, which commands the approach to Savannah from the ocean; and this order was executed on the 3d of January.

On the 4th, Governor Moore, of Alabama, seized the United States Arsenal at Mt. Vernon, and on the 5th occupied Forts Morgan and Gaines, which guard the approach to Mobile. In announcing the fact to the President, he said that he had seized these forts because "it would have been an unwise policy, suicidal in its character, to have permitted the Government of the United States to make, undisturbed, preparations within the State to enforce by war and bloodshed an authority which it was the fixed purpose of the people of Alabama to resist to the uttermost of their power."

Florida for like reasons seized the United States Arsenal at Apalachicola on the 6th, and Fort Marion at St. Augustine on the 7th.

On the 9th of January the President laid before Congress the correspondence which had taken place between himself and the South Carolina commissioners. He also informed that body that forts, arsenals, and magazines of the United States had been seized by several of the States which had not yet seceded, and declared that the fact could no longer be disguised that the country was "in the midst of a great revolution."

The responsibility for this condition of affairs rested, he said, upon Congress alone, and it was for Congress to adopt such measures as would secure peace and union to a distracted country. He therefore implored them, in heaven's name, to submit the Crittenden Compromise to a vote of the people, so that the people might, as they surely would, "redress the serious grievances which the South have suffered," and bring back peace and harmony to the country.

While reiterating the opinion which he had expressed in his annual message, that neither he nor Congress had any right to make aggressive war upon any State, he now asserted the "clear and undeniable right" of the Federal Government "to use military force defensively against those who resist the Federal officers in the execution of their legal functions, and against those who assail the property of the Government."

But while admitting that it was *his* duty, and declaring that it was *his* purpose, to collect the public revenues and to protect the public property everywhere, so far as might be practicable, he said that it was for Congress to enact the laws which would give him the power to execute this duty; and that it should do this promptly.

He would take care meanwhile that the peace of the District of Columbia should not be disturbed during the remainder of his term of office.

Neither Congress nor the country paid any attention to the peaceful recommendations of the President; for on that very day the first gun of the war was fired, and the *Star of the West*, which had been sent to the relief of Sumter, was driven back to sea by the batteries which South Carolina had erected for the defence of the harbor of Charleston.

The news sped over the land with the rapidity of thought. The President's message was read by the light of the lurid glare of that Southern cannonade. Northern men thought, not of conciliation, but of resenting the insult to the flag of the Union. Southern men were enraged by what they believed to be the President's duplicity, and his attempt to overawe them. Both read the message to see what the President would do. Both saw in it his fixed purpose to make war upon the South, reluctantly, sadly, and almost in despair, but to make war, nevertheless, because he believed that it was his duty to execute the laws and to protect the property of the Federal Government.

Louisiana, warned by her senators at Washington that reinforcements were on the way to Fort St. Philip and Fort Jackson, which guard the entrance to the Mississippi and are the only defences of New Orleans in that direction, took possession of the arsenal at Baton Rouge on the 10th of January and occupied the forts the next day.

Mississippi had seceded on the 9th. Florida seceded on the 10th, and as her troops were already gathering at Pensacola, Lieutenant Slemmer, commanding the forts in that harbor, transferred his forces from the mainland to Fort Pickens. Florida immediately occupied the abandoned barracks, forts, and navy-yard.

On the 11th (January) Alabama seceded and invited all of the slave-holding States to meet the people of Alabama by their delegates in convention on the 4th of February at the city of Montgomery, for the purpose of consulting with each other as to the most effectual mode of securing concerted and harmonious action in whatever measures might be deemed most desirable for their common peace and security.

Such was the reply of the *Cotton States* to the President's attempt to reinforce Fort Sumter, and to his threat to coerce the South into obedience to the Federal laws.

The North was just as prompt and decisive in resenting the insult to the flag of the Union, and in declaring its determination to sustain the Government. On the 11th of January the Legislature of New York adopted the following preamble and resolutions:

"*Whereas*, treason, as defined by the Constitution of the United States, exists in one or more of the States of this Confederacy; and whereas, the insurgent State of South Carolina, after seizing the post-offices, custom house, moneys, and fortifications of the Federal Government, has, by firing into a Government vessel, ordered by the Government to convey troops and provisions to Fort Sumter, virtually declared war; and whereas, the forts and property of the United States Government in Georgia, Alabama, and Louisiana have been unlawfully seized with hostile intention; and whereas, further, Senators in Congress avow and maintain these treasonable acts; therefore,

"*Resolved*, That the Legislature of New York, profoundly impressed with the value of the Union, and determined to preserve it unimpaired, hail with joy the recent firm, dignified, special message of the President of the United States; and that we tender to him through the Chief Magistrate of our own State whatever aid in men and money he may require to enable him to enforce the laws and uphold the authority of the Federal Government; and that in defence of 'the more perfect Union,' which has conferred prosperity and happiness on the American people, renewing the pledge given and redeemed by our fathers, we are ready to devote 'our fortunes, our lives, and our sacred honor' to upholding the Union and the Constitution."

The Legislatures of Ohio, Pennsylvania, Minnesota, Wisconsin, and Illinois spoke out in similar tones, and made it plain that every Northern State would exert its whole power to maintain the Union by force.

There were, however, in every Northern State many men who shrank from the thought of a bloody war, and who believed that the Union could not be preserved by violence.

On the 31st of January a great meeting was held in the city of New York to consider the condition of the country. At this meeting James S. Thayer, an old line Whig, made a speech, in which he said:

"We can, at least, in an authoritative way and in a practical manner, arrive at the basis of a peaceable separation (cheers). We can, at least, by discussion, enlighten, settle, and concentrate the public sentiment of the State of New York upon the question, and save it from that fearful current which, circuitously but certainly, sweeps madly on through the narrow gauge of 'the enforcement of the laws' to the shoreless ocean of civil war! (Cheers.) Against this under all circumstances and in every place and form we must now, and at all times, oppose a resolute and unfaltering resistance. . . .

"It is announced that the Republican Administration will enforce the laws against, and in, all the seceding States. . . .

"You remember the story of William Tell. . . . Let an arrow winged by the Federal power strike the heart of an American citizen, and who can number the avenging darts that will cloud the heavens in the conflict that will ensue? (Prolonged applause.) What then is the duty of the State of New York? What shall we say to our people when we come to meet this state of facts? That the Union must be preserved! But if that cannot be, what then? *Peaceable separation.* (Applause.)"

Ex-Chancellor Walworth said:

"It would be as brutal, in my opinion, to send men to butcher our own brothers of the Southern States, as it would be to massacre them in the Northern States. We are told, however, that it is our duty to enforce, and that we must enforce, the laws. But why? And what laws are to be enforced? There were laws that were to be enforced in the time of the American Revolution. Did Lord Chatham go for enforcing those laws? No! he gloried in the defence of the liberties of America. He made that remarkable declaration in the British Parliament: 'If I were an American citizen, instead of being, as I am, an Englishman, I never would submit to such laws, never, *never*, NEVER!'"

Edward Everett, speaking at Faneuil Hall on February 2d, said:

"To expect to hold fifteen States in the Union by force is preposterous. The idea of a civil war accompanied, as it would be, by a servile insurrection, is too monstrous to be entertained for a moment. If our sister States must leave us, in the name of Heaven let them go in peace!"

The border slave-holding States were outspoken against coercion.

On the 6th of January, Governor Hicks, in an address to the people of *Maryland*, assigning his reasons for refusing to convene the Legislature, said: "Maryland is with the South in sympathy and feeling. She demands from the North the repeal of its offensive unconstitutional statutes, and appeals to it for new guarantees. She will wait a reasonable time for the North to purge her Statute Book, so as to do justice to her Southern brethren, and if her appeals are vain, she will make common cause with her sister States in resistance to tyranny, if need be."

The Virginia Legislature met on the 7th. Governor Letcher, while condemning the action of South Carolina, insisted that the North had brought about the present condition of affairs, and that it was for it to end the rising strife. He declared that he would regard any attempt of Federal troops to pass across Virginia for the purpose of coercing a Southern State as an act of invasion to be repelled by force. On the 19th the Legislature resolved: That if all efforts to reconcile the differences between the two sections of the country should prove abortive, then, every consideration of honor and interest demanded that Virginia should unite her destinies with those of her sister slave-holding States." This resolution was unanimously adopted, and $1,000,000 were appropriated for arming and equipping the militia.

The Legislature of Tennessee called a State Convention on the 12th of January, and on the 18th adopted these resolutions:

"That this General Assembly has heard with profound regret of the resolutions recently adopted by the State of New York, tendering men and money to the President of the United States, to be used in coercing certain sovereign States of the South into obedience to the Federal Government.

"That this General Assembly receives the action of the Legislature of New York as the indication of a purpose on the part of the people of that State to further complicate existing difficulties by forcing the people of the South to the extremity of submission or resistance; and so regarding it, the Governor of the State of Tennessee is hereby requested to inform the Executive of the State of New York, that it is the opinion of this General Assembly that whenever the authorities of that State shall send armed forces to the South for the purpose indicated in said resolutions, the people of Tennessee, uniting with their brethren of the South, will, as one man, resist such invasion of the soil of the South at all hazards and to the last extremity."

On the 17th, Governor Magoffin said to the General Assembly of *Kentucky* that though Kentucky disapproved of the hasty and inconsiderate action of the seceding States, Kentuckians would never stand by with folded arms while those States were struggling for their Constitutional rights, and were being subjugated by an antislavery Government. On the 21st, the Legislature adopted the Tennessee Resolutions.

Missouri seemed to be on the very verge of secession. Even St. Louis denounced the coercion of the South. At a great Union meeting held there on the 12th of January, a meeting composed of men who " believed that the rights and property of all sections of the country could be better protected within the American Union than by destroying the Government "—a meeting called and controlled by such staunch loyalists as Nathaniel Paschall, Hamilton R. Gamble, James E. Yeatman, and Robert Campbell—resolutions were unanimously adopted declaring that

"6. The possession of slave property is a Constitutional right, and, as such, ought to be recognized by the Federal Government. And if the Federal Government shall fail and refuse to secure this right, the Southern States should be found united in its defence, in which event Missouri will share the common duties and common dangers of the South.

"8. . . . We cordially approve of the principles of adjustment contained in what are known as the Crittenden Propositions. . . .

"10. In the opinion of this meeting, the employment of the military forces of the Government to enforce submission from the citizens of the seceding States will inevitably plunge the country in civil war. . . . We therefore earnestly entreat, as well the Federal Government as the seceding States, to withhold and stay the arm of military power, and on no pretext whatever to bring on the nation the horrors of civil war until the people themselves can take such action as our troubles demand.

"11. The people of Missouri should meet in convention for the purpose of taking action in the present state of the nation's affairs, at the same time to protect the Union of the States and the rights and authority of this State under the Constitution."

On the 14th *The Republican*, the great conservative journal of the State, the mouth-piece of her rich men and merchants, in a leader addressed to

Abraham Lincoln, urging him to save the Union by advising his followers to assent to the re-enactment of the Missouri Compromise, said:

"Six States have already gone out of the Union so far as their own action is concerned, hastily, and without sufficient cause, as we believe, but still they have assumed an attitude of independence of the Government of the United States, and what is to be done? To attempt to coerce them back by military force will bring ruin upon every State in this Union. One-half of your own State will resist any attempt to organize or march an army for the subjugation of Missouri or any of the revolting States; and Kentucky and Tennessee, when the worse comes to the worst, will again become 'the dark and bloody ground,' before they will suffer their soil to be polluted by the tread of armed hosts marching to the slaughter of their neighbors and friends and kinsmen in the Southern States."

The General Assembly was not slow to respond to the feeling of the people.

The bill to call a Convention to consider whether Missouri should secede, and to adopt measures for vindicating the sovereignty of the State, and the protection of her institutions, was reported back to both Houses on the 9th of January, and passed both Houses on the 18th. In the Senate only two votes were recorded against its passage. In the House

105 members voted for it and only eighteen against it. Of these latter, eleven were from St. Louis.

The passage of the bill by such a majority was a great triumph for the Southern Rights men, and they, in order to emphasize the fact, now determined to proclaim the sympathy of the State with the South, by a bold act, which should intensify the enthusiasm of their own adherents, and rally to their support the timid and irresolute, of whom there were not a few in every county. The opportunity to do this in a marked way had been afforded them by the arrival at the capital of a commissioner, whom the State of Mississippi had sent to ask the co-operation of Missouri in the adoption of "measures for the common defence and safety of the slave-holding States." Accordingly, Governor Jackson, immediately upon the passage of the bill, notified the Legislature that this commissioner, Mr. Russell, would be pleased to confer with them as to the objects of his mission. A joint committee was at once appointed to wait upon him, and invite him to address the General Assembly; and the ceremony was arranged for that very evening.

At the appointed hour the Senate, preceded by its officers, entered the hall of the House of Representatives, and took the seats which had been assigned to them. And then the Governor and other chief officers of the State, and the Judges of the

Supreme Court were announced, and took their seats within the bar.

And now a little scene was enacted, which, trifling in itself, illustrates the temper of the time, and the then disposition of the Legislature and the people.

The committee being about to bring in the commissioner, the President of the Joint Convention (Lieutenant-Governor Reynolds) said:

"When the Commissioner from the State of Mississippi is announced, the members of the General Assembly will rise to receive him."

John D. Stevenson, a Republican representative from St. Louis, sprang to his feet.

"Are we here, Mr. President, to do homage to the ambassador of some foreign potentate?"

President.—"I understand, sir, that this is a joint session of the General Assembly, to listen to an address from the Commissioner of the State of Mississippi, and I hope, for the honor of all parties, that the member from St. Louis will take his seat."

Stevenson.—"Shall I have a chance?"

President.—"Take your seat."

A voice.—"Good!"

Stevenson.—"I desire to have a chance."

President.—"Take your seat."

A voice.—"Better!"

Stevenson.—"Mr. President, I can read, sir, the rules that govern this body, and I suppose, if I am well informed, that when the President rules me out of order, it is his duty to state why he so rules."

President.—" The business of this session is to hear a speech from the Commissioner from Mississippi, and all other business is out of order."

Stevenson.—" I understand that the President commands the members to rise."

President.—" I will change it to a request, and I hope that no member of this General Assembly will have the indecency to refuse to rise."

Stevenson.—" Oh! that will do, sir."

The commissioner was thereupon introduced, the members rising from their seats to receive him.

He made a long address, the substance of which was that he had been charged by the General Assembly of Mississippi to inform the people of Missouri that Mississippi had formally dissolved her connection with the United States, and, in conjunction with other slave-holding States, was about to organize a Southern Confederacy; that the old Union had even now ceased to exist, and could never be reconstructed; that war between the North and the South was inevitable, and would be begun within ninety days; that the guns which had driven back the *Star of the West* from the harbor of Charleston had already given the signal for the strife; and that in view of all these facts the people of Mississippi earnestly invited the people of Missouri to unite with their Southern kindred for their common defence and their common safety.

This address was listened to with the greatest attention, and received with every manifestation of approval and sympathy. At its conclusion the joint session was dissolved; but the demonstration in favor of an alliance with the South was noisily kept up till almost dawn.

Mr. Halliburton had already (16th January) offered in the Senate a resolution against coercion, similar to that which Virginia had adopted. But the matter was brought more formally before the General Assembly, on the 28th, by Mr. Vest (the Patrick Henry of resistance in Missouri), who then reported from the Committee on Federal Relations a preamble and resolutions, which, while following for the most part those of the Tennessee Legislature, differ from them in some important particulars.

"Whereas we have learned with profound regret that the States of New York and Ohio have recently tendered men and money to the President of the United States for the avowed purpose of coercing certain sovereign States of the South into obedience to the Federal Government,

"*Therefore, Resolved,* That we regard with the utmost abhorrence the doctrine of coercion, as indicated by the action of the States aforesaid, believing that the same would end in civil war, and forever destroy any hope of reconstructing the Federal Union. So believing, we deem it our duty to declare that, if there is any invasion of the slave States for the purpose of carrying such doctrine into effect, it is the opinion of this General Assembly, that the people of Missouri will instantly rally on the side of their Southern brethren to resist the invaders at all hazards, and to the last extremity.

"*Resolved*, That the Governor of this State be requested to transmit to the Governors of New York and Ohio the above resolutions."

These resolutions were ably supported by Vest, Harris, and Cunningham, and opposed vigorously by Partridge and Peckham. They were adopted on the 29th, eighty-nine members voting for them and fourteen against them.

The Senate, having been notified of the passage of these resolutions by the House, accepted them as a substitute for the less vigorous resolutions of Senator Halliburton, and finally took them up and concurred in them (February 15th), only one Senator (Dr. Morris of St. Louis) voting against them.

By this action of her General Assembly, Missouri was solemnly pledged, so far as her Representatives could pledge her, to resist the coercion of the seceding States, at all hazards, and to the last extremity.

But behind all this remained the yet unanswered question, whether the General Assembly expressed the feelings and pronounced the purpose of *the people of Missouri.*

CHAPTER III.

THE PEOPLE.

Canvass for the Convention—Secessionists, Union Men, Unconditional Union Men—Georgia, Louisiana, and Texas Secede—Organization of the Confederate Government—Peace Conventions: They Distract the Border States, and Divide the Southern Men of Missouri—Rollins—Hall—Blair and the Wide Awakes—The Union Men and Submissionists carry the State—The Secession Majority in the Legislature gives way—Postponement of the Bill to arm the State—The Convention meets; Sterling Price its President—Governor Jackson, Parsons, and Vest still Defiant—The Commissioner from Georgia—Vest's Speech—The North and the South prepare for War—The General Assembly Submits—Failure of the Military Bill—The Debate in the House.

THE Act calling a State Convention provided that the delegates should be chosen on the 18th of February, and that they should convene at Jefferson City on the last day of that month.

The canvass was straightway opened by each of the three parties into which the people of the State were divided— Secessionists, Conditional Union men, and Unconditional Union men.

Conspicuous among the *Secessionists* were the Governor and Lieutenant-Governor of the State, a majority of the Members of the General Assembly, both United States Senators (James S. Green and Trusten Polk), and General David R. Atchison.

They were earnestly supported by the Jefferson City *Examiner*, the St. Louis *Bulletin*, and other journals. They did not desire the disruption of the Union. Few of them believed in the right of secession. All of them deplored the precipitate action of South Carolina, and the now apparent determination of the other Cotton States to follow in her footsteps. But believing that the withdrawal of all those States from the Union would soon be an accomplished fact; that they would establish a Southern Confederacy; that all of the other slave-holding States would eventually be forced to enter this Confederacy; and that war between it and the Government of the United States would necessarily follow; they thought that it was the duty of Missouri to declare emphatically that in that event she would take her stand with the South, to which she was bound by every tie that holds a people together—race, sympathy traditions in common, a common history, like institutions, and like interests—and with it fight against the North.

The only formidable opponents of the Secessionists were the *Conditional Union men*. These gradually fell under the leadership of Hamilton R. Gamble, Alexander W. Doniphan, James S. Rollins, William A. Hall, John S. Phelps, ex-Governor Stewart, Sterling Price and the St. Louis *Republican*, then conducted by Nathaniel Paschall, a man of mature age, great experience, strong intellect, and consummate common sense. Under the guidance of these astute managers the Conditional Union men assumed a position which, from the moment of its adoption, began to divide the Secessionists. Few of these, as has been said, were primarily in favor of secession. All of them regarded the dissolution of the Union with sorrow and apprehension. They would have gladly persuaded the seceding States to return into the Union, and to trust to peaceful methods for the protection of their rights and the maintenance of their honor. They were not particularly devoted to the institution of slavery, nor were they deeply interested in the maintenance of that system. They were Secessionists, *only* because they believed that the Union had been dissolved, that its reconstruction was impossible, that war was inevitable, and that in war the place of Missouri was by the side of the Southern States, of which she was one. But all around them were Southern-born men and many Northern-born citizens, who, while ready to declare that Missouri would resist every attempt on the part of the United States Government to coerce the seceding States back into the Union, believed that the North, rather than involve the country in a disastrous war, would concede to the South her clear Constitutional rights, and thus re-establish the

Union upon a firmer basis than it had ever rested upon.

This belief, or rather this *hope*, was the foundation on which Gamble and Hall and Paschall builded their party. In their resolutions, and speeches and addresses, they declared that Missouri was firmly attached to the Union, and would adhere to it so long as there was reason to hope that the North would adopt the Crittenden Proposition, or give other Constitutional guarantees to the South that the United States would protect slavery wherever it lawfully existed; but that if the North refused to give such guarantees within a reasonable time, it would be the duty of Missouri to secede from the Union and to unite with the South for the protection of Slavery and the defence of their common interests. They also declared that if the North, pending attempts to adjust matters peaceably, should make war upon any Southern State, Missouri would at once take up arms in defence of such State. By this wise action the Conditional Union men won the sympathy of the slave-holders of Missouri, and of her mercantile and manufacturing classes, and rich land owners, all of whom regarded war as the greatest of evils. The zeal, the earnestness, and the ability with which they conducted the canvass, together with the course of events outside of the State, soon brought into their ranks many Secessionists, who had taken hope again.

The Unconditional Union men, still calling themselves Republicans, took the ground that they would support the Government in whatever measures it might adopt to maintain the Union and to force the Southern States to obey its laws. The one leader of this party was Francis P. Blair, Jr. Up to this time it had been composed almost exclusively of Germans, a few antislavery men of New England origin, and the personal followers of Blair, Bates, and Brown. The Presidential election had shown that they numbered only one-tenth of the voters of the State. Blair saw in the action of the Conditional Union men an opportunity to greatly increase his own following, by drawing to it those supporters of Bell, Douglas, and Breckinridge who were unwilling to vote for the secession of Missouri, even if the North should refuse to adopt the Crittenden Compromise. There were many such men; but they looked upon the Republicans as the cause of all the troubles in which the country was involved, and felt an unconquerable repugnance to joining that party. They were Union men, but they would not be Republicans.

Blair determined to make their co-operation with the Republicans easy, by organizing both as the *Unconditional Union* party. In this he was violently opposed by the less intelligent of the Republicans, but, with the support of Broadhead, Glover, Filley, and How, he carried his point, and when the time for selecting candidates for the Convention came, the call for the meetings which were to choose members of the nominating conventions was addressed to "all Unconditional Union men." In these meetings a great many anti-Republicans took part, and united in the selection of delegates to the nominating conventions.

When the St. Louis convention met, "the Irreconcilables" renewed their opposition to Blair's wise course, and contended that no one should be nominated as a candidate for the State Convention who had not voted for Lincoln. Blair said in reply that he cared little to what party men *had* belonged. What he wanted was men who were *now*, and who would *hereafter*, under all circumstances, and in every emergency, be for the Union; that he himself intended to stand by it to the end; to oppose in every way the secession of Missouri; and if Missouri should secede, to still try to hold St. Louis fast to the Union, and that he desired the help of every man who was resolved to do likewise; that this was no time to struggle for a party; but it was now the first and chief duty of every man to struggle for the Union. His counsels prevailed, and a composite ticket was nominated — seven

Douglas Democrats, three Union men who had voted for Bell, and four that had voted for Lincoln.

The canvass, being thus opened, was conducted with great zeal, and in the midst of ever-increasing excitement, for during its progress events of the gravest importance were occurring every day both within and without the State.

Georgia seceded on the 18th of January, Louisiana on the 26th, and Texas on the 1st of February; and on the 4th of February, delegates from these three States, and from Florida, Alabama, Mississippi and South Carolina met in Convention at Montgomery and began to create the Government of the Confederate States.

Sane men had long foreseen that war between the North and the South was inevitable unless some plan of conciliation acceptable to both sections could be devised and agreed upon before the 4th of March, on which day Lincoln would become President, with a Republican Congress to sustain him in whatever measures he might adopt to preserve the Union. The scheme which had met with the most favor in the border slave-holding States was that these should hold a convention at Nashville on the 4th of February to formulate the conditions upon which they would themselves remain in the Union and try to bring the seceded States back into it ; and that these conditions should then be submitted to a Convention of all the States, to meet at Wheeling on the 11th of February.

This scheme was abandoned, however, in favor of a proposition made by Virginia. The General Assembly of that State (January 19) invited all the other States to send commissioners to a convention which was to meet in Washington on the 4th of February, in order "to consider, and, if practicable, to agree upon some suitable adjustment" of the difficulties between the slave-holding and the non-slave-holding States, and to report the same to Congress. The Legislature at the same time sent ex-President Tyler to Washington, and Judge John Robertson to South Carolina to procure from the United States Government and from that of South Carolina a mutual agreement to abstain, pending the deliberations of the Convention, from the doing of any act which would produce a collision of arms.

South Carolina readily acceded to this request of Virginia; but the President, conceiving that he had no power to make such an agreement, submitted the matter to Congress. That body treated it with the utmost indifference. Nevertheless, all the border slave-holding States, and most of the Northern States, appointed commissioners to the convention. Missouri sent Alexander W. Doniphan, Waldo P. Johnson, Harrison Hough, John D. Coalter, and A.

H. Buckner. It met at Washington on the 4th of February.

The Conditional Union men of Missouri made the most of this convention, and of the hopes that it held out to those who were in favor of "peace at any price."

James S. Rollins used his persuasive eloquence and great popularity to bring the wavering to the side of the Union. He appealed to them in speeches and in letters to stand by it as long as there was any hope of preserving it. "There was every reason," he said, "to believe that the Peace Convention would bring about a settlement, and even if it failed to do this, it would still be the duty of the Border States to stick together till every other hope of adjustment had failed." To win their confidence, and hold them fast, he told them again and again that whilst he was himself always "in favor of the Union, the Constitution, and the enforcement of the Laws," he was unalterably opposed to the doctrine of coercion, and would to his very utmost resist the sending of Federal troops into any State that had seceded, with the purpose to force it back into the Union. He was the more willingly listened to because he was known to be one of the greatest slave-holders in Missouri, and had always been faithful to her institutions.

Listening to the honied words of Rollins made

those who heard him more willing to listen to the stern logic of a man of stronger intellect and more earnest convictions than he—William A. Hall—one of those honest, hard-headed, plain-speaking men whom New England had sent to Missouri. He told them in his earnest, sensible way that the question which they had to decide was "not one of sentiment, but of sense. We hold our power," said he, "as a trust for others. We hold it for the benefit of our wives and our children; for the protection of the aged, the infirm, and the helpless. We have no right to consult our feelings when the interests of others are in our keeping, and when their happiness is dependent on our action. . . .

"What are we to gain by dissolving the Union? The Fugitive Slave Law is a law of the United States. To destroy the Union is to annul the Fugitive Slave Law, bring Canada to our borders, and make our slave property valueless. But this is not the worst of it. While sacrificing our property by an attempt to save it, we will bring upon ourselves war, which, if it come, will destroy all our property and expose us and our families to miseries such as, happily, we have never known, but of which the pages of history are full. . . . The geographical position of Missouri makes her essential to the North, and even if the North should consent to the secession of every other slave-holding State, it will never consent to the secession of Missouri. She lies in its pathway to the West. She commands the navigation of the Missouri and all its tributaries, of the Upper Mississippi, the Illinois, the Ohio, the Tennessee, and the Cumberland. . . . Never will the North and the North-west permit the navigation of these great rivers to be controlled by a powerful foreign nation, for their free navigation is essential to the prosperity of those regions. They might let the mouths of the Mississippi be held by a weak Confederacy of Cotton States, but never by a powerful people of which Missouri would form part.

"Our feelings and our sympathies strongly incline us to go with the South in the event of a separation; but passion and feeling are temporary, interest is permanent. The influence of geographical position will continue so long as the face of the Earth remains as it is, and the position of Missouri and the navigation of the Mississippi will be great and important interests long ages after the feelings and passions which now dominate the country shall have passed away and been forgotten."

The Conditional Union men had already lowered their tone. They no longer threatened war against the United States if the Government should refuse to protect slavery, or even if it should dare to lead its armies into the seceding States in order to coerce them into obedience to the laws of the Union. Their entreaties grew stronger every day; their threats grew weaker. Many of them—most of the rich land owners, and of the great slave-holders—were fast learning the duty of submission. It is an old saying that "Nothing is so timid as wealth." The war demonstrated that of all wealth, property in slaves was the most timid and the most cowardly. Nor was it only the rich Union man who now began to cower in the horrid presence of war; but many a blatant Secessionist, who owned neither land nor negroes, many a one who had for years been stirring up strife between the North and South, and boasting that "One southern man could whip half a dozen Yankees," now saw that to stand in the way of those "Yankees" meant danger to the limbs and to the life of him who should be brave enough to dare to do it; and they put up their bowie-knives and bridled their tongues till the war was ended, and they could again safely loosen the one and brandish the other.

The changed tone of the Conditional Union party, and its ever-increasing tendency toward submission, kept within its ranks thousands of voters who would otherwise have gone over to the Unconditional Union men. Blair saw this, but it did not disturb him, for he knew that sooner or later they would come to him. He went on busily organizing and consolidating his forces, preparing systematically, earnestly, and intelligently for war, and doing everything that a statesman and soldier could do to hold Missouri loyal to the Union, which he believed to be the source of all her prosperity.

The Germans were the nucleus of his power. They were—every one—unconditionally for the Union. Knowing nothing of the peculiar relations of the States to the Federal Government, nothing of the circumstances of its formation, nothing about the Constitution, they could not comprehend that South Carolina had any more right to secede from the Union than St. Louis had to secede from Missouri. Knowing nothing of the causes which endeared Virginia to her sons; feeling none of that State pride which a New Englander or a South Carolinian felt; owing his own citizenship to the United States and not to any State, he could not comprehend that to a Virginian loyalty and patriotism meant devotion to Virginia, and not to the Union. Hating slavery, he was anxious to destroy it rather than to protect it; and having neither kindred nor friends in the South, he could not sympathize with its people in their unequal contest with the Union, nor feel that it was his duty to stand by them in the hour of danger.

During the Presidential election they had been organized as Wide-Awakes. Blair had since been converting them into semi-military companies of Home Guards. He now redoubled his exertions in this direction, drilled and disciplined the men, and armed them as fast as his means permitted. In obtaining funds for this purpose he was greatly helped by Isaac Sherman of New York, and other Eastern men. These companies had, before the day of election (February 18), become so numerous and arrogant as to arouse the fear that they might, by interfering with the election, provoke a riot that day. Governor Jackson was appealed to by many prominent citizens for protection. Having no authority to call out the militia during the session of the General Assembly, he submitted the matter to that body. The Senate at once, by a vote of 18 to 4, authorized him to call out the militia, but the proposition was vigorously opposed in the House by John D. Stevenson, the leader there of the Unconditional Union men, himself a Virginian, and it was, despite the fervid appeals of Vest, defeated.

The election passed off quietly. Not a single avowed Secessionist was chosen. In St. Louis the Unconditional Union candidates were elected by over 5,000 majority, and the State declared against secession by a majority of 80,000.

The result was a surprise to every one, and a bitter disappointment to the South.

The immediate and all-important effect which the

election had upon the course of affairs in Missouri, was the overthrow of the Secession majority in the House of Representatives, and the consequent defeat of all measures for organizing, arming, and equipping the militia, and for getting the State ready for war. Bills having those objects in view had been reported to both Houses early in February, and were under discussion on the day that the election took place. When they were taken up the next day, Senators and Representatives, who had up to that time been clamorous for arming the State, announced that they interpreted the late vote as declaring that the people of Missouri were overwhelmingly opposed to the enactment of any warlike measures, and that consequently they would themselves vote against these bills.

It was in vain that the Governor and his adherents urged that war was inevitable, and that the first duty of the General Assembly to the people of the State was to prepare her for it; that if they were themselves willing to falsify their repeated pledge to resist the coercion of the seceding States, they should at least arm the State for her own defence, for the maintenance of peace within her own borders, and for the safety of her own people; in vain it was that Churchill, and Parsons, and Rains in the Senate, and Vest, Freeman, and Claiborne in the House, taunted them with cowardly " submission to a Black Republican potentate;" in vain that Harris, still a Union man, begged them to at least discuss his carefully prepared bill, so as to understand its provisions and to see that it contained nothing for which the most loyal of Union men ought not to vote—nothing could overcome the terror that had taken possession of their souls. Panic-stricken, they sought safety in the ranks of the Submissionists, and turned Missouri over, unarmed and defenceless, to Frank Blair and his Home Guards.

In spite of all this, Governor Jackson maintained the same bold attitude which he had taken on the day of his inauguration, and was sustained in it by Parsons and a majority of the Senators, and by Vest and nearly one-half of the Representatives. They could do nothing, but they lost no opportunity to revive the courage of their followers, and to hold them in readiness for the conflict that was sure to begin sooner or later.

The convention met at Jefferson City on the 28th of February.

The next day (March 1st) an opportunity was offered to the Secessionists to make a demonstration, and they took advantage of it. The State of Georgia had sent a commissioner—Luther J. Glenn —to Missouri to ask her to secede and become one of the Confederate States. Arriving at Jefferson City on the 1st of March, he presented his credentials to the Governor the same afternoon. The city was crowded with Unionists, all of them exulting over their great victory at the polls and the meeting of a Convention to which not a single Secessionist had been elected. Nearly every distinguished Union man in the State was there, either as a member of the Convention or to witness its deliberations, and to hold the vacillating firm in their loyalty to the Union. To all appearance, Missouri was about to commit herself irrevocably to the maintenance of the Union, and to assume a position which would eventually force her to make war upon the Southern people. Had Governor Jackson now wavered in his devotion to the South, had he in that hour of great trial proved recreant to the principles which had always controlled his actions, that position would have been surely taken. But, with a courage as great as was ever shown upon any battlefield, Jackson raised aloft the banner of the State, and called upon the Southern men of Missouri to rally under its folds, fearless of the gathering forces of those who were rebelling against her, and careless of the deserters that were flocking to their camp.

The Secessionists determined to serenade the Commissioner from Georgia. When he stepped upon the balcony to thank them for their sympathy, the Governor of the State stood beside him, and presented him to the people in a defiant speech, in which he reiterated that the honor and the interests of Missouri both required her to stand firmly with the Confederate States "in resistance to the abolitionized North," and to instantly secede and entei the Confederacy if Lincoln should undertake, as he surely would, to make war upon the South.

The next day, Saturday, March the 2d, the Governor notified the General Assembly that the commissioner desired to confer with that body upon the subject of his mission. Some opposition being made in the House to the adoption of a resolution which the Senate had passed inviting him to address both Houses that evening in joint session, Harris and Vest supported the resolution warmly. The latter said:

"I stand here to-day, come weal, come woe, sink or swim, survive or perish, to cast my political fortunes for all time, to give all that I have, and all that I am, to that people which is mine by lineage, by birth, and by institutions—the people of the South; and should the time come for battle, for storm, or for wreck, I will be with that Southern people. Coerce them back? Representatives of Missouri! let me tell you now, sneer at them as you may! let me tell you now, that the God who protected our forefathers, will protect that Southern people.

"Thrice have we to Clan Alpine come in friendship's guise,
When next we come 'twill be with banner, brand and bow,
As clansman meets his mortal foe."

"Sirs! we have appealed to the North, begged it, and besought it. We might as well have prayed to the winds. You talk of peace. There is no peace. The Republican party must cease its eternal and everlasting warfare upon our property, or in the red glare of battle, and in the shock of contending armies, we will appeal to the God of Battles, and ask Him to protect us.

"I say here to-day in face of a dominant majority of 80,000 Submissionists, I say to you and I say to these Submissionists, that if they intend to justify the coercion of the seceded States, I shall myself be in favor of the instant separation of Missouri from the North, and will stake my life on the result.

"We, who live on the broad prairies of Missouri, with but few slaves around us, cannot appreciate the dangers that environ the men of the South, their wives and their children; the horrors of a servile insurrection; their fear, and their hatred of a party which has elected to power a man who declares that slavery must be confined to the slave States, so that it may, like a scorpion, sting itself to death. How? In the blood and carnage of African lust and African rage. And yet we are told that these people must stand still and allow all these terrors to be brought upon them! . . . I would rather—a hundred times rather—settle this question *now*, upon the battle-field. If I were a citizen of one of those Southern States, I would do as they have done, and as a Missourian, I am willing and ready to follow Old Virginia, wherever she may lead, and no one can doubt that she will go with the South."

The resolution was adopted, and that evening the Commissioner for Georgia addressed the General Assembly, explaining the causes which had impelled Georgia to secede, and urging Missouri to unite with her and the other slave-holding States in the formation of a Southern Confederacy.

While matters were thus drifting towards civil strife in Missouri, the only State in which the contest did, during the first year or two, or at any time, assume that character, the North and the South were both getting ready for war.

Jefferson Davis had been inaugurated President of the Confederate States on the 18th of February; measures to organize an army were adopted on the 28th of February, and provision was made for the transfer to the Confederate Government of the troops that had been raised by the several States, for their own defence. South Carolina had already occupied all the forts in Charleston Harbor, except Sumter, and was erecting powerful batteries to command and reduce that fortress when the time should come, and was enlisting, organizing and drilling men in every county and in every neighborhood. General McCulloch had, with an overwhelming force, surrounded the United States troops at San Antonio, and by authority of the State of Texas compelled General Twiggs, the commander of the United States forces in that department, to surrender to the State all the United States property within her limits, and to agree to withdraw every Federal soldier from her territory. Georgia had called her militia into active service under the command of those veterans, Twiggs, Hardee and Walker. Bragg and Beauregard were mustering an army in Louisiana, and the streets of New Orleans were crowded with enthusiastic volunteers. Van Dorn had succeeded Jefferson Davis in command of the army that Mississippi was raising, and its ranks were rapidly swelling. Florida had been in arms since the beginning of the year, and was still strengthening her forces in all directions, while throughout Alabama there was not a Federal soldier, and everywhere the enlistment of volunteers was hurrying. Even Arkansas had risen in overwhelming force, and driving Captain Totten and his command out of the State, had taken possession of the United States Arsenal at Little Rock.

The Northern States were no less active. Massachusetts had already tendered to the President twenty-six regiments for the defence of the capital, and nearly every other loyal State was emulating her example. Even Congress had begun to discuss the employment of force in order to compel the seceding States to restore the property which they had captured and to obey the laws of the United States.

And most important of all, the whole power of the Government of the United States, its army and navy, together with its treasury and all its great resources, had passed out of the unwilling hands of Buchanan, into the firm grasp of Abraham Lincoln; out of the control of the South and its Northern friends into that of the anti-slavery North, and was thenceforth to be wielded for the preservation of the Union and the enforcement of its laws and the conquest of all its enemies.

Encouraged by the brave attitude of Jackson, and incited by the preparations for war that were making all around them, the Southern Rights' members of the Missouri Legislature made a supreme effort to pass the bill for arming the State. It was taken up on the 5th of March.

L. M. Lawson, of Platte, the youngest member of the House, and a native of the State, spoke against the bill. It was unnecessary, he said, because no one was proposing to attack Missouri, or to assail her honor, or to do any injury to the persons or property of her people; it was oppressive, because it would burden the State with enormous taxation at a time when the troubled condition of the country and the fear of war was bankrupting every one; it was dangerous, because it would place in the hands of the Governor the power and the means to involve the State in war and to bring upon her inhabitants the unspeakable horrors of fratricidal strife. Missouri had no cause to secede from the Union, no ground upon which to arm herself against the Federal Government; no reason to apprehend war unless she should, by her own folly, bring it upon herself and her people. Let her be loyal to the Union, and the Union would still protect her, as it had always done.

Conrow, replying to Lawson, said that Lincoln's inaugural had removed from his mind the last hope for the safety of the Union. If he carried out his threat to coerce the South into obedience to the laws of the Federal Government, the country would soon blaze with the flames of civil war. Missouri would not submit to Lincoln's domination. If she did, he would never again call himself a Missourian.

N. C. Claiborne said: " The gentleman from Platte (Lawson) thinks that we are appealing to the fears of members. There are times when the brave fear. The universal gloom, which hangs like mourning drapery around our once happy country, deepened by Lincoln's inaugural, which plainly sets forth the plan of coercion, will cause every patriot heart to quail with fear. His determination to hold, occupy, and possess the Southern forts strangles the hopes of all those who have prayed for the preservation and reconstruction of the Union. He means war. Long before the echo of the first cannon fired by his minions against a Southern city shall have died away, those who have been seeking to compromise our difficulties on just and honorable terms, will have buckled on their armor and planted themselves upon the ramparts of the Constitution, in defence of Southern rights. . . . It has been said that Missouri will submit, that her Convention will submit. He who says so slanders the members of that Convention, and outrages the people of Missouri. Tell me not that this State will tolerate the odious doctrine of coercion. Never, NEVER will she tolerate it. Seventeen thousand Republicans, nine-tenths of them foreigners living in the city of St. Louis, cannot warp the judgment of 150,000 freemen and control the destinies of this State. The thing is absurd. Missouri will share the destinies of the South. For my own part, I will never abandon the home of my adoption, I will remain upon the western border of Missouri, and will battle there for her honor and her rights."

Harris again urged the House to pass the bill. It was no longer a question of policy, but of duty, and a necessity to put the State in condition to protect her people and their possessions; and to secure to her that influence among the other States to which she was entitled by reason of her greatness and her position, so that she might use this influence to stay the hand of violence and war, and to preserve the peace and maintain the Union. "If she failed to do this, humiliating disaster and dire ruin would come upon her, and she ought therefore to set about it at once." His anxiety was not inspired, he said, "by sympathy with the seceded States. They had withdrawn from the Union without adequate preparation to maintain their independence, and in doing this had shown more temper than statesmanship. What he desired was not so much to defend *them* against the consequences of their own rashness and folly as to maintain the dignity of Missouri, and to protect the persons and property of her citizens."

The House refused to pass the bill. In this the South sustained a defeat more disastrous to its independence than any which thereafter befell its arms, down to the fall of Vicksburg.

CHAPTER IV.

THE CONVENTION.

The State Convention—Gamble's Report and Resolutions—Amendments Proposed—Debates—William A. Hall—John B. Henderson—Prince L. Hudgins—John T. Redd—James O. Broadhead—Adoption of the Report and Resolutions—The General Assembly—Election of a United States Senator—Defeat of James S. Green—Blaine's Opinion of Him—The Metropolitan Police Bill—Vest's Adverse Report on the Action of the Convention—His Speech—The Legislature Rejects the Recommendations of the Convention and Adjourns—The Revival of Secessionism—Defeat of the Coercionists in St. Louis—Election of a Conservative Mayor.

THE State Convention met at Jefferson City on the last day of February. Ex-Governor Sterling Price, a Union man, was chosen President, receiving the votes of seventy-five Union men, while the votes of fifteen Southern Rights' men were given to Nathaniel W. Watkins, a half-brother of Henry Clay. As soon as the Convention completed its organization it adjourned its session to St. Louis, whose loyal atmosphere it preferred to that of the capital.

Of its ninety-nine members fifty-three were natives of either Virginia or Kentucky; and all but seventeen had been born in the slave-holding States.

Only thirteen were natives of the North. Three were Germans, and there was one Irishman. The President of the Convention, the Chairman of the Committee on Federal Relations Judge Gamble, the leader of the Unconditional Union men on the floor James O. Broadhead, and the most conspicuous opponent of Secession John B. Henderson, were all Virginians.

The Convention reassembled at St. Louis on the 4th of March, the day of Lincoln's inauguration, and went straight to work. On the 9th the Committee on Federal Relations made a long report through its chairman, Judge Gamble. In this report, after reviewing the condition of the country, they said:

"To involve Missouri in revolution, under the present circumstances, is certainly not demanded by the magnitude of the grievances of which we complain; nor by the certainty that they cannot be otherwise and more peacefully remedied, nor by the hope that they would be remedied, or even diminished by such revolution.

"The position of Missouri in relation to the adjacent States, which would continue in the Union, would necessarily expose her, if she became a member of a new Confederacy, to utter destruction whenever any rupture might take place between the different republics. In a military aspect secession and connection with a Southern Confederacy is annihilation for Missouri.

"The true position for Missouri to assume is that of a State whose interests are bound up in the maintenance of the Union, and whose kind feelings and strong sympathies are with the people of the Southern States, with whom we are connected by the ties of friendship and blood. . . . To go with those States—to leave the government our fathers builded—to blot out the star of Missouri from the constellation of the Union is to ruin ourselves without doing them any good. We cannot follow them, we cannot give up the Union, but we will do all in our power to induce them to again take their places with us in the family from which they have attempted to separate themselves. For this purpose we will not only recommend a compromise with which they ought to be satisfied, but we will endeavor to procure an assemblage of the whole family of States in order that in a General Convention such amendments to the Constitution may be agreed upon as shall permanently restore harmony to the whole nation."

The committee also submitted to the Convention resolutions conformable to these opinions, and which in substance were,

1. That there was no adequate cause for the withdrawal of Missouri from the Union.

2. That believing that the seceded States would return to the Union if the Crittenden Proposition were adopted, the Convention would request the General Assembly to call a Convention of all the States to consider that proposition.

3. That they would entreat the Federal Government not to employ force against the seceding States, and the latter not to assail the Government, while this proposition was under consideration.

Mr. Bast moved that the Convention should further declare that if the Northern States should refuse to assent to the Crittenden Compromise, and the other border slave States should thereupon secede, Missouri would not then hesitate to take a firm and decided stand in favor of her sister States of the South.

For this proposition only twenty-three members voted. Among them were Sterling Price, Robert A. Hatcher, Harrison Hough, Prince L. Hudgins, John T. Redd, and Nathaniel W. Watkins. Among the seventy who voted against it were General Doniphan, Judge Gamble, James H. Moss, William A. Hall, John B. Henderson, and James O. Broadhead.

While Mr. Moss, who was, by the way, a man of ability and character, would not vote to declare that Missouri would, under any circumstances, secede, he was opposed to coercion, and therefore offered a resolution declaring that Missouri would "never furnish men or money for the purpose of aiding the General Government in any attempts to coerce a seceding State."

In advocating this resolution he said:

"I submit to every man of common sense in this Assembly to tell me whether Missouri will ever furnish a regiment to invade a Southern State for the purpose of coercion. Never! *Never!* And, gentlemen! Missouri expects this Convention to say so. . . . I believe it to be the duty of Missouri to stand by the gallant men of southern Illinois, who have declared that they will never suffer a Northern army to pass the southern boundary of Illinois for the purpose of invading a Southern State."

To this William A. Hall replied with unanswerable argument that if Missouri remained in the Union it would be her duty to furnish both men and money to the General Government when properly called upon for them, whether to coerce a State into submission, or for any other purpose. To say that she would not do this, would be an idle threat at best, and a mischievous one. Threats on the part of Northern men or communities might have a good effect by showing the willingness of some men at the North to be just to the South. But such threats coming from a Southern State would only encourage the seceding States and enrage the North.

The Convention voted down the proposition of Mr. Moss; and "the pitiless logic of facts" forced him afterwards to raise and command a regiment for the subjugation of the South!

While *acting* consistently with their new-born determination to stand by the Union, the Conditional Union men still *talked* as they had been wont to talk when they were soliciting the votes of the Southern people of Missouri. Even John B. Henderson, daring and reckless as he had become in his newly awakened zeal and loyalty, opposed Moss's resolution only because it was *useless*.

"Does any man suppose," said he, "that the President of the United States will so far disregard his duties under the Constitution, or forget the obligation of his oath, as to undertake the subjugation of the Southern States by force? Will the abstract principle of the enforcement of the laws ever be carried by the President to the extent of military subjugation? If so, this Government is at an end. Will you tell me that Mr. Lincoln will send Don Quixotes into the Southern States with military force to subjugate those States? Certainly not. . . . He who dreams that this Government was made or intended to subjugate any one of the States dreams certainly against the spirit, against the intent, and against the whole scope of our institutions. . . . The President has no more power to use force than you or I. Why, then, should Missouri declare that she will under no circumstances lend means or money to the enforcement of the laws by the Federal Government?"

There were a few who still dared to speak as Southern men in a Missouri Convention, and to express in the presence of Blair's Home Guards and of United States troops and in the centre of the loyal city of St. Louis, the opinions which they had expressed during the canvass to their Southern-born constituents. Among these were Prince L. Hudgins and John T. Redd. The former, in the course of an able and impassioned argument in support of Moss' proposition, said:

"I do not believe that a State has a constitutional right to secede; but seven States claim to have seceded, and I, for one, am anxious to bring them back. You cannot do this by threats, nor by force, nor by abuse. They have done what they thought best for themselves, for their children, and for their children's children. They have done it deliberately and after great consideration. . . . If Missouri wishes to bring them back, she must remember that they are our brethren; that they must be treated not as traitors, but as patriots; and that they can only be brought back upon fair and honorable terms. . . . The Federal Government has no right to force them back; and if it had such a right, this Convention should say that it *ought* not to be, and in the language of Virginia and Kentucky, *must* not be, used. It has been settled beyond the power of refutation that the Government has no right to march an armed force into a State in order to subjugate it. If this be so, cannot Missouri have the courage to say that, if Abraham Lincoln, in violation of the Constitution, and in violation of his oath, march an army into the South, she will not aid him with men and money?

"It is strange that any man who lives in Missouri, and believes in her institutions, should hesitate to declare that she will not engage in such a war. It would be a dreadful thing to do, even if the Constitution, and the flag of our country, and our own honor required us to do it—to make war upon the land in which we were born, and whose churchyards are filled with the graves of our ancestors; to desolate the homes and to shed the blood of our kindred. It is too horrible to contemplate. Missouri never will do it. . . .

"Nor can I believe for one moment that Missouri intends, or that this Convention will say that is her duty, to submit to Northern aggression, to give up her institutions, and to sacrifice her honor. Let our slaves go if they must, let all our property be sacrificed, but let us maintain our honor—the honor of freemen. If ever the President command

Missourians to shed the blood of their Southern brothers, they should take the halter in one hand and the sword in the other and tell him that when he had taken the one he might use the other. I have no submission blood in my veins. If I had I would let it out with a knife."

John T. Redd, of Marion, was even more emphatic than Hudgins. They were both men of ability, and of high standing, and their words had weight with the people of Missouri. It is a pity to offer the reader only a dry summary of their speeches. They ought to be read in full by every one who wishes to comprehend the motives which governed the conduct of the men who took up arms against the Federal Government.

"If the General Government send troops upon Southern soil to retake the forts now in the hands of those States, to retake the custom-houses for the purpose of collecting the revenue, or for any other purpose, the Union is gone. If it be once dissolved it can never be reconstructed, because between the sundered sections there will be a gulf of blood.

"It is my opinion that if the General Government will not wait till the country can, by conciliation and compromise, save the Union, Missouri should and will take the stand with her Southern sisters; and that, having failed to obtain their rights, having failed to obtain any guarantee from that great anti-slavery party which has so long trampled the Constitution under foot, she and they should take their stand outside of the Union, taking with them the Constitution, and that glorious banner which they have baptized in the blood of a hundred battle-fields, and fight, if need be, for their rights and institutions, as their fathers fought, and until the last drop of blood be spilled. . . . If she is to remain in the Union at the sacrifice of her institutions and her rights, she should change the device of her coat-of-arms, remove from it the grizzly bears, whose rugged nature was never animated by a craven spirit, and substitute in their place a fawning spaniel, cowing at the feet of its master, and licking the hand that smites it.

Even Broadhead, an Unconditional Union member from St. Louis, did not believe that the Federal Government had a right to coerce a State; but he found in the power which it had to call out the militia in order to execute the laws, to suppress insurrection, and to repel invasion, abundant authority to use force for the preservation of the Union.

Argument and declamation had, however, little to do with the settlement of the question, and with determining the action of the Convention. It was a *fact* which decided the matter and *persuaded* that body to declare that Missouri would adhere loyally to the Union. *This fact* was bluntly announced to the Convention and to the people of the State by Broadhead, who was not only a delegate to the Convention but a member of the Union Safety Committee of St. Louis and a trusted counsellor of Mr. Lincoln, at the conclusion of his speech, in these words: "Missouri cannot go out of the Union if she would. I think I know what I say when I speak it, *Missouri has not the power to go out of the Union if she would."* What he meant will appear in the sequel. He did know what he was saying.

The Convention adopted Gamble's report and resolutions, and a few days afterwards (March 21) adjourned subject to the call of a committee, which it named.

Early in the session, the General Assembly had refused to elect a United States Senator in place of James S. Green, whose term was to expire on the 3d of March. It had done this upon the ground that it was better to learn first whether Missouri would remain in the Union or not. It being now obvious that the State would not secede, the General Assembly proceeded to the election of a Senator (March 12th). The Democrats nominated Green for the place, but found it impossible, after several days' balloting, to elect so pronounced a Secessionist as he. Waldo P. Johnson was thereupon elected. It is a noteworthy fact that Green, who was relegated to private life because he was a Secessionist, did not raise his hand or his voice in behalf of the South during the war, while Johnson, who had been elected because he was a good Union man, quickly resigned his seat in the Senate, entered the army, and fought for the Confederacy till the end of the war.

Of Green, Mr. Blaine, who rarely permits himself to write justly or fairly about any Southern man says: "No man among his contemporaries had made so profound an impression in so short a time. He was a very strong debater. He had peers, but no master, in the Senate. Mr. Green on the one side, and Mr. Fessenden on the other, were the Senators whom Douglas most disliked to meet, and who were best fitted in readiness, in accuracy, and in logic to meet him. Douglas rarely had a debate with either in which he did not lose his temper, and to lose one's temper in debate is generally to lose one's cause. Green had done more than any other man in Missouri to break down the power of Thomas H. Benton as a leader of the Democracy. His arraignment of Benton before the people of Missouri in 1849, when he was but thirty-two years of age, was one of the most aggressive and most successful warfares in our political annals."

After serving several years in the House of Representatives, he had been elected to the United States Senate in January 1859, and became the leader of the pro-slavery men in the Congressional contest for the possession of Kansas. He bore himself there with so much dignity and courtesy, and was so able in argument and brilliant in debate, that he won the admiration of every one and deserved even higher praise than that which Mr. Blaine accords to him.

Although the Secessionists had, through defection of some of their number, lost control of the House of Representatives, and could not consequently enact any measure looking toward the secession of the State, they could, nevertheless, bring to their support a majority of the House, whenever they attacked the Republican party and not the Union; for many men who were devoted to the Union were bitterly hostile to the Republicans, and especially hostile to that party as it was constituted in St. Louis. In that city, it consisted almost wholly of Germans, though their leaders were chiefly Kentuckians and Virginians. They were in possession of the City Government, and their Mayor was a stern and uncompromising partisan, a member of the Union Safety Committee, and a man who would not hesitate to use the police force and all the power and resources of the city to repress any movements on the part of the Secessionists. He was sustained also by the powerful semi-military organization of Home Guards, and could, in the moment of need, call them to his aid as special constables and, by investing them with the panoply of the law, thrice arm them for the fight. These companies, as has already been told, had, previous to the election of the 18th of February, become so turbulent and aggressive as to alarm the peaceful residents of the city, and recent events had made them more arrogant and more dangerous still. It had therefore become a matter of supreme importance to the Secessionists to take these great powers from the Mayor, and accordingly a law was now enacted for creating a Board of Police Commissioners and authorizing a police force for the city of St. Louis. This bill, which passed the Senate on the 2d of March, and the House on the 23d, authorized the Governor, with the consent of the Senate, to appoint four commissioners, who, along with the Mayor of the city, should have absolute control of the police, of the Volunteer Militia of St. Louis, and of the sheriff and all other conservators of the peace. This act summarily took away from the Republican Mayor and transferred to the Governor through his appointees, the whole police power of the city of St. Louis. This was its expressed intention. It had other and more important purposes which were carefully concealed.

On the 22d of March, the President of the Convention transmitted to the General Assembly the resolution requesting that body to take the proper steps for calling a Convention of all the States to propose amendments to the Constitution.

Mr. Vest reported (March 27th) from the committee to whom the resolution was referred, that "Going into council with our oppressors before we have agreed among ourselves, can never result in good. It is not the North that has been wronged, but the South, and the South can alone determine what securities in the future will be sufficient. The interests of Missouri, all her sympathies and the affections of her people render her destiny the same with that of the Border Slave States. Mediation by one State alone will amount to nothing. Let us first agree with those whom God and Nature have made our associates in council, and then, in a temperate but firm manner, make known our united decision to the people of the North. If such a demand, coming from the people of eight sister States, swelling in a tone of grandeur and power which *should* sway the destinies of the universe, shall be disregarded, then, indeed, all hopes of reconstruction would be ended, and appealing to the civilized world a united South, with common lineage, common feelings and common institutions, would take their place among the nations of the earth. With these opinions the committee beg leave to report that it is inexpedient for the General Assembly to take any step towards calling a National Convention."

In the course of the debate upon this report, Vest said: "The Convention has been guilty of falsehood and deceit. It says that there is no cause for separation. If this be so, why call a Convention? In declaring that if the other Border Slave States seceded Missouri would still remain within the Union, these wiseacres have perpetrated a libel upon Missouri. So help me God! if the day ever comes when Missouri shall prove so recreant to herself, so recreant to the memories of the past and to the hopes of the future, as to submit tamely to these Northern Philistines, I will take up my household gods and leave the State. Make another Constitution and these Northern Vandals will trample it under foot. . . . I appeal to the people of Missouri to maintain their rights. I defy the Convention. They are political cheats, jugglers, and charlatans, who foisted themselves upon the people by ditties and music and striped flags. They do not represent Missouri. They have crooked the pliant hinges of the knee that thrift might follow fawning. As for myself, two grandfathers who fought for our liberties rest in the soil of Virginia, and two uncles who fought in the Revolution, sleep in the land of the Dark and Bloody Ground. With such blood in my veins, I will never, *never*, NEVER submit to Northern rule and dictation, I will risk all to be with the Southern people, and, if defeated, I can with a patriot of old exclaim,

> ' More true joy an exile feels,
> Than Cæsar with a Senate at his heels.' "

The Legislature, having adopted the report, adjourned the next day, March the 28th.

The Secessionists now began to gather strength again. The Governor had never wavered in his determination to hold the State firm to her pledge to resist the coercion of the South. And now many of those who had in January and February and in the early days of March been deluded into the belief that it was still possible to prevent war had at last come to the conclusion that war was inevitable, that a collision would sooner or later take place between the Federal Government and the South, and that Missouri would have to take part in the conflict; and they were now taking sides with the Governor. In St. Louis, particularly, a strong revulsion of feeling had set in against Blair and his followers. Their open preparation for war alarmed the great land owners and rich merchants of St. Louis, who preferred peace to everything else, and it frightened thousands of others whose prosperity depended on the continuance of Southern trade, which would be instantly stopped by war. It was plain now that the South was for peace, and the North for war. The Secessionists had thus become the party of peace, and they were joined by every man who wanted that above all things. It was useless for Mr. Lincoln to say that he was averse to war. All men knew that, but they also knew that it was *only by war* that he could maintain the Union. The common sense of the people recognized this fact, and that they acted upon it was abundantly proven when the Municipal Election took place in St. Louis on the 1st of April, and the Unconditional Union men, who had carried the city in February by a majority of 5,000, were defeated by a majority of 2,600.

This was a declaration in favor, not of secession, but of peace, and against making war upon the South; and there were still men—thousands of men—in St. Louis, and throughout Missouri—who continued to believe that war might yet be averted; and there were others who foolishly fancied that, even if war raged from the Lakes to the Gulf and from the Atlantic to the Pacific, Missouri could, in the midst of the bloody strife, remain neutral and enjoy unbroken peace.

There were, however, two classes of men in Missouri who had never indulged in these baseless hopes; who had seen at the outset that war was inevitable, and had then begun to prepare for war. At the head of the one stood the Governor of the State, Claiborne F. Jackson; at the head of the other Francis P. Blair, Jr. Never did either of them quail in the presence of any danger, nor shrink from the performance of any duty, however difficult or perilous, which he was called upon to encounter, or to undertake, in defense, or in maintenance, of the principles to which he had devoted his life. Under the banner of the State upheld by the one or under the flag of the Union uplifted by the other, all earnest men had at last begun to rally. What these men *did* is what must now be told.

II. MILITARY.

CHAPTER V.

FRANK BLAIR REBELS AGAINST THE STATE.

The Department of the West—General William S. Harney—The St. Louis Arsenal—Major William H. Bell—Isaac H. Sturgeon—Federal Troops brought to St. Louis—Frank Blair organizes Rebellion against the State—The Home Guards—The Minute Men—Basil W. Duke—Frost's Brigade—Daniel M. Frost—His Negotiations with Major Bell—General Scott removes Bell—Major Hagner in Command.

AT the beginning of 1861 that part of the United States west of the Mississippi was divided into five Military Departments—*The West, Texas, New Mexico, Utah,* and *The Pacific.*

The most important of these, *The Department of the West*, embraced all the country lying between the Mississippi River and the Rocky Mountains, except Texas, New Mexico, and Utah. It was under the command of Brigadier-General William S. Harney, and its head-quarters were at St. Louis.

Harney was an officer of large experience and great gallantry. Appointed to the army from civil life in 1818, he had done hard and conspicuous service in the Florida War, and had fought under Scott in Mexico, and won distinction on many fields; had been brevetted brigadier-general for his conduct at

Cerro Gordo, and had been promoted to that full rank in 1858. Though more than sixty years old he was still in the vigor of his robust manhood, very tall, broad-shouldered, and as straight as an arrow, and his bronzed features were flushed with the glow of an exuberant vitality. He had married long before in St. Louis, and was living there in luxury; for he was a man of wealth, fond of society and addicted to its pleasures. Possessed of no great intellect, he had, nevertheless, what often supplies its place among soldiers, energy, courage, and a high sense of honor. He was, moreover, devoted to the service, adventurous and fearless—was, in fact, an ideal dragoon. Though a Louisianian by birth, and himself a slave holder, though his family and intimates were Southern people and slave holders, and though he himself sympathized with the South in its struggle against the North, he loved the Union, and knew no other country, and was absolutely loyal to the flag under which he had served so many years and so gallantly.

In the southern part of the city, on the shore of the Mississippi, was the St. Louis Arsenal. It contained about sixty thousand stand of arms and a large supply of other munitions of war, and the workshops were extensive and well equipped. In addition to the artisans employed in these shops there were at the post several ordnance officers and a few men detailed from the troops at Jefferson Barracks. These barracks were ten miles farther down the river, and were occupied by a small force, mostly recruits, commanded by Major Macrae.

The commandant of the arsenal was Major William H. Bell, a North Carolinian. On graduating at West Point in 1820, he had been assigned to ordnance duty, and had ever since belonged to that branch of the service. St. Louis was virtually his home; for, in the course of his long service in the army, he had been stationed there many years, and by prudent investments had amassed a considerable fortune in town lots and suburban property; and there, too, he had formed the chief friendships of his life. He was a capable officer, and bore a high character both in the army and among his friends in civil life.

The seizure by the seceding States of the Federal forts and other public property within their limits during the last days of December, and in the early days of January, had naturally turned the thoughts of every man in Missouri to this arsenal, whose great stores of arms and ammunition were of incalculable value at that juncture. There was also gold to the amount of $400,000 in the vaults of the Assistant Treasurer at St. Louis. That official, Isaac H. Sturgeon, a Kentuckian, had lived many years in St. Louis, and was well known there as an active, shrewd, and cunning politician, of no mean ability. He had always been identified with the Southern Rights wing of the Missouri Democracy; had resisted the mild free-soilism of Colonel Benton; had vigorously opposed the squatter sovereignty theories of Stephen A. Douglas; was a follower of President Buchanan, who had appointed him to office; and had earnestly supported Breckinridge during the late canvass. He generally consorted with Southerners, and was believed by the semi-secessionists of the city and State to be one of themselves. From them he learned what were the plans, or rather the talk, of the more reckless members of that party, and fancied that an attack was about to be made by them not only upon the arsenal, but upon the Government funds in his own custody.

He accordingly wrote on the 5th of January a guarded letter to the President (of whose sentiments he was not quite sure), and in it said that he was greatly concerned for the safety, not only of the public funds in his own hands, but of the munitions of war at the arsenal, as it was plain that "*both* parties had their eyes fixed upon those two points;" and that he would, therefore, "venture to suggest" to the President the propriety of concentrating troops at the arsenal, for the protection of the property there, and of the "treasure" in his own custody.

This letter having been referred by the President to General Scott, the latter forthwith sent Lieutenant Robinson with a detachment of forty men, from Newport Barracks to St. Louis, "to be placed by the department commander at the disposal of the Assistant Treasurer." This detachment reached St. Louis on the morning of the 11th of January, and was quartered in the Government Building, wherein were the custom house, the post office, the Federal courts and the Assistant Treasury.

This absurd display of force by the Government provoked the intensest excitement throughout the city. Extras were issued by the papers; great crowds began to gather around the post office; and an outbreak would have followed, had not General Harney wisely ordered the troops to the arsenal, and thereby quieted the people. No one seemed to be able to explain the coming of these Federal soldiers. The Assistant Treasurer kept himself prudently out of view.

As soon as the fact had been telegraphed to Jefferson City, the Governor called the attention of the General Assembly to it, and Senator Parsons offered these resolutions:

"*Resolved*, That we view this act of the administration as insulting to the dignity and patriotism of this State, and calculated to arouse suspicion and distrust on the part of her people towards the Federal Government.

"*Resolved,* That the Governor be requested to inquire of the President what has induced him to place the property of the United States within this State in charge of an armed Federal force."

The removal of the troops from the post office to the arsenal caused the General Assembly to drop the matter. But the incident had important consequences nevertheless, the very reverse, however, of what had been intended by Mr. Sturgeon; for it set both Union men and Secessionists to making serious and diligent preparation to get possession of the arms in the arsenal.

It was now that Blair first began to convert the Wide-Awakes into Home Guards, and to drill, discipline, and arm them. He saw that the time for action had come. The State Government had, with the new year, passed into the hands of a Governor, who was an avowed sympathizer with the seceding States, and was pledged to resist all attempts of the Federal Government to enforce its laws within those States, and he was supported by a General Assembly, one House of which was almost unanimously, and the other very decidedly, in accord with him. A law had already passed the Senate, and was pending in the House, to take away from the Republican Mayor of St. Louis all authority over the Volunteer Militia of that city, and to confer that power upon the Governor instead; and Blair knew that the object of this law was not only to deprive the Mayor of the means with which to help the Federal Government, in case of disturbances in St. Louis, but also to range the military companies of the city on the side of the Secessionists, if the latter should undertake to seize the arsenal, or if any conflict should take place between them and the Union men.

Blair did not hesitate. He never did. But, availing himself of the excitement produced by the bringing of Federal troops to St. Louis, he began the formation of companies of Home Guards, that self-same night. The work, once begun, was carried on actively by him, with the assistance of a committee of safety of which Oliver D. Filley, Mayor of the city, was chairman, and James O. Broadhead, secretary. Its other members were Samuel T. Glover, a Kentuckian, John How, a Pennsylvanian, and Julius J. Witzig, a German. Filley was a New Englander and Broadhead a Virginian.

The first company which they enrolled was composed of both Germans and Americans, and Frank Blair was elected captain. Eleven companies, aggregating about seven hundred and fifty officers and men, nearly all of them Germans, were soon drilling and getting ready for active service. Some of them were armed (partly by Governor Yates of Illinois, and partly by private contributions), but most of them were still unarmed, at the time that the election of delegates to the State Convention took place.

The Governor and other Southern Rights men viewed these Home Guards with just apprehension; and consequently they put into the military bill, then before the Legislature, a clause which was intended to disband them. This clause required the commanding officer of each of the several military districts into which the State was divided to disarm every organization within his district, which had not been "regularly organized and mustered into the service of the State;" and to confiscate the arms of such organizations to the use of the State. Had this bill become a law in February, the course of events in Missouri might have been essentially changed.

The St. Louis Secessionists were no less active than the Union men. They were few in number; but most of them were young, ardent, and full of zeal. They regretted the determination of the Cotton States to secede. They would rather have had them remain within the Union, and fight within it for their constitutional rights. But they believed nevertheless that these States had the right to secede and to establish a separate Government if they chose to do so. Whether this was a constitutional right, or a revolutionary right they did not care; nor ought they to have cared. For the God-given right of revolution is a higher and a more sacred right than any which is based upon the mere bargainings and concessions of men. The people who abandon it or fear to assert it always lose their freedom sooner or later and sink surely to the condition of serfs or slaves. To the exercise of this natural right in 1776 the Republic owes its existence. To the assertion of it by the South in 1861 the Republic owes its present grandeur, and its perfect unity.

When South Carolina seceded these young St. Louisians no longer doubted that all the Cotton States would secede and form a Southern Confederacy, that between this Confederacy and the Union war would ensue, and that in this war the whole country would take part. For themselves they were resolved to fight with and for the South, among whose people and upon whose soil most of them had been born.

Throwing aside all vain regrets and bravely accepting the inevitable, they began at once to fit themselves for war; began to learn the rudiments of the art in the school of the soldier. They were very few, however, till Sturgeon's folly set fire to the passions of men and lit the flames of civil war on the soil of Missouri. Many then joined their ranks—many who had hitherto held aloof for love of the Union or for the sake of peace, but who now despaired of both.

Among these was Basil Wilson Duke, a young lawyer from Kentucky. He was about twenty-five years of age, able, enterprising, and bold; giving promise, even then, of those soldierly qualities which eventually made him John Morgan's most trusted lieutenant and the brilliant commander of a Confederate cavalry brigade. In the presidential election he had supported Douglas with great zeal and some eloquence, and since then had earnestly deprecated disunion and striven to stay the current that was setting toward secession in Missouri. Now he awoke suddenly to the conviction that the North was going to make war upon the South. That was enough for him. To go with his people when they were attacked; to stand by them when they were in danger, uncaring whether they were right or wrong; to share *their* perils, and to fight with them against *their* foes, was with him an instinct and a duty. He at once joined the small band of secessionists and became their most conspicuous leader. Among them he found men as brave and as earnest as he; some of them with ability equal to his own, and talents as useful, perhaps, though not so brilliant and attractive.

One of these, Colton Greene, was a prosperous young merchant, hardly as old as Duke. A South Carolinian by birth, he sympathized earnestly with the people of that State and justified their conduct in seceding. With a rather delicate physical organization, and of a retiring disposition, he possessed fine sensibilities, a cultivated intellect which was both sharp and strong, courage, and determination. He was, withal, painstaking, laborious and earnest, upright and honorable.

These two, with Rock Champion a great-hearted young Irishman, and a few others as daring, were as quick to organize the Secessionists into *Minute Men* as Blair had been to organize his Wide-Awakes into *Home Guards;* and they did it boldly and openly, beginning it the very day that the Federal troops arrived at St. Louis.

Never was there a finer body of young fellows than these *Minute Men*. Some were Missourians; some from the North; some from the South; and others were Irishmen. Among them all there was hardly a man who was not intelligent, educated, and recklessly brave. Some who had the least education were as brave as the bravest, and as true as the truest. Most of them fought afterwards on many a bloody field. Many of them died in battle. Some of them rose to high commands. Not one of them proved false to the cause to which he then pledged his faith.

They established their head-quarters at the old Berthold mansion, in the very heart of the city, at the corner of Fifth and Pine Streets, and also formed and drilled companies in other parts of the city, against the time that they could arm and equip themselves. They were hardly three hundred in all, but they were so bold and active, so daring and ubiquitous, that every one accounted them ten times as numerous.

Like Blair and the Home Guards, they had their eyes fixed upon the arsenal, and expected out of its abundant stores to arm and equip themselves for the coming fight. In that arsenal were sixty thousand good muskets, while in all the Confederate States there were not one hundred and fifty thousand more. They were barely three hundred men, and more than ten thousand stood ready to resist them; but for love of the South, and for love of the right, and for the honor of Missouri, they were willing to peril their lives any day to get those muskets. And they would have gotten them or perished in the attempt but for the advice of their leaders at Jefferson City.

These counseled delay. They believed that it was better to wait till the people should, in their election of delegates to the Convention, declare their purpose to side with the South. They never doubted that the people would do this; never doubted that they would elect a Convention which would pledge Missouri to resist the subjugation of the South, and would put her in position to do it. Sustained by the voice of the people, and instructed by their votes, the Governor would then order General Frost to seize the arsenal in the name of the State, and he, with his brigade and the *Minute Men*, and the thousands that would flock to their aid, could easily do it.

In anticipation of all this and of the passage of the military bill, one of whose provisions required, as has been told, the disbandment of all unauthorized military companies, the *Minute Men* were now organized, according to law, and five companies duly mustered into the State service by General Frost on the 13th of February.

These companies—Captains Barret, Duke, Shaler, Greene and Hubbard—were then formed into a battalion, of which Captain James R. Shaler was elected major, and were assigned to Frost's Brigade. They afterwards formed part of Bowen's Regiment.

Daniel M. Frost was a native of New York. Graduating at West Point, in 1844, he had served creditably in the Mexican War, and afterwards on the frontier. Marrying in St. Louis, in 1851, he soon afterwards resigned his commission in the army and engaged in business in that city. Turning his attention to politics, he was elected to the

State Senate, and, as a member of that body, procured the enactment of the law under which the militia of the State was now organized. Under the provisions of that law he enlisted in 1858–9 the troops which constituted the First Brigade of Missouri Volunteer Militia, and, having béen appointed brigadier-general, was assigned to the command of it. This brigade consisted of a regiment of infantry and some separate companies, and aggregated about five hundred and eighty officers and men.

It had recently returned from the western border of the State, whither it had been sent in November to repel the incursions of a band of Kansas desperadoes, who, under lead of a Captain Montgomery, were ravaging the frontier counties of Missouri. On this expedition the men had learned something of the duties of an army in the field, and, uneventful as the campaign was, had acquired much of the spirit and bearing of regular troops, and looked upon themselves and were regarded by others as veterans, which, indeed, many of them in fact were.

Frost, in view of the threatening aspect of affairs, took every means to foster and strengthen this soldierly spirit of his men, and to prepare them thoroughly for war. In all this, he was zealously aided by both officers and men; and towards the 1st of February, his little brigade—a complete army in itself, with infantry, artillery and dragoons—was fully equipped, well drilled and disciplined, and ready to take the field.

Neither he nor his men had any very precise idea of the part which they would be called upon to take in the event of war between the North and the South. Like himself, they were, for the most part, Union men, but opposed to the subjugation of the South. Few of them expected to use their arms against the United States; fewer still to use them against the South. They were citizens and soldiers of Missouri and were ready to fight for her. Further than that they did not then look, or care to look.

The Governor trusted Frost fully, and he trusted him rightly. For Frost was not only an accomplished soldier, well instructed in the art of war and experienced in all of its lesser duties, and one of the best of organizers and disciplinarians, but he was also perfectly true to the State, whose officer he was, and ready to defend her against all assailants, whoever they might be, and under whatever guise they might appear. It was for her to decide, in Convention, what position she would take if war should happen. Till then, it was his duty to obey the orders of his commander-in-chief, her Governor. One thing, however, he would not do. He would not make war upon the South. Virginians like Gamble and Bates and Broadhead, and Kentuckians like Blair and Brown and Glover, might, under the influence of a sublime patriotism, and a Brutus-like devotion to the Union, send down armies to lay waste their native land, and slay their brothers, and widow their sisters, and drive them far away from their ruined homes, but he, Northern-born though he was, would not help them to do it.

Whatever judgment history shall, in the distant future, pass upon the conduct of those Northern men, who, living in the South, like Frost, stood by the South in her hour of great peril, and bared their swords in her defence, fighting for the weak against the strong, the people for whom these men fought should always hold them in honor, and in the most grateful remembrance.

No one comprehended more clearly than General Frost the necessity which compelled Missouri to keep the arsenal and its stores within her grasp, if she would arm and equip her people; as arm them she must, sooner or later, whether to fight for the Union, or against it, or to maintain her own neutrality. This necessity he made manifest to the Governor, and was by him authorized to seize the arsenal, whenever the occasion might require such decisive action.

In the performance of the duty thus entrusted to him, Frost came to an understanding with Major Bell, the commandant of the arsenal. In communicating this fact to the Governor the General wrote on the 24th of January:

"I have just returned from the arsenal. . . . I found the Major everything that you or I could desire. He assured me that he considered that Missouri had, whenever the time came, a right to claim it as being on her soil. He asserted his determination to defend it against any, and all irresponsible mobs, come from whence they might, but at the same time gave me to understand that he would not attempt any defence against the proper State authorities.

"He promised me, upon the honor of an officer and a gentleman, that he would not suffer any arms to be removed from the place without first giving me timely information; and I promised him, in return, that I would use all the force at my command to prevent him being annoyed by irresponsible persons.

"I, at the same time, gave him notice that, if affairs assumed so threatening a character as to render it unsafe to leave the place in its comparatively unprotected condition, I might come down and quarter a proper force there to protect it from the assaults of any persons whatsoever, to which he assented. In a word the Major is with us, where he ought to be, for all his worldly wealth lies here in St. Louis (and it is very large), and then again, his sympathies are with us. . . .

"I shall be thoroughly prepared with the proper force to act as the emergency may require, but the use of force will only be resorted to when nothing else will avail to prevent the shipment or removal of the arms.

". . . The arsenal, if properly looked after, will be everything to our State, and I intend to look after it; very quietly, however. I have every confidence in the word of honor pledged to me by the Major, and would as soon think of doubting the oath of the best man in the community. . . . Of course I did not show him your order, but I informed him that you had authorized me to act as I might think proper to protect the public property."

It must be remembered that though Missouri was at that time within the Union, the right of the several States to the Federal property within their limits had not then been as clearly defined as it has since been by the high court of war, the supremest of all earthly tribunals.

But the United States Government was now getting ready to defend the arsenal against *Home Guards*, *Minute Men*, and the *State*.

Sturgeon, elated by the success of his first attempt to direct the movements of the United States army, and encouraged by the less pacific attitude which the President had latterly assumed toward the South, wrote again, and less guardedly, to the President, on the day after Lieutenant Robinson's arrival at St. Louis (January 12).

"The secession paper of the city," said he, "and those who follow it seemed to think it highly improper that the Government should send troops here to guard its public property from seizure. All Union men, however, are gratified that the Government has taken this precautionary measure. I wish it was about two hundred instead of forty men."

To General Scott he wrote the same day, and, as was becoming, wrote somewhat as one soldier might write to another:

"About two hundred (200) men, well officered and well armed, should be kept in the arsenal to furnish a nucleus around which the Union-loving, law-abiding, and conservative elements of the city might rally to prevent any unlawful proceeding."

These letters from Sturgeon, and perhaps others from other people, turned General Scott's attention to St. Louis, and a few days later Major Peter V. Hagner was ordered to relieve Major Bell as commandant of the arsenal, and the latter was ordered to New York. Instead of obeying this order, Major Bell resigned his commission in the army and retired to his farm in St. Charles County, Missouri. Major Hagner assumed command of the post on the 24th of January.

Hagner was a native of Washington city. He

graduated at West Point in 1836, and during the Florida War served in the artillery. He was transferred to the ordnance department in 1838. In the war with Mexico he was brevetted captain for gallant and meritorious conduct at Cerro Gordo. For his conduct at Chapultepec he was brevetted major. At the St. Cosme gate he was wounded while gallantly fighting. His commission as captain of ordnance was dated July 10, 1851. His brevet rank of major dated from September 13, 1847. The significance of these dates will appear in the course of this story. He was now about forty-eight years of age, and was recognized by every one as an officer of ability, experience, integrity, and honor, and worthy of all confidence.

CHAPTER VI.

NATHANIEL LYON.

Nathaniel Lyon—A Sketch of the Man and of his Career—He is ordered to the St. Louis Arsenal—Asserts his Right to the Command there—The President Sustains Hagner—Lyon wins Blair's Confidence—Drills and Disciplines the Home Guards—Renews his Contest with Hagner—Reinforcement of the Arsenal—The State Election—Overwhelming defeat of the Secessionists—Their Momentary Submission—Lyon and Blair again urge Hagner's Displacement—Lyon denounces Hagner's "Imbecility or Damned Villany," and General Scott's "Sordid Partisanship and Fondness for Toadies"—What He would do—The Minute Men try to Provoke a Riot in St. Louis—Lyon Assigned to Command of all the Troops at the Arsenal, but not over Hagner and the Arsenal—The St. Louis Election—Defeat of the Union Men—Their Alarm—Lyon in Command at St. Louis—He distrusts Lincoln, but has faith in "Almighty Truth."

NATHANIEL LYON was born in Ashford, Connecticut, on the 14th of July, 1818. He entered West Point in 1837, and graduating in 1841 was assigned to the Second Infantry. With that regiment he served in Florida till 1842, and with it he took part in the war with Mexico. On the march from Vera Cruz to the city of Mexico he was promoted to the first lieutenancy of his company and as such commanded it during that campaign. At Cerro Gordo he was with Harney. For his gallant conduct in the battles of Churubusco and Contreras, he was, with three other officers, commended to the "special notice" of his brigade commander, and was brevetted captain on the 20th of August, 1847. On entering the city he was slightly wounded.

From 1849 to 1853 he was on duty in California, and while there made a successful campaign against the Clear Lake Indians of Northern California. General Persifor F. Smith, in his report to the War Department, says, "That all the officers in the expedition united in awarding the highest praise to Captain Lyon for his untiring energy, zeal, and skill, and attribute his success to the rapidity and secrecy of his marches, and to his skilful dispositions on the ground."

Many stories are told of his adventures in this wild region. On one occasion when all alone, he was attacked suddenly by three mounted Indians. His presence of mind and quickness of movement saved him. With a bullet he emptied the saddle of the foremost. Turning upon the next with his sabre, he buried its blade in the Indian's body. The third savage was glad to get away unharmed.

Returning to Benicia toward the end of September, 1851, Captain Lyon enjoyed a much-needed rest. He pictures himself, at this time, as continuing in his "usual and long established customs, growing old, indeed, but not ashamed to own it; proud, perhaps, but not haughty; prudent, it may be, in worldly affairs, yet not crafty for wealth; desirous enough of fame, but not infatuated with blind ambition; and, in general, taking the world as it comes, enjoying richly its many blessings, sympathizing with the unfortunate, and laughing with the indifference of cool philosophy at the sore disappointments with which selfishness and cupidity are ever torturing their victims."

During the greater part of 1852 he was on leave of absence in the Eastern States, and took great interest in the then pending presidential election. He was at that time a staunch Democrat, and so enthusiastic an admirer of Franklin Pierce, that on his way back to California he made a speech in his favor to his fellow-passengers on the steam-ship.

The next year he returned to the East with his regiment and spent a part of the winter at Washington. While there he listened eagerly to the debates in Congress on the question of slavery in the Territories, for the Kansas-Nebraska bill was then under consideration. His earnest nature was deeply impressed by what he heard, and his sympathies were aroused in behalf of the negro.

The next year (1854) he was sent with his company to Fort Riley, some 120 miles west of Kansas City, and there he got into the very midst of that bitter contention and savage warfare, with which North and South were then struggling for the possession of Kansas—for supremacy in the Union, and for freedom or slavery.

Lyon was not slow to espouse the cause of the slave, and to 'maintain it with all the earnestness of his Puritan disposition; and he did all that an officer of the army dared do for the success of the party of freedom, and for the triumph of the Free-State men.

Extracts from letters which he wrote about this time show how he was being educated for the work that he was to do in Missouri.

In March, 1855, he writes that "preparations are now in progress to resist the arrogant and insolent imposition of Missourians. Whether they will prove effective may be seen in the result. Indeed it is fully apprehended that the aggressions of the pro-slavery men will not be checked till a lesson has been taught them in letters of fire and blood."

In December, "I have seen so much of the overbearing domination of the pro-slavery people in Kansas toward the Free-State men that I am persuaded that the latter have either to fight in self-defence or submit ignobly to the demands of their aggressors. . . . I despair of living peaceably with our Southern brethren without making disgraceful concessions, but rest assured that this will not always be, and in this view I foresee ultimate sectional strife, which I do not care to delay." And about the same time he speaks of the then Secretary of War, as "that heartless villain, Jefferson Davis."

In 1856, he seriously considered whether it were not better to resign his commission, and quit the army, than, as one of its officers, aid in enforcing the laws of the United States in Kansas. He looked upon "the course of the General Government as selfish, partial and corrupt," and " could not submit to the self-debasement and humiliation of being employed as a tool in the hands of evil rulers for the accomplishment of evil ends." From the necessity of resigning he was saved by being ordered out of Kansas.

But he was in Kansas again in 1859, and taking as active an interest as ever in the contest between slavery and freedom; was with General Harney, in December 1860, when Frost's Brigade was sent by the Governor of Missouri to co-operate with Harney in arresting Montgomery, and protecting the country adjacent to Fort Scott; and was left by Harney at Fort Scott, after Montgomery and his band had dispersed and escaped.

From that post he wrote, January 27, 1861:

"I do not consider troops at all necessary here, and should much prefer to be employed in the legitimate and appropriate service of contributing to stay the idiotic fratricidal hands now at work to destroy our Government. . . . It is no longer useful to appeal to reason, but to the sword, and trifle no longer in senseless wrangling. I shall not hesitate to rejoice at the triumph of my principles, though this triumph may involve an issue, in which I certainly expect to expose, and very likely shall lose, my life. I would a thousand times rather incur this, than recall the result of our presidential election. We shall rejoice, though, in martyrdom if need be."

Four days later he was ordered to St. Louis, with his company.

He was now in the forty-third year of his age; of less than medium height; slender and angular; with abundant hair of a sandy color, and a coarse reddish-brown beard. He had deep-set blue eyes; features that were rough and homely; and the weather-beaten aspect of a man who had seen much hard service on the frontier. What manner of soldier he was will soon be seen.

His first act on reaching the arsenal was characteristic of the man, of his contentious spirit, and aggressive disposition, of his resolute purpose to have his own way, of his distrust of all conservative men, like Major Hagner. Though the latter was five years his senior in the service, his commission as captain was twenty days junior to Lyon's; for promotion in the ordnance was slower than in the infantry, to which Lyon belonged. But he had been assigned to duty at the arsenal according to his brevet rank of major, and that made him senior to Lyon.

No regard for Hagner's greater age, or longer service; no feeling of courtesy towards an older brother in arms, weighed with Lyon for a moment against the fact that Hagner was not an Abolitionist, that his wife was the daughter of a slaveholder, and himself the friend and associate of Southern sympathizers. Such a man was not, in his opinion, to be trusted with so important a command as the St. Louis arsenal; such a man was not fit to have authority over a true and loyal soldier like himself. He at once asserted his own right to the command, by virtue of his senior commission as captain. The question was submitted to General Harney. He sustained Hagner, and Lyon thereupon appealed to the President. He, too, sustained Hagner, and Lyon had to submit for the time.

This struggle with Hagner had not diverted his attention from what was happening around him, nor had it kept him out of the greater struggle to which it was merely subsidiary. He at once established the closest relations with Blair, and the other influential Union men of St. Louis, and by his zeal, intelligence and boldness won their instant and perfect confidence. They saw that he was the very man that they needed; that he had been sent to them, as it were, by Providence or by Fate to save Missouri to the Union.

Practical always, he went straight to work to organize, drill and discipline the Home Guards, and to convert them into soldiers upon whom he could rely to defend the arsenal and to fight the Secessionists. He frequented their drill-rooms and armories; instructed the officers and men; inspired them with confidence in himself; taught them too to have faith in themselves and in the cause for which they were going to battle; fired their enthusiasm; and inflamed their patriotism.

The election of delegates to the State Convention was to take place on the 18th of February. The whole Commonwealth was profoundly agitated. In St. Louis the wildest excitement prevailed. The Secessionists were confident of success, and openly boasted that if they carried the State they would seize the arsenal, and out of its stores arm equip and supply the State Guard, which the General Assembly would then authorize to be enlisted, and called into active service.

Blair and Lyon appreciated the danger, and redoubled their efforts to meet it. They believed that if they could get absolute control of the arsenal and its stores, they need not fear any force which the State or the Secessionists could bring against it; for they could then arm and equip the Home Guards and their other adherents, with these stores, and send what was left to Illinois where they would be safe.

Under no circumstances would Hagner distribute the arms to the Home Guards. He could not do it without violating the laws of his country and his oath as an officer; and these were things that he could not do. He had not yet learned that *war silences law* and burns up in its flames all formal oaths.

Lyon had learned this, and he knew that the country was on the verge of war; that armed men were gathering at the North and at the South to begin the deadly conflict; and he had made up his mind to issue the arms to the Home Guards in case of need, despite both Hagner and Harney. He would not let a law, which was intended for the safety of the Union, be used for the destruction of the Union; he would not stand idly by and let the arms which belonged to the Union be turned against the Union by its worst enemy. But he did not wish to be forced into an unlawful course, if it could be avoided; not that he cared much about it himself, but there were a great many law-abiding Union men in Missouri, whom it would be unwise to offend or to alarm. Their feelings and their prejudices must be consulted, or they might take part with the State and against the Federal Government. He and Blair resolved, accordingly, to try again to have himself placed in command of the arsenal. This would be accomplished if the President would order Hagner to be assigned to duty, without reference to his brevet rank.

"I should care nothing," said Lyon, "for the decision against me, as I have told Major Hagner, if he would take proper precautions for defence. The place is in imminent danger of attack, and the Governor of Missouri will no doubt demand its surrender if the State shall pass an ordinance of secession. The prospect is gloomy and forebodes an unnecessary sacrifice of life, in-case of hostile demonstrations. But I do not despair of an effective defence, and I hope to administer a lasting rebuke to the traitors who have thus far had their own way."

As the Buchanan administration would not listen to Blair and himself, they got Sturgeon to write again, on the 9th of February, to General Scott, and to advise him to reinforce the arsenal with all the troops that were at Jefferson Barracks, and to place Lyon in command of both them and the arsenal.

Scott ordered the troops to the arsenal, but he left Hagner in command; and on the 16th of February—two days before the election—203 officers and men were, in obedience to this order, brought to the arsenal, which was further reinforced a few days later, by 102 officers and men. These reinforcements increased the troops at the post to nine officers and 484 men. General Harney now informed the War Department in a report made on the 19th of February that there never had been any danger of an attack upon the arsenal, and that if one should be made "the garrison would be promptly rescued by an overwhelming force from the city."

Whatever danger may have existed had in fact passed. For the State had, in the election of delegates to the Convention, declared against secession by an overwhelming majority, and had affirmed the loyalty of her citizens to the Union. The Secessionists were for the moment utterly disheartened. The General Assembly sullenly submitted to the will of the people, and postponed the consideration of every measure looking to the preparation of the State for war, or for the maintenance even of her own neutrality.

Lyon and Blair were not deceived by these delusive signs of peace, nor did they relax their efforts to get ready for war. They knew that it would break out sooner or later, and that whoever then held the arsenal would hold St. Louis, and that whoever held St. Louis and the arsenal would in the end hold Missouri.

They did not even wait for the inauguration of

Lincoln, now only a few days off, but Blair himself hastened to Washington in order to beg Mr. Buchanan to immediately assign Lyon to the command of the arsenal; stopping, however, at Springfield to explain the condition of affairs to Mr. Lincoln, and to prepare him to act promptly on assuming office. But neither Mr. Buchanan nor General Scott would give heed to Blair's entreaties. For they distrusted both him and Lyon, and would not give them the power to inaugurate civil war in Missouri. Moreover, they had implicit confidence in both Harney and Hagner, and felt sure that they would do all that could be done for the safety of the arsenal, and for the maintenance of the Federal authority in Missouri.

Lyon meanwhile kept urging Hagner to strengthen the defences of the arsenal, and suggested many ways in which this could be done. Hagner paid no attention to his suggestions. Lyon, losing all patience, wrote to Blair on the 25th of February:

"Major Hagner refuses to do any of these things and has given his orders not to fly to the walls to repel an approach, but to let the enemy have all the advantages of the wall to lodge himself behind it, and get possession of all outside buildings overlooking us, and to get inside, and under shelter of *our* outbuildings, which we are not to occupy before we make resistance. *This is either imbecility or damned villany;* and in contemplating the risks we run, and the sacrifices that we must make in case of an attack, in contrast to the vigorous and effective defence we are capable of, and which (in view of the cause of our country and humanity, and the disgrace and degradation to which the Government has been subjected by pusillanimity and treachery) we are now called upon to make, I get myself into a most unhappy state of solicitude and irritability. With even less force and proper dispositions I am confident we can resist any force that can be brought against us; by which I mean such force as would not be overcome by our sympathizing friends outside. These needful dispositions, can, with proper industry, be made within twenty-four hours. There cannot be, as you know, a more important occasion, or a better opportunity to strike an effective blow at this arrogant infatuation of secessionism than here; and must all this be lost by either false notions of duty, or covert disloyalty?

"As I have said, Major Hagner has no right to the command, and, under the Sixty-second Article of War, can only have it by a special assignment of the President, which I do not believe has been made; but that *the announcement of General Scott that the command belongs to Major Hagner is his own decision and done in his usual sordid spirit of partisanship, and favoritism to pets, and personal associates, and toadies;* nor can he, even in the present straits of the country, rise above this in earnest devotion to justice and the wants of his country. If Mr. Lincoln chooses to be deceived in this respect, as I fear he will be, he will repent it in misfortune and sorrow; for neither supercilious conceit nor unscrupulous tyranny was ever a veil for patriotism or ability. Major Hagner is not accustomed to troops, and manages them here awkwardly, but this is nothing compared to the great matter on hand, and *this*, as I have plainly told him, is of much more importance than that either he, or I, should conduct it. A simple order, countermanding that assigning him to duty according to brevet rank, would give me command. With a view to defence here, it would, however, be well to add that I should assume control, and avail myself of all means available for the purpose. . . . If I should have command I would have no trouble to arm any assisting party, and perhaps, by becoming responsible for the arms, etc., I might fit out the regiment we saw at the Garden the other day."

An event which happened on the day that Lincoln was inaugurated, and on which the State Convention began its sessions at St. Louis (March 4th), came very near precipitating the conflict in Missouri, and gave Blair and Lyon good cause to press their demands upon the Government.

During the preceding night some of the Minute Men (Duke, Greene, Quinlan, Champion, and McCoy) raised the flag of Missouri over the dome of the Court-house, and hoisted above their own head-quarters a nondescript banner, which was intended to represent the flag of the Confederate States. The custodian of the Court-house removed the State flag from that building early in the morning; but the secession flag still floated audaciously and defiantly above the Minute Men's head-quarters, in the very face of the Submissionists' Convention, of the Republican Mayor, and his German police, of the department commander, and of Lyon and his Home Guards; and under its folds there was gathered as daring a set of young fellows as ever did a bold, or a reckless deed. They were about a score at first, but when an excited crowd began to threaten their quarters, and the rumor to fly that the Home Guards were coming to tear down their flag, the number of its defenders grew to about one hundred. They all had muskets of the latest and very best pattern. On the floors of the upper rooms were heaps of hand grenades. In the wide hall was a swivel, double-shotted, and so planted as to rake the main entrance if any one should be brave enough to try to force it. At every window there were determined men, with loaded muskets, and fixed bayonets; behind them were others, ready to take the place of any that might fall; and in all the building there was not a man who was not ready to fight to the death, rather than submit to the rule of Abraham Lincoln; nor one who would have quailed in the presence of a thousand foes, nor one of them that survives to-day, who would not fight just as willingly and just as bravely for the flag of the Union. Outside, too, throughout the ever-growing crowd, other Minute Men were stationed, to act as the emergency might require.

Before the hour of noon had come all the streets in the vicinity were thronged with excited men, some drawn thither by mere curiosity and by that strange magnetism which mobs always exert; some to take part with the Minute Men, if "the Dutch" should attack them; some to tear down "the rebel flag," and to hang "the traitors," who had dared to raise it on the day of Lincoln's inauguration.

Everything betokened a terrible riot and a bloody fight. The civil authorities were powerless. It was to no purpose that they implored the crowd to disperse; in vain that they begged the Minute Men to haul down their flag. The police could do nothing. The Home Guards did not dare to attack, for their leaders knew that the first shot that was fired would bring Frost's Brigade, which was largely composed of Minute Men, to the aid of their friends, and that they would also be reinforced by the Irish, between whom and the German Home Guards there was the antipathy of both race and religion. Only once did any one venture to approach the well-guarded portals of the strong-hold. The rash fools that did it were hurled back into the street, amid the jeers and laughter of the crowd. Blair and the Republican leaders, unwilling to provoke a conflict, kept their followers quiet, and finally towards midnight the crowd dispersed. The next day's sun shone upon the rebel flag still flying above the roof of the Minute Men's quarters. But Duke and Greene were unhappy, for they had hoped to bring on a fight, in which they would have been reinforced by Frost's Brigade, and the Irish and many Americans, and in the confusion to seize the arsenal, and hold it till the Secessionists of the State could come to their aid. They were, nevertheless, greatly elated because the people believed more than ever that there were thousands of Minute Men, instead of hundreds.

Blair used the incident with effect at the War Department, and a few days later (March 13) Lyon was assigned to the command of all the troops at the arsenal and of its defences. General Harney, however, still thwarted the desires of Blair and Lyon, by instructing the latter that the order of the War Department did not confer upon him any authority over Major Hagner, or any control over the arms and other material of war in the arsenal, which was the very thing that Blair and Lyon needed in order to issue arms to the Home Guards. For the full consummation of their desires they had still to wait.

Various causes which have been set out in a previous chapter, and among these the enactment of the law which placed the police, and all other conservators of the peace, and also the volunteer militia of St. Louis, under the orders of commissioners appointed by and in sympathy with the Governor, wrought a complete change in the political status of that city; and at the Municipal Election, which was held on the 1st of April, Daniel G. Taylor, the candidate of those who were opposed to Lincoln's administration and to war against the South, was chosen mayor by a majority of 2,658 votes, over John How, the candidate of the Unconditional Union men.

As Mr. How was an exceptionally popular man, a leading member of the Union Safety Committee, and a devoted supporter of Blair and Lyon, his defeat by so large a majority was in itself enough to alarm the Union men. But the matter was made worse for them by the fact that through this election the whole organized power of the city was taken from the Union men, and given to their enemies. The Governor had already put the police under the control of Duke, the leader of the Minute Men, James H. Carlisle and Charles McLaren, two avowed Secessionists, and John A. Brownlee, who, though a Northern man, was strongly opposed to the subjugation of the South.

This new danger only caused Lyon, who fully realized its magnitude, to become more resolute, and to work more earnestly. To some Union men, who expressed to him their fears that the Southern men would now try to seize the arsenal, he said that in that event he would issue arms to the Home Guards and Union men, law or no law; and that if Major Hagner interfered he would "pitch him into the river." To Blair, who was again in Washington, he wrote on the 6th of April that the Government should forthwith give him entire control of everything at the arsenal without exception of men or means. His desire had been already realized and in a way which was unexpected, for General Harney, who seems to have at last begun to recognize the fact that there was at least a possibility of war, had that very day made an order which virtually placed Hagner and the arsenal and everything in it under his command.

Lyon was now master of St. Louis. But, far from being content with the vantage that he had gained, he was only anxious to use it for the accomplishment of greater things. Impatient, earnest, and eager to get at the throats of "the traitorous slaveholders," he ill-brooked the slowness with which Lincoln seemed to be moving. He feared "that the President lacked the resolution to grapple with treason and to put it down forever;" that "he was not the man for the hour," and that "our political triumph had been in vain. If matters go on as they do, we shall soon have" (so he wrote) "a formidable array of hostile troops upon us. When this comes, it will, I trust, arouse the supine and timid North to a patriotic resolution, which shall, in spite of Executive tamperings, do something to retrieve her present degradation. If Mr. Lincoln does one tithe of his duty, as he has promised, we must have hostilities with the South. . . . I do not see how war is to be avoided. Under quack management it may be long and bloody, yet I have no apprehensions about the final triumph of Almighty Truth, though at the cost of many unnecessary sacrifices. But let them come! I would rather see the country lighted up with flames from its centre to its remotest borders, than that the great rights and hopes of the human race should expire before the arrogance of Secessionists. Of this, however, there is no danger. They are at war with nature and the human heart, and cannot succeed."

CHAPTER VII.

THE ARSENAL.

Bombardment of Fort Sumter—The President calls for Seventy-five Thousand Troops—The Reponse of the North—Its effect at the South and in the Border States—The Missouri *Republican*—Governor Jackson's Reply—Frost's Advice—The Legislature Convened—A plan to Capture the Arsenal—Commissioners sent South for Siege Guns—Frost's Brigade Ordered into Encampment—The Plan Divulged to Harney and Lyon—Lyon Calls on the Governor of Illinois for Troops, and occupies the Hills around the Arsenal—Bowen ordered to Report with his Command to Frost—Lyon authorized to Arm the Home Guards—Harney Countermands the Order—Seizure of Liberty Arsenal by Secessionists—Harney ordered to Washington City—Lyon arms the Home Guards, and sends the Surplus Arms to Alton.

WHILE these things were being done in Missouri, delegates from South Carolina, Georgia, Florida, Alabama, Louisiana, and Texas, had met at Montgomery Alabama, on the 4th of February; had adopted a Provisional Constitution for "the Confederate States of America" on the 8th; and had elected Jefferson Davis to be President and Alexander H. Stephens Vice-President of this Provisional Government on the 9th.

Mr. Davis, who was at that time in command of the army which Mississippi was raising for her defence, seems to have been reluctant to accept the Presidency. For he had at last come to believe, contrary to the common opinion of the Southern people, that war was at least likely to ensue; and, fancying himself better fitted for the field than for the Cabinet, preferred the command of an army to the Presidency. He and Mr. Stephens were, nevertheless, inaugurated on the 18th of February.

The Provisional Congress had already (February 12) taken under its charge the questions and difficulties then existing between the several Confederate States and the Government of the United States, relating to the occupation of forts, arsenals, navy yards, and other public establishments; and had also (February 15) requested the President elect to send three commissioners to Washington city to treat with the Federal Government as to those matters, and to establish friendly relations with the United States.

These commissioners opened informal negotiations with the Administration on the 12th of March, with relation chiefly to the evacuation of Fort Sumter), and succeeded at last in getting from the Government an assurance that it would not undertake to supply that fort without first giving notice to the Confederates. On the 8th of April this notice was given to General Beauregard, who had been assigned (March 1) to the command of all the troops near Charleston. The fact having been communicated to his Government by Beauregard, he was ordered (April 10) by the Secretary of War to demand the evacuation of the fort. This demand was made the next day. The negotiations which followed were, at 3.30 o'clock on the morning of the 12th, terminated by a notice from General Beauregard that unless the fort were surrendered within an hour, he would open fire upon it. At 4.30 A.M. a signal shell was accordingly thrown into Sumter, and a few moments later fire was opened from all the Confederate batteries. Major Anderson returned the fire about 7 A.M. It was then kept up continuously by both sides for nearly thirty-four hours until, at about two o'clock in the afternoon of the 13th, the fort was surrendered.

"The effect of the assault on Fort Sumter," says Mr. Blaine, "and the lowering of the national flag to the forces of the Confederacy acted upon the North as an inspiration, consolidating public sentiment, dissipating all differences, bringing the whole people to an instant and unanimous determination to avenge the insult, and to re-establish the authority of the Union. Yesterday there had been division. To-day there was unity."

The President issued a proclamation on the 15th, calling on the militia of the several States to the number of seventy-five thousand, to "suppress combinations in South Carolina, Georgia, Florida, Alabama, Mississippi, Louisiana, and Texas, too powerful to be suppressed by the ordinary course of judicial proceedings; . . . to maintain the honor, the integrity, and the existence of our National Union, and the perpetuity of popular government; . . . and to repossess the forts, places, and property which have been seized from the Union."

On the same day the Secretary of War telegraphed to the governors of all the States which had not seceded, requesting them to detail from the militia of their several States enough men to make up the total of seventy-five thousand troops called for by the President, "to serve as infantry, or riflemen, for a period of three months." The quota to be furnished by each State was set forth in these telegrams.

"The proclamation," to use once more the picturesque words of Mr. Blaine, "was responded to in the loyal States with an unparalleled burst of enthusiasm. On the day of its issue hundreds of public meetings were held from the eastern border of Maine to the extreme western frontier. Work was suspended on farm and in factory, and the whole people were aroused to patriotic ardor, and to a determination to subdue the Rebellion and restore the Union, whatever might be the expenditure of treasure or the sacrifice of life. Telegrams and congratulations of sympathy fell upon the White House like snow flakes in a storm."

Northern Democrats talked no more of "resisting the march of a Black Republican army to the South," nor of "offering their dead bodies as an obstruction to its progress." They became instantly and earnestly "loyal," and their great leader, Stephen A. Douglas, promptly waited on Mr. Lincoln, and expressing his deepest sympathy, tendered his active co-operation.

The effect upon the South was no less instantaneous and decisive.

Throughout the seceded States the wildest enthusiasm took possession of every one. They had fought the United States, and had won the fight. They had, after a bombardment the like of which few living men had ever seen, taken the strongest Federal fortress in all the Confederacy. They suddenly awoke "to a sense of power and became wild with confidence in their ability to defy the authority of the United States."

In the border slave-holding States, which till now had remained steadfast in their allegiance to the Union, the sympathy of the people with their Southern kindred was carried to the highest pitch, and their Governors, in responding to Mr. Lincoln's call for troops to invade the South, gave utterance to this universal feeling: Virginia would furnish no militia "to the powers at Washington for the subjugation of the Southern States." North Carolina "would be no party to the wicked violation of the laws of the country, and to the war upon the liberties of a free people." "Tennessee would not furnish a single man for coercion, but would raise fifty thousand men for the defence of her rights and those of her Southern brethren." "The people of Arkansas would defend to the last extremity their honor and their property against Northern mendacity and usurpation." Kentucky "would furnish no troops for the wicked purpose of subduing her sister States of the South."

Missouri was intensely excited. The Secessionists were exultant, and even the Submissionists took heart again and became defiant. The St. Louis *Republican*, whose columns reflected with wonderful fidelity the ever-varying phases of public opinion, the wishes, the fears and the hopes of the rich men of Missouri, of her slave-holders, of the owners of her great landed estates, of the proprietors and managers of her banks and railways and other great corporations, of her merchants and of her manufacturers, said the day after the surrender of Sumter and before the President had called out the militia:

"No matter what may be the expenditure of life and money, the seceding States never can be conquered. A more unrighteous and unpopular war was never inaugurated. And we look to the people of the free States, now, on the instant, to put forth their solemn protest against the prosecution of this unnatural war. . . . If the Union is to be riven asunder by the mad policy of Mr. Lincoln, all they have to do is to encourage him in the war which he has commenced. No one doubts, we apprehend, the ability of the Confederate States to defend themselves against any force which Mr. Lincoln may send to attack them. But this calamity should be averted before it spreads and takes in, as it will, the border free States, as well as the slave States."

The Columbia *Statesman*, edited by another eminent conservative, William F. Switzler, was equally outspoken. It said on the 15th of April:

"Let them (the border States) stand as a wall of fire between the belligerent extremes, and with their strong arms and potential counsel keep them apart. Let them stand pledged, as they now are, to resist any attempt at coercion, plighting their faith, as we do not hesitate to plight the faith of Missouri, that if the impending war of the Northern States against the Southern shall, in defiance of our solemn protest and warning actually occur (which God in his mercy forefend!) we shall stand by Virginia and Kentucky and our Southern sisters—sharing their dangers, and abiding their fortunes and destiny—in driving back from their borders the hostile feet of Northern invaders. *Of* the South, we are *for* the South."

The *Republican*, commenting the next day (April 16) on the President's proclamation, said:

"We make no doubt that there are fanatics, and fools, and vagabonds enough in the North, who if collected together, might make a good-sized army in point of numbers; but how far they will be ready to encounter the dangers of a march through any of the border slave States of the Union is a question which admits of easy solution. Not one of those States, whether in or out of the Union, will ever permit an army, mustered in the free States, to pass over its territory with the design of invading either of the States now in rebellion against the Federal Government. If Governor Curtin of Pennsylvania wishes to test it, let him put himself at the head of his troops and attempt to march through Virginia.

"And so, Mr. Lincoln may as well understand at once, will it be with all the *hordes* that he may send into the field for this purpose. Their track will be marked with their own blood, shed by the people of the slave States, in defence of their own territory, and of what they conceive to be the rights of the South, and in anticipation that the same fate is intended for themselves, if this war shall be successful.

"We need not wait for the answer of the Governor of Missouri to this demand upon the State for her quota of troops. The people are ready to respond *now*, that they will not contribute one regiment, nor one company for any such purpose. They will not make war upon the South, nor aid in the attempt to retake Fort Sumter, or any other fort in the possession of any one of the States, which have asserted their independence.'

Governor Jackson had never wavered in his determination to place Missouri on the side of the South in the impending war, and had done and was still doing all that could possibly be done with the insignificant means at his command to prepare the State for hostilities. As soon after the adjournment of the General Assembly as his duties at the capital would permit, he had gone to St. Louis to confer with General Frost and others as to what was best to be done. At the conferences which they held some of the most active Secessionists of the city were present. Among them were John A. Brownlee, President of the Police Board, Judge William M. Cooke, and Captains Greene and Duke. They all agreed that the most important and the first thing to be done was to seize the arsenal, so as to obtain the means for at once arming and equipping the State Militia. How this could be done was to be shown by General Frost in a memorial which he promised to draw up forthwith and present to the Governor.

Events moved more rapidly than any one anticipated, and General Frost had not yet completed his *memorial*, when the fall of Fort Sumter changed the aspect of affairs, and compelled him to consider other matters in connection with the seizure of the arsenal. Consequently on the 15th of April he submitted to the Governor, with the indorsement of Mr. Brownlee, a written memorandum, in which he pointed out the strategic importance of St. Louis, and the fact that Lyon had not only greatly strengthened the defences of the arsenal, but was erecting batteries and mounting heavy siege guns and mortars with which to command the river approaches to the city, and the city itself, and would soon have St. Louis at his mercy, and be able to dictate the course of the State.

"I fully appreciate," he went on to say, "the very delicate position occupied by your Excellency, and do not expect you to take any action, or to do anything that is not legal and proper to be done, under the circumstances, but I would nevertheless suggest the following as both legal and proper."

1. Convene the General Assembly at once.

2. Send an agent to the South to procure mortars and siege guns.

3. Prevent the garrisoning of the United States arsenal at Liberty.

4. Warn the people of Missouri "that the Presi-

dent has acted illegally in calling out troops, thus arrogating to himself the war-making power, and that they are, therefore, by no means bound to give him aid or comfort in his attempt to subjugate by force of arms a people who are still free, but, on the contrary, should prepare themselves to maintain all their rights as citizens of Missouri."

5. Order him (Frost) "to form a military camp of instruction at or near the city of St. Louis; to muster military companies into the service of the State; and to erect batteries and do all things necessary and proper to be done in order to maintain the peace, dignity, and sovereignty of the State."

6. Order Colonel Bowen to report with his command to him (Frost) for duty.

It was intended that the camp of instruction should be established on the river bluffs below the arsenal in such position that, with the aid of the siege guns and mortars which were to be brought from the South, Frost, and his brigade reinforced by Bowen's command and by volunteers would be able to force Lyon to surrender the arsenal and all its stores to the State.

While considering these matters the Governor received (April 16) the requisition of the Secretary of War for four regiments of infantry—Missouri's quota of the seventy-five thousand men called for by the President. To this requisition he replied (April 17):

"Your dispatch of the 13th instant making a call upon Missouri for four regiments of men for immediate service, has been received. There can be, I apprehend, no doubt but these men are intended to form a part of the President's army to make war upon the people of the seceded States. Your requisition, in my judgment, is illegal, unconstitutional, and revolutionary in its objects, inhuman and diabolical, and cannot be complied with. Not one man will the State of Missouri furnish to carry on such an unholy crusade."

Commenting upon this reply the next day the *Republican* said: "Nobody expected any other response from him, and the people of Missouri will indorse it. They may not approve the early course of the Southern States, but they denounce and defy the action of Mr. Lincoln in proposing to call out seventy-five thousand men for the purpose of coercing the seceding States. Whatever else may happen, he gets no men from the Border States to carry on such a war."

On the same day that the Governor refused to comply with the requisition for troops, he sent Captains Greene and Duke to Montgomery, with an autograph letter to the President of the Confederate States, requesting him to furnish those officers with the siege guns and mortars which General Frost wanted for the proposed attack upon the arsenal; and Judge William M. Cooke was sent to Virginia upon a similar errand.

He also summoned the General Assembly to meet at Jefferson City, on the 2d of May, "for the purpose of enacting such measures as might be deemed necessary and proper for the more perfect organization and equipment of the militia, and to raise the money, and provide such other means as might be required to place the State in a proper attitude of defence."

To have ordered General Frost to establish a military camp of instruction at St. Louis, and given him the extraordinary powers which he asked for, would have been too open a defiance of the United States Government, and would have also disclosed prematurely the purpose of the encampment, and justified Lyon in taking whatever measures he pleased to prevent the accomplishment of that purpose. The Governor, therefore, adopted the more prudent and strictly legal expedient of ordering the commanding officers of the several militia districts of the State to assemble their respective commands, in obedience to a law enacted in 1858, at some convenient place, each within his own district, on the 3d of May, and to go with them into encampment for six days, to the end that the officers and men might attain a greater degree of efficiency in drill and discipline. This order of course authorized General Frost to establish his camp wherever he pleased within the city or county of St. Louis.

Lieutenant-Colonel Bowen was then ordered to disband the South-west Battalion (which was still guarding the western counties of the State against marauders from Kansas), with the exception of a light battery and one company of mounted riflemen, and to report with these and all officers and men belonging to the St. Louis Militia District, to General Frost, at his encampment in St. Louis.

The United States arsenal at Liberty, in the western part of the State, had already been taken (April 20) by the Secessionists, and its munitions of war, among which were four brass guns, had been appropriated to their own use.

The plans of Governor Jackson and General Frost for the capture of the arsenal came to the knowledge of General Harney almost as soon as they were formed, and on the 16th of April he wrote to General Scott:

"The arsenal buildings and grounds are completely commanded by the hills immediately in their rear, and within easy range, and I learn from sources which I consider reliable that it is the intention of the Executive of this State to cause batteries to be erected on these hills, and also upon the island opposite to the arsenal. I am further informed that should such batteries be erected, it is contemplated by the State authorities, in the event of the secession of the State from the Union, to demand the surrender of the arsenal.

"The command at the arsenal at present consists of nine officers and about four hundred and thirty enlisted men. . . . While this force would probably be able to resist successfully an assaulting party greatly superior to itself in numbers, it could not withstand the fire of batteries situated as above indicated. Under these circumstances, I respectfully ask instructions for my guidance."

Lyon did not ask, or wait for, instructions. He wrote that very day (April 16) by a trustworthy messenger to Governor Yates of Illinois and asked him to obtain authority from Washington to hold in readiness for service at St. Louis the six regiments which Illinois had been called upon to furnish. There were, he said, quarters for 3,000 men at Jefferson Barracks, and 1,000 or 2,000 could be quartered at the arsenal. He also suggested to Governor Yates that, as the arms at the arsenal were the main object of the threatened attack upon that post, it might be well for him to make requisition for a large supply of arms, and get them shipped thence to Springfield. Governor Yates submitted the matter immediately to the President, and was on the 20th of April instructed to send two or three regiments of the Illinois quota "to support the garrison of the St. Louis arsenal." Lyon was, at the same time, ordered to equip these troops with arms, accoutrements, and ammunition, "and moreover to issue ten thousand additional stands of arms and accoutrements to the agent of the Governor of Illinois, together with a corresponding amount of ammunition."

Blair returned from Washington to St. Louis on the 17th of April. He comprehended the situation clearly, and acted with his accustomed wisdom, boldness, and decision. By his advice Colonel Pritchard and other anti-secession officers of Frost's Brigade resigned their commissions, and were followed out of that organization by all the positive Union men. On the 19th he telegraphed to the Secretary of War: "Send order by telegraph at once for mustering men into service to Captain N. Lyon. It will then be surely executed, and we will fill your requisition" (that which had been made upon Missouri for four regiments) " in two days. Relieve Hagner. Answer immediately."

He had already procured from the War Department an order placing five thousand stand of arms at the disposal of Lyon for arming " loyal citizens "— that is to say the Home Guards—in case of necessity, and now hastened, by his counsels and encouragement, the recruitment of the four regiments which he had tendered to the Government, and which he was resolved to have ready by the time that the order for mustering them into the service could be received. An incident which occurred at this time came opportunely to his aid.

Lyon, with that utter disregard of the mere letter of the law, which was one of his most marked characteristics, had for the better security of the arsenal and also for the convenience of the men, occupied with his patrols the streets adjacent to the arsenal. This was a clear violation of the city ordinances, and a direct interference with the duties of the Board of Police Commissioners. The Board complained of it to Captain Lyon, and demanded that he should obey the laws. He refused to comply. As the Board could not enforce his obedience, the matter was referred to General Harney. The Commissioners at the same time protested against the issue of United States arms by Lyon to men not in the military service, as these men might thereby be made dangerous to the peace of the city, which it was the duty of the Board to maintain.

Harney immediately (April 18th) ordered Lyon to withdraw his patrols into the limits of the arsenal, and forbade him to issue arms to any one without his own (Harney's) previously obtained sanction.

This determined Blair to demand the removal of Harney from the command of the Department of the West, and he accordingly wrote the following letter (April 19th) to his brother, Judge Montgomery Blair, Postmaster-general, and forwarded it by a special messenger:

"Dr. Hazlitt will hand you this letter. He goes to Washington for the purpose of urging the removal of General Harney from this post, and giving us some one to command who will not obstruct orders of the Government intended for our assistance. Harney has issued orders, at the instance of the Secessionists, refusing to allow us to have the guns which the Government had ordered to be given to us. We also want an order to Captain Lyon to swear in the four regiments assigned to Missouri. If you will send General Wool, or some one who is not to be doubted, to take command of this district, and designate an officer to swear in our volunteers; and arm the rest of our people who are willing to act as a civic or home guard, I think that we shall be able to hold our ground here. I consider these matters of vital importance, . . . and ask you to see Cameron (Secretary of War), immediately, in regard to the business."

The seizure of the United States arsenal at Liberty hastened the action of the Secretary of War upon Blair's requests. Harney was (April 21) relieved of the command of the Department of the West and ordered to repair to Washington city and report to the General-in-chief. On the same day Lyon was instructed to "immediately execute the order previously given to arm loyal citizens, to protect the public property, and execute the laws," and was also ordered to "muster into the service the four regiments which the Governor had refused to furnish."

These orders were received at St. Louis on the 23d of April. Harney relinquished the command of the department the same day, and left the next for Washington city. The command was to devolve upon the senior officer in the department; but Captain Lyon, strange to say, acted and was recognized by the Government as commanding the department.

He proceeded quickly to organize the four regiments, and, while doing this, sent away from St. Louis all the surplus munitions of war which were still there. This last was done on the night of the 26th of April, when the steamer *City of Alton*, dropping unnoticed down to the arsenal, took the arms and other munitions aboard, and transferred them to Illinois. This ended the contest for the arsenal.

CHAPTER VIII.

CAMP JACKSON.

Douglas and the Northern Democrats Declare for the Union—The North Unanimous—Missouri Threatened on Three Sides by Federal Armies, and St. Louis full of Federal Soldiers—The Border States Hesitate—The Confederacy Does Nothing—Missouri Helpless and Submissive—The Governor still Resolute—He Purchases Arms and Powder—Camp Jackson—Lyon Authorized to Enlist Ten Thousand Men and to Proclaim Martial Law in St. Louis—Elected Brigadier-General of the Home Guards—Arms from the Confederacy taken to Camp Jackson—Lyon Visits the Camp in Disguise—Capture of Camp Jackson and the State Troops—Rioting and Bloodshed—The General Assembly Enacts the Military Bill and Confers Dictatorial Powers on the Governor—A Panic in St. Louis—Harney Resumes Command and Establishes Order in the City—Missourians See the Danger of Seceding and Begin to Submit.

THE enthusiasm of the Southern Rights' people of Missouri quickly subsided in view of the unanimity with which the North was responding to the President's call for troops, and in contemplation of the dangers which they would have to encounter who should dare to take up arms against the Federal Government.

The North had become united, while the South was still divided. For more than a generation the Democrats of the North had stood by the South with a constancy and a courage that deserve all praise. In obedience to the Constitution, which they revered, and for the sake of the Union which they loved, they had maintained the rights of slave-holders under the Constitution long after the enjoyment of those rights had come into conflict with the humane spirit of the age and with the civilization of the North ; they had maintained those rights even when they led to the enactment of a law whose requirements were abhorrent to their feelings; and they had continued to maintain them even when the South, appealing to those rights, broke the compact whereby a part of the national domain had been consecrated to freedom forever. They had stood by the South even then ; and throughout all the savage struggle for Kansas, and during the Presidential election of 1860, and until they had themselves been swept out of power in every non-slave-holding State because of their obedience to the Constitution, and their friendship for the South. And even after South Carolina and other States had seceded, they still felt kindly towards them, and sought to bring them back into the Union, not by force, but by assuring to their people the enjoyment of every right to which they could justly lay claim under the Constitution. But when the South, in the exercise of the right of secession or of revolution or whatever else one may choose to call it, established a separate government and took up arms against the Union, they could no longer stand by it, but rallied, as they ought to have done, under the flag of their own country.

That the North was thoroughly united, Missourians did not have to look far to see. Just across the river, that State with which their own was most closely bound, not only by geographical contiguity, but by community of origin, by common interests, by daily intercourse, and by every tie which holds two States together, was rushing to arms in response to the appeals of her Douglas, no less than to the call of her Lincoln, and was assembling armies all along the eastern boundary of Missouri; while on her northern border Iowa was gathering her volunteers to attack her, if she should venture to rebel against the Government; and on her western frontier the free-State men of Kansas were mustering under the leadership of desperadoes like Montgomery, and of soldiers like Dietzler, to renew on the soil of Missouri their bitter war against the "border ruffians" of the South. The Government was also concentrating its regulars at Fort Leavenworth under Sturgis and Steele, within sight of the richest and most populous counties of the State; and Blair and Lyon had at St. Louis more than five hundred regulars, and five thousand well armed volunteers, many of them veterans. Worse than all, the State was divided against herself, and one-fourth of her own people were ready to take up arms against their Governor; who, to resist all these gathering armies, had no troops but Frost's fractional brigade, many of whose officers and men would throw down their arms rather than use them against the Union; and a few widely scattered companies of militia, some of which were composed chiefly of "loyal" men.

The Southern Rights' men of Missouri saw all this, and that there was no one to help them if they should resist the Government. Their own State seemed to be powerless. The Confederacy had shown no disposition to aid them. Virginia had seceded, but North Carolina and Tennessee were hesitating; Arkansas still clung to the Union, Maryland had been subjugated, and Kentucky was about to submit without striking a blow, without even raising her arm to strike. To resist, thus circumstanced, the Federal Government, was to provoke its wrath; to involve their State in civil war; to ruin their own fortunes; to impoverish their families; and to expose themselves to all the hazards of war. What could they do? The *Republican* which felt as they felt, advised them to do that which they wanted to do. Like them, it had been defiant on the 18th of April; like them it was submissive on the 22d. Missouri, it now said, must take her stand, not with South, but with Kentucky: "Let us take the same position that Kentucky has taken—that of armed neutrality. Let us declare that no military force levied in other States, shall be allowed to pass through our State, or camp upon our soil. Let us demand of the opposing sections to stop further hostile operations until reason can be appealed to in Congress, and before the people; and when that fails it will be time enough for us to take up arms. Why should we, all unprepared, rush out of the Union, to find a doubtful and reluctant reception in the Confederate States?"

As soon as the Governor learned that the arms with which he had been hoping to equip the State troops had been removed from the arsenal, he directed General Harding, the Quarter-master General, to proceed to St. Louis, and procure for the State all the arms and ammunition that he could find in that city. That officer had in February reported to the Governor that the only munitions of war which the State owned, except a few muskets in the hands of the militia, were two 6-pounder guns, without limbers or caissons; about one thousand muskets; forty sabres; and fifty-eight swords. The latter were, he said, of an antique Roman pattern and "would not be as useful in war as so many bars of soap." In St. Louis he now purchased, partly by force, several hundred hunting rifles, some camp and garrison equipage, and about seventy tons of gunpowder; all which were shipped to Jefferson City on the 7th of May under guard of Captain Kelly's company, detailed for that duty by General Frost.

Though the removal of the arms from the arsenal had taken away the motive which caused the Governor to order the militia into camp at St. Louis, it was determined to hold that encampment, nevertheless. The intention of holding it on the hills near the arsenal, was, however, abandoned. For to camp there now would be an idle threat at best, and besides, and this was a still more potent reason, those very hills had been quietly occupied by Lyon with both infantry and artillery. Frost, therefore, selected a camp in a wooded valley, known as Lindell Grove, near the intersection of Olive Street and Grand Avenue, in the western part of the city, and called it Camp Jackson, in honor of the Governor. And there his brigade, aggregating a little more than seven hundred men, went into encampment on Monday, the 6th of May.

Besides the officers and the men of the brigade, there were a number of young men in the camp, who had come from all quarters of the State to learn something of the art of war, and to take part in any hostile movement which Frost might undertake.

From this little force one company, Captain Kelly's, was detached on the 7th and ordered to Jefferson City, leaving Frost about six hundred and thirty men.

Blair and Lyon, who had been kept well informed as to everything that the Governor and Frost were doing, had been meanwhile quietly getting ready to capture the camp, together with Frost and all his command. No longer obstructed by Harney, they had, by the 30th of April, mustered into the service five regiments of infantry, all of them well armed and fully equipped. On that day (April 30) Lyon wrote to the Secretary of War: "The State is doubtless getting ready to attack the Government troops with artillery. I have sent three volunteer companies with Captain Totten's battery to occupy buildings outside of the arsenal, hired for this purpose both to give them shelter and to occupy commanding positions which the Secessionists had intended to occupy themselves, and upon which they openly avowed that they would plant siege batteries to reduce this place, the arsenal. This exasperates them and has given rise to a singular correspondence which, when convenient, I will lay before the War Department."

On the same day (April 30) the following extraordinary paper was transmitted to St. Louis, addressed by "Simon Cameron, Secretary of War," to

"Captain Nathaniel Lyon, commanding Department of the West."

"The President of the United States directs that you enroll in the military service of the United States loyal citizens of St. Louis and vicinity, not exceeding, with those heretofore enlisted, ten thousand in number, for the purpose of maintaining the authority of the United States and for the the protection of the peaceable inhabitants of Missouri, and you will, if deemed necessary for that purpose by yourself and Messrs. Oliver D. Filley, John How, James O. Broadhead, Samuel T. Glover, J. J. Witzig, and Francis P. Blair, Jr., proclaim martial law in the city of St. Louis."

This remarkable document was indorsed, "It is revolutionary times, and therefore I do not object to the irregularity of this. W. S." (Winfield Scott.) It bore this indorsement besides, "Approved April 30, 1861. A. Lincoln."

Upon receiving this authority Lyon mustered into the service on the 7th and 8th of May four more regiments of infantry, which, with a fifth that was mustered in on the 11th, constituted what became known as the United States Reserve Corps, or Home Guards. The five regiments that had been organized in April were known as Missouri Volunteers. The First Regiment of Missouri Volunteers was composed largely of natives of this country and

Irishmen. Francis P. Blair, Jr., was its colonel, George L. Andrews, its lieutenant-colonel; and John M. Schofield (now major-general), its major. The other nine regiments were composed almost exclusively of Germans. The officers of the five regiments of Missouri Volunteers urged Blair to accept the command of that brigade, but he insisted upon their electing Lyon instead, and of course, his wishes were obeyed. Lyon was thenceforth known as Brigadier-general Lyon, though he was not commissioned as such till the 17th of May, to rank from the 18th. Chester Harding was made adjutant-general of the brigade. Captain Thomas W. Sweeny of the Second Infantry was chosen brigadier-general of the brigade composed of the five regiments of Home Guards, and was commissioned as such on the 20th of May. He had served in the Mexican War as captain of a company of New York volunteers, and at the close of that war had entered the regular army.

Blair and Lyon were now ready to strike. They had more than 7,000 well armed men, and within two miles of them lay encamped nearly all the militia of the State—less than 700 men. Capture these men, and take away their arms, and the Governor would have no organized force, no arms, nothing with which to resist the occupation of the State by Federal troops, and within a week they would hang "the traitor," or drive him out of the State. There was no time to waste, for not only would the militia disperse to their homes on the last day of the week, but by that time Harney would be back in St. Louis, and again in command of the department, and nothing would then be done to harm the Secessionists. It was therefore agreed on the 7th of May between Blair, Lyon, Harding, and Franklin A. Dick, to take the camp at once.

A thing now happened which gave them a good pretext to do what they wanted. Such things are always happening to those who know how to take advantage of them.

It will be remembered that Governor Jackson had sent Captains Duke and Greene to Montgomery for siege guns and mortars, with which Frost was to take the arsenal. On reaching the Confederate capital they laid their requests before the President and his Cabinet, and explained to them the purpose for which they wanted the guns and mortars. Mr. Davis, who had, at one time, been stationed at St. Louis, and was familiar with the ground, approved the plan, and ordered the commandant of the Baton Rouge Arsenal to supply the requisition. He also wrote to the Governor of Louisiana, and asked him to render such assistance as he could to the Missouri officers.

To Governor Jackson he wrote (April 23):

". . . After learning, as well as I could, from the gentlemen accredited to me, what was most needful for the attack on the arsenal, I have directed that Captains Greene and Duke should be furnished with two 12-pounder howitzers and two 32-pounder guns, with the proper ammunition for each. These, from the commanding hills, will be effective against the garrison, and to break the enclosing walls of the place. I concur with you as to the great importance of capturing the arsenal and securing its supplies, rendered doubly important by the means taken to obstruct your commerce and render you unarmed victims of a hostile invasion.

"We look anxiously and hopefully for the day when the star of Missouri shall be added to the constellation of the Confederate States of America.

"With the best wishes, I am,

"Very respectfully yours,

"JEFFERSON DAVIS."

The arms and ammunition were procured at Baton Rouge and shipped to St. Louis as merchandise, and consigned to well-known Union men. At St. Louis they were turned over (May 8) to Major Shaler, of Frost's Brigade, and taken to Camp Jackson. The fact was made known to Blair and Lyon as soon as the thing was done, and they determined to act at once. The next day Lyon, disguised as an old woman, drove through the camp, and satisfied himself, by personal inspection, that the men had in their possession arms and ammunition which had been taken from the United States Arsenal at Baton Rouge, and which, therefore, rightfully belonged, in his opinion, to the Federal Government. Returning to the arsenal, he summoned the Committee of Safety to meet him there at once, and told them that it was "necessary to seize the camp, and every man in it, and to hold them as prisoners of war." Blair, Broadhead, Filley, and Witzig, concurred with him; but Glover and How objected that the camp had a legal existence for six days, and should not be attacked during that time; that those in command of it recognized the authority of the United States Government and kept the national flag flying over the encampment, and had not committed any breach of the peace; and that, if there was any property there of the United States, the proper way to reach it was through a writ of replevin, which the United States Marshal could enforce, if necessary, by calling on General Lyon for troops.

Lyon replied that he knew the camp to be a nest of traitors; that the Legislature was in secret session, and might have already put a new military law in operation, or certainly would do so in a day or two; that advices from all parts of the State were discouraging to the Union men; that the rebels were gathering strength; that Harney would arrive on Sunday, and no one could tell what he would do; and that Camp Jackson must, therefore, be taken forthwith. Glover and How yielded at last, with the understanding that the United States Marshal should head the column which was to march against the camp. Lyon had, nevertheless, made up his own mind to use no subterfuge. He meant "to capture the camp and the men in it, both the officers and the enlisted men, with all its material of war; to demand a surrender, with his men in line of battle and his cannon in position, and if the demand were not complied with at once to fight for it." And he got ready to do this the next morning Friday the 10th of May.

Frost, who had during the last day or two heard frequent rumors that Lyon was going to capture the camp, received positive information Friday morning that the attack was to be made that day. He thereupon addressed to Lyon a letter in which he positively denied that either he, or any part of his command, had any hostile intentions towards the United States Government, or its property, or representatives. "I trust," said he, "after this explicit statement, we may be able by fully understanding each other to keep far from our borders the misfortunes which unhappily afflict our common country." This communication was sent to Lyon through Colonel Bowen. Lyon refused to receive it, and immediately put his column in motion. After surrounding the camp he sent one of his staff to Frost with a demand for the immediate and unconditional surrender of his whole command. As his force was more than ten times as great as Frost's, the latter had to surrender. Both Grant and Sherman saw all these things.

The militia having stacked their arms, were formed into line, and conducted out of the camp on their way to the arsenal. They had moved but a short distance when they were halted, and kept standing in a line parallel with and a few yards from Olive Street, which was occupied by Lyon's troops. During the halt, which lasted several hours, great numbers of men, women, and children gathered around the prisoners and their captors. They were, of course, intensely agitated and, as the excitement grew, began to jeer at and abuse "the Dutch Blackguards" (so called in derision because one of the German companies called itself *die Schwartze Garde*). Suddenly a few shots were fired, and were followed almost immediately by volley after volley, extending in regular succession down the line of troops, until apparently a full regiment had thus fired by company. Twenty-eight people lay dead or mortally wounded. Among them were three prisoners and an infant in the arms of its mother. The march was quickly resumed, and the prisoners were safely secured within the grounds of the arsenal. The next night (May 11) all of them except Captain Emmett Macdonald were released on their parole not to bear arms against the United States. Macdonald refused to give his parole, but was, after many adventures, released through the intervention of the courts.

The General Assembly had met on the 2d of May. The Governor, after calling its attention to the state of the country, repeated, what he had often said, that the interests and sympathies of Missouri were identical with those of the other slave-holding States, and that she must therefore unite her destiny with theirs; that while she had no war to prosecute, she would be faithless to her honor, and recreant to her duty, if she hesitated a moment to make the amplest preparation for the protection of her people against all assailants; and that, therefore, the General Assembly should "place the State at the earliest practicable moment in a complete state of defence."

Both Houses went into secret session, and began to consider bills to carry out these recommendations. They had, however, made but little progress, when, during the afternoon of the 10th of May, the Governor, entering hastily the Hall of Representatives, informed some of the members that Lyon had captured Camp Jackson, and was holding the State troops as prisoners of war. The Military Bill was under discussion at the moment, its passage resisted at every step by the opponents of secession. In an instant all resistance gave way and within less than fifteen minutes the bill had passed both Houses and was awaiting the Governor's signature.

Towards midnight all Jefferson City was aroused by the ringing of the church bells. The Legislature met and was notified by the Governor that he had been informed that "two of Mr. Blair's regiments were on the way to the capital." In the midst of the wildest excitement an act was rushed through both Houses authorizing "the Governor to take such measures as he might deem necessary or proper to repel invasion or put down rebellion," and $30,000 were appropriated to enable him to execute the dictatorial powers thus conferred upon him. Other acts intended to prepare the State for war were also introduced.

The Governor meanwhile sent detachments of men in all haste to hold the railroad bridges over the Gasconade and the Osage, over which "Mr. Blair's two regiments" would have to pass on their way from St. Louis. In the excitement of the hour the detachment which was sent to guard the Osage Bridge set it on fire and partially destroyed it.

The powder which the Governor had purchased

in St. Louis and stored at Jefferson City was hurriedly removed to various hiding places, more or less remote; and the funds in the State treasury were secreted. Every man armed himself as best he could with shot-guns, rifles, sabres, and ancient swords, and there was much talk of "resisting the invaders." The story is told of one ardent patriot, a "cockade man" (a cockade on the hat of a Secessionist meant, in those days, what a chip on the shoulder of an Irishman is supposed to mean when his blood is up), who declared that he was going to the Moreau, all alone if no one would go with him, and would fight Lyon and his "Dutch cut-throats" there, all by himself. It is said, however, that he did not go to the Moreau either then or the next day, and, what is more, that he never left home during all the war.

While these things were going on at Jefferson City, the excitement at St. Louis grew apace. During the afternoon of the 10th and the evening of that day the streets were crowded with anxious and angry people. The capture of Camp Jackson; the detention of Frost and his men as prisoners of war; the cruel shooting down of unoffending women and children by Lyon and his German Home Guards, had aroused Americans and Irish to a state of frenzy. Towards morning the crowds grew denser and more dangerous, particularly in the central part of the city, where the people of native birth chiefly resided, and, as the day advanced, evinced a determination to put an end to the domination of the Germans.

Late in the afternoon as a regiment of Home Guards was returning from the arsenal to its barracks in the northern part of the city, it encountered near Walnut Street a crowd, which had gathered there to see it pass. Halting for a moment as if to resent the hooting of the multitude, it had resumed its march, when some one fired a shot into its ranks. The head of the column turned and poured a volley into the crowd, and into its own rear ranks. Eight men were killed, two of them soldiers, and many were wounded. The people fled, and the regiment continued on its way. This occurrence inflamed the Germans to such a degree of fury, that they now made open threats to exterminate the Secessionists, and on Sunday, the 12th of May, these threats became so loud as to alarm the American population, whose only organized defenders, the Volunteer Militia, had been disarmed, and were prisoners of war. What could unarmed men do against Lyon and his ten thousand German soldiers thoroughly armed and equipped?

The Mayor and the Police Commissioners were powerless. In their fright the people begged General Harney, who had resumed command at St. Louis, to send the Home Guards out of the city. This he promised to do; but Blair soon convinced him that as these regiments had been enlisted to serve *within* St. Louis, they could not be sent away.

When the people learned that Harney could not send the Home Guards away, they inferred that it was because these regiments had revolted against him, and were going to carry out their threats to exterminate the "Secesh." A panic took possession of the city. Thousands of women and children were sent across the Mississippi, and other thousands were getting ready to follow, when Harney brought two companies of United States Artillery, and two companies of Regular Infantry into the city, and issued a proclamation wherein he pledged his "faith as a soldier," to preserve the public peace, and to protect the lives and property of the people. This wise and timely proceeding quieted the apprehensions of every one, and most of the fugitives returned to their homes.

CHAPTER IX.

BOTH SIDES PREPARE FOR WAR.

Harney approves the Capture of Camp Jackson—Occupies St. Louis—Asks for troops from Iowa and Minnesota "for Operations in Missouri."—Adjournment of the Legislature—Sterling Price offers his services to the State—Is appointed Major-General—Appointment of Brigadier-Generals—Volunteers at Jefferson City—Marmaduke—McCulloch, and McIntyre—Organization of the State Guard Begun—The Price-Harney Agreement—Dissatisfaction of Blair and Lyon—They procure Harney's Removal—Lyon in Command of Missouri.

HARNEY soon made it plain to every one that, while he was anxious to maintain peace within the State, and to abstain from all acts of violence, he was resolved to hold her faithful to the Union, and to compel her people to obey the laws of the United States.

On the 13th of May he wrote to General Scott that "Captain Lyon's conduct in capturing the State troops" met with his own entire approval; and the next day he published a *Proclamation to the People of Missouri*, in which he denounced the Military Bill, which had just been enacted by the General Assembly, as "an indirect secession ordinance ignoring even the forms resorted to by other

States," and declared that, inasmuch as "its most material provisions were in conflict with the Constitution and laws of the United States, the act was itself a nullity, and not by any means to be obeyed by the people of Missouri," and that "in any event the whole power of the United States would, if necessary, be exerted to maintain the State in her present position in the Union."

As to Camp Jackson, he said that its "main avenue had the name of Davis, and a principal street the name of Beauregard; that a body of men" (the Minute Men) "had been received into the camp by its commander, which had been notoriously organized in the interests of the Secessionists, the men openly wearing the dress and the badge distinguishing the army of the so-called Southern Confederacy;" and that a quantity of arms "unlawfully taken from the United States Arsenal at Baton Rouge," had also been taken there; that there could therefore be no doubt "as to the character and ultimate purpose of that encampment;" and that "no government in the world would be entitled to respect that would tolerate for a moment such openly treasonable preparations."

The proclamation closed with this remarkable declaration:

"Disclaiming, as I do, all desire or intention to interfere in any way with the prerogatives of the

State of Missouri or with the functions of its Executive, or other authorities, yet I regard it as my plain duty to express to the people in respectful but at the same time decided language that within the field and scope of my command and authority the supreme law of the land must and shall be maintained, and that no subterfuges, whether in the form of legislative acts" (the Military Bill) " or otherwise, can be permitted to harass or oppress the good and law-abiding people of Missouri" (that is to say the Union men and Submissionists). "I shall exert my authority to protect *their* persons and property from violations of every kind, and I shall deem it my duty to suppress all unlawful combinations of men" (the State Guard), "whether formed under pretext of military organization or otherwise."

He had already taken military possession of the city of St. Louis, by stationing troops at all important points.

The *Republican*, commenting the next day on this *Pronunciamento*, and on the occupation of the city by Federal troops, had the courage to say, with the last free breath that it drew in four long years: "We are bound hand and foot; chained down by a merciless tyranny; are subjugated and shackled."

Having made up his mind to subjugate the State of which he was a citizen and to fight against the people among whom he was born, and of whom he was one, General Harney did not content himself with publishing proclamations, but began to get ready, like the true soldier that he was, to compel obedience to them. On the 17th of May he telegraphed to General Scott for ten thousand stand of arms, "for issue to reliable Union men" in other counties than St. Louis, and asked that the Governors of Iowa and Minnesota (which States were within the Department of the West) should be called upon to furnish him nine thousand men "for operations in Missouri." He wanted, besides, authority to enlist in St. Louis a regiment consisting exclusively of Irishmen. The scent of the blood with which the streets of the city were reeking, had aroused the spirit of "the bold dragoon," and, as in the days of his youth, he was eager to fight, and ready to strike whomever he was *ordered* to strike, whether it were Indian or Mexican, Northman or Southman, stranger or kinsman.

The General Assembly had adjourned on the 15th of May after creating a military fund into which the school fund and all other available moneys of the State were ordered to be paid, together with a loan of $1,000,000, which the banks were expected to subscribe, and also the proceeds of $1,000,000 State bonds, which the Governor was authorized to sell.

It had also passed *unanimously* resolutions denouncing bitterly the conduct of Blair and Lyon; requesting the Governor to instantly call out the militia; and declaring that "the people of Missouri would rally as one man, to perish, if necessary, in defending their Constitutional rights."

The unanimity with which these resolutions were adopted attests the almost universal indignation and anger with which the capture of the State troops and the shooting down of unoffending men, women, and children had filled the hearts of the people of Missouri. Many who till now had never wavered in their fidelity to the Union, now determined to stand with their State, and to resist the government of Abraham Lincoln. Conspicuous among these were ex-Governor Sterling Price, President of the State Convention, and John B. Clark. They both hastened to Jefferson City, and tendered their services to the Governor. Their accession was hailed with unbounded delight by the Secessionists and it helped in a great degree to check the tendency to submit, which was spreading from St. Louis all over the State.

Sterling Price was born of a good family in Prince Edward County, Virginia, in 1809. He was carefully educated in the schools near by, and at Hampden Sidney College, and afterwards attended the law school of one of the most eminent of Virginia's jurists, her venerable chancellor, Creed Taylor.

Moving with his father's family to Missouri in 1831, he had resided ever since on the same farm in Chariton County. Elected to the Legislature in 1840, he was at once chosen Speaker of the House, a distinction rarely conferred upon a man so young and wholly unused to deliberative assemblies. But he was a born leader of men. Tall, handsome, well educated and accomplished; a gentleman of commanding presence and dignified manners; a man of character and worth, and richly endowed with that best of all mental gifts—common sense—he was also instinctively a parliamentarian, comprehended as by intuition the rules that govern legislative bodies, and enforced them with promptness and vigor. After serving four years as Speaker, he was elected to Congress. But hardly had he taken his seat when in the spring of 1846 war was declared against Mexico. Resigning his place in Congress he returned instantly to Missouri, raised a mounted regiment, and led it to New Mexico, to the command of which he had been assigned. The next year, the President, in recognition of his services and of his civic and military ability, promoted him to brigadier-general. At the close of the war he returned to Missouri, and in 1852 was elected Governor of the State, and occupied that office till the beginning of 1857.

In 1860, he had supported Douglas for the Presidency, because he was himself devoted to the Union, and did not like the threat of secession, which was involved in the candidacy of Breckinridge. In the late election of delegates to the State Convention he had taken ground against the secession of Missouri, and had been elected with great unanimity, as he would have been, had he taken the contrary position, for his neighbors had unbounded confidence in his patriotism and good sense. He was made President of the Convention, and had throughout its entire session borne himself as a sincere friend of the Union, opposed under all circumstances to its dissolution, and just as earnestly opposed to making war upon the South. To this position he had continued to adhere even after the President's call for seventy-five thousand men to invade the South. But the attack of Blair and Lyon upon Camp Jackson, their capture of the State troops, and their killing of helpless women and children, aroused within him the deepest indignation, and determined him to draw his sword against the men who had dared to do such things, and against the Government which sustained them.

He was unquestionably the most popular man in Missouri. With none of Doniphan's splendid talents and brilliant wit; with none of Gamble's passionless logic; with none of Green's power in debate, and none of Rollins' persuasive speech; with none of that rare blending of Christian graces with stalwart strength of mind, which gave Trusten Polk the victory over Benton in 1856; with none of Edward Bates' bland eloquence, and with little of Governor Jackson's devotion to abstract principles, and still less of his fiery zeal; he was more trusted by Missourians than any of them, more than *all* of them *now*, when Missouri wanted a warlike leader.

The recently enacted Military Bill provided for the enlistment of the Missouri State Guard, and authorized the Governor to appoint eight brigadier-generals to command the military districts into which it divided the State. The Legislature also empowered the Governor to appoint a major-general, who should have command of this entire force when called into active service. To this office General Price was, as the Legislature intended, appointed on the 18th of May.

On the 21st the Governor announced the appointment of the following brigadier-generals, Alexander W. Doniphan, Monroe M. Parsons, James S. Rains, John B. Clark, Merriwether Lewis Clark, Nathaniel W. Watkins, Beverly Randolph, William Y. Slack, and James H. McBride, all of them men of high character and known ability and devoted to Missouri. Doniphan, Parsons, M. L. Clark, and Slack had all distinguished themselves in the war with Mexico. Their commissions were forthwith transmitted to all, with orders to enroll at once the men within their respective districts, and get them ready for active service.

In all that part of the State west of Jefferson City, and particularly in the counties bordering on the Missouri (whose population was composed almost entirely of Southern people), the work of enrolment was pushed vigorously. Volunteers had indeed begun to flock to the capital as soon as it was seen that the Governor and the General Assembly intended to resent "the outrages" that had been perpetrated at St. Louis, and that men like Sterling Price and John B. Clark were drawing their swords in defence of the State.

By the 18th of May more than a thousand of these volunteers had gathered at Jefferson City, and were impatiently waiting to be mustered into the State Guard, and to take the field under the command of Price. Among them were some companies from Cooper brought thither by Captain Robert McCulloch, and some from Callaway brought by Captain D. H. McIntyre. The *Independence Grays* came from Jackson, with full ranks, bringing with them the four brass 6-pounders, which had been taken from the United States Arsenal at Liberty; guns, which, after many strange adventures, were gallantly fought against the Government to which they belonged. Kelly's St. Louis company was still there.

The regiment first organized was composed of eight companies from Parsons' district, which embraced the counties adjacent to Jefferson City. It was known as the First Regiment of Rifles, and John S. Marmaduke was its colonel.

Marmaduke was a native of Missouri, a son of one of her former Governors, and a nephew of Governor Jackson. He had graduated at West Point in 1857, and was a lieutenant of infantry when the President called for troops. Resigning his commission at once, he began to enlist the regiment which he now offered to the State. He was a young man of very decided ability and a fine soldier. It is a noteworthy fact that he is now Governor of the State, that McCulloch is Treasurer, that McGrath who was a private in Kelly's company is Secretary of State, and that McIntyre was recently Attorney-General of the Commonwealth.

The active preparations for war which General Harney was making at St. Louis, and which the Governor and General Price were making at Jefferson City and throughout the State, alarmed some very conservative citizens, who still believed that the neutrality of Missouri might be maintained if General Price and General Harney would consent to it. They accordingly induced General Harney to invite Price, in whom he and they justly had great confidence, to meet him at St. Louis, in order to ascertain whether they could not agree upon some plan for preventing a conflict. As the State was wholly unprepared for war, General Price, with the Governor's approval, readily accepted General Harney's invitation, and on the 21st of May these two officers made what is known as the Price-Harney Agreement, wherein, avowing that the object of each was "to restore peace and good order to the people of the State in subordination to the laws of the General and State governments," General Price, as Major-General of the Missouri State Guard, undertook, with the Governor's express sanction, "to maintain order within the State, among the people thereof;" and General Harney declared that if this were done he could have no occasion (as he had no wish) to make any military movements within the State.

While General Price was still in St. Louis, General Harney said to him through a friend, that as the State Guard might come within the meaning of the President's proclamation requiring officers of the United States Army to disperse all armed bodies hostile to the supreme law of the land, he hoped that General Price would discover some way to suspend the organization of the State Guard until the constitutionality of the act creating it could be passed upon by some competent authority.

General Price replied that he had no right to nullify or to disobey a law of the State, and could not, of course, suspend the organization of the State Guard. But upon returning to Jefferson City he ordered (May 24) all of the troops which had come thither from other military districts to return to their homes, there to be organized by their respective district commanders into companies and regiments as required by law. Captain Kelly's company alone was excepted from the operation of this order.

The action of General Harney in this matter gave great offence to Blair and Lyon. His interference with their plan for overrunning the State immediately after the capture of Frost's Brigade, had already decided them to insist upon his removal from the command of the Federal forces in Missouri, and Blair had sent his brother-in-law Franklin A. Dick, and Lyon had sent Dr. Bernays, the editor of the *Anzeiger des Westens*, to Washington city to urge the matter upon the President.

In a written memorandum which he gave to Dr. Bernays for his guidance Lyon said: "Tell him all about our situation here. I have no confidence whatever in Harney, or in Major McKinstry" (quarter-master of the department). "I feel that they are against us, and that they will throw all kinds of difficulties in our way. They already do so. I never can obtain in time what I need from the quarter-master's department, and all the precautions that I take against the rebels are frustrated by the proceedings of General Harney. Tell the President to get my hands untied, and I will warrant to keep this State in the Union."

Dick reached Washington city on the 16th of May, and obtained, that very day, an order for the appointment of Lyon as brigadier-general of volunteers; and also persuaded the President, against the advice of Attorney-General Bates, Judge Gamble, and other influential citizens of St. Louis, to make an order relieving General Harney of the command of the Department of the West. Not wishing, however, to offend his attorney-general, who was a St. Louisian, the President directed Postmaster-General Montgomery Blair, a brother of Frank, to inclose the order to the latter with instructions that it was to be delivered, *at his discretion*, to General Harney; adding, however, that it was "better to mortify Harney than endanger the lives of many men, and the position of Missouri in the present conflict." The President also wrote a private letter to Colonel Blair (May 18) saying that he was doubtful of the propriety of the order, and therefore wished him to withhold it, unless, in his judgment, the necessity to the contrary was very urgent. "But," said he, "if in your judgment it is indispensable, let it be so." Blair, after consulting with Lyon, decided to let Harney retain command until he could satisfy the President that he ought to be removed; and straightway went to work to accomplish that result. Inspired by him, the Safety Committee forwarded to Washington city a vigorous protest (written by James O. Broadhead), against the continuance of the Price-Harney agreement (May 22).

"It seems," they say, "to leave the Union men in the hands of the very power which imperils their safety;" it does not repudiate secession: it impliedly recognizes the right of the State authorities to arm the State under the provisions of the military law, which law sets at defiance the Constitution of the United States, and the authority of the General Government: it does not require the disbandment of the military companies which have been organized under that law: and it only "puts off the evil day until such time as the enemy shall be better prepared to make resistance." It would be better, they said, that the General Government should maintain its authority by the stern enforcement of military rule. For its enforcement the Government had sufficient troops in the State, if it would only instruct the commanding general to distribute them at various points, where they could be used to protect loyal citizens, and to prevent the organization of the State Guard.

Two days later (May 24) Blair wrote to the Secretary of War denouncing Governor Jackson as a "traitor;" and declaring that the agreement between Price and Harney had disgusted himself, and was giving great dissatisfaction to all Union men. The newspapers were flooded with letters and telegrams from all parts of the State, giving accounts of "outrages" that were pretended to have been committed by the Secessionists, with the countenance of Governor Jackson and General Price, upon the "loyal" inhabitants of the State. These accounts were all sedulously collected, embellished, and multiplied, and then laid with the indorsement of "strong" men before the President; who, believing them, wrote to Harney (May 27) through the adjutant-general that it was "his duty summarily to stop, with the force under his command, and *such troops as he might require from Kansas, Iowa, and Illinois*, the outrages which were being perpetrated on loyal citzens. The professions of loyalty to the Union by the State authorities of Missouri are not to be relied upon. They have already falsified their professions too often, and are too far committed to secession to be entitled to your confidence: and you can only be sure of their desisting from their wicked purposes, when it is out of their power to prosecute them. *The authority of the United States is paramount, and whenever it is apparent that a movement, whether by color of State authority or not, is hostile, you will not hesitate to put it down."*

Before these instructions reached St. Louis, Blair had already delivered to General Harney the order relieving him of the command of the Department of the West. In explaining his action to the President he wrote on the 30th of May, that he had become satisfied that unless the Government occupied the State in force without further delay, the Union men would be crushed, or driven out, entirely, "and the State itself be completely given over to the hands of the rebels;" that Harney, by reason of his agreement with Price, could do nothing; and that it had, consequently, become indispensable to remove him.

Harney, upon receiving the order, relinquished command of the Department (May 30), and it was the next day assumed by Brigadier-General Lyon.

CHAPTER X.

LYON DECLARES WAR.

Blair and Lyon outline their plan of Campaign—Federal Forces in and around Missouri—Defenceless Condition of the State—The Governor and Price prepare for War—Attempts to preserve the Neutrality of the State—The Planters' House Conference—Lyon Declares War against the State—The Governor's Proclamation—He calls out the Militia—Determines to make a stand at Booneville and to hold the Missouri—Abandons Jefferson City and retires to Booneville—General Price goes to Lexington.

THERE was nothing now to prevent Blair and Lyon from executing the plan of campaign upon upon which they had agreed before the capture of Camp Jackson.

Blair outlined this plan to the President in the letter which he addressed to him on the 30th of May. He said therein that the blow struck at Camp Jackson, had "greatly intimidated the leaders of the rebellion," and that if it had been followed up then, as he and Lyon had intended, by blows struck in other parts of the State, the rebellion would have been speedily and effectually crushed in Missouri, at small cost of life and treasure; but that under Harney's policy the Government had been losing ground so rapidly, and its enemies becoming so active and formidable, that the Union men were now in danger of being driven out of the State; that to prevent this and to meet the force with which the Confederates were preparing to invade the State from Arkansas and the Indian Territory, the President ought to authorize the enlistment in Missouri of a sufficient number of troops to hold Jefferson City, Lexington, St. Joseph, Hannibal, Macon City, Springfield, and other points, and should at the same time order the United States troops at Fort Leavenworth and the regiments that were being raised in Kansas to co-operate with General Lyon in resisting any invasion of the State from the Southwest. "We are well able," he said, "to take care of this State without assistance from elsewhere, if authorized to raise a sufficient force within the State; and after that work is done we can take care of the Secessionists from the Arkansas line to the Gulf, along the west shore of the Mississippi."

Lyon, less confident than Blair that the Union men of Missouri could hold the State without the aid of a force from other States, urged the Secretary of War also to direct the Governors of Illinois and Iowa to furnish him the troops which they had been instructed to send to Harney, and said that if this were done and the Government would look after Cairo, he would himself move into the Southwest to meet McCulloch, who was said to be advancing into Missouri from Arkansas with a large army. Orders conformable to these suggestions were instantly made by the President, and Lyon found himself early in June at the head of a considerable force, thoroughly organized, well armed, and equipped for active service.

At St. Louis besides about five hundred Regulars, including Totten's Battery, he had of Missouri Volunteers, ten regiments of infantry, a battalion of artillery, one company of sappers and miners, and one company of rifles, aggregating about ten thousand officers and men. He had also several thousand Home Guards in different parts of the State, where the Germans were numerous and the Union sentiment predominant, and they were generally well armed and equipped. At Fort Leavenworth there were four companies of infantry, four of cavalry, two of dragoons, and a number of recruits, the whole aggregating about one thousand men, all belonging to the United States Army. There were also in the same vicinity two regiments of Kansas Infantry, Dietzler's and Mitchell's, nearly two thousand strong. Two Iowa regiments (Bates' and Curtis') were on the northern border of the State and ready to invade it at a moment's notice; and Illinois was concentrating troops at Quincy, Alton and Cairo, whence they could enter Missouri in an hour.

To oppose this formidable force the State had

scarcely one thousand partially organized troops, and most of these were armed with shot guns and rifles. Except a few muskets and half a dozen field-pieces and some powder, it had no munitions of war, nor any supply of food, nor any transportation, nor any military stores of any kind, nor any money.

But all this did not dismay either the Governor or General Price. On the contrary, as soon as they learned that Harney had been removed and that Lyon was in command, General Price published an order to the brigadier-generals of the several military districts, in which he said that, while it was still the desire of the Governor and himself to maintain the neutrality of Missouri and keep the peace until her Convention should decide what position the State would take in the impending conflict, and were themselves still carrying out in good faith the agreement made with General Harney, the removal of that officer from the command of the Federal forces in Missouri and the manifest intention of his successor, General Lyon, to arm the Union men of the State, which was itself a palpable violation of the Price-Harney agreement and one that ought to be resisted to the last extremity, had aroused grave fears that the people were to be forced by the terrors of a military invasion to take a position not of their free choice;

that it was his own intention to prevent the consummation of such an outrage; and that they need have no fear that a million such people as the citizens of Missouri could be subjugated.

Secret orders were at the same time sent to them to hasten the organization of the troops in their respective districts, and to get them ready for active service. Each regiment was instructed to adopt the State flag, which was to be "made of blue merino with the arms of the State emblazoned in gold gilt on each side."

The imminence of the danger led those who still hoped to save Missouri from the horrors of war to make one more effort to prevent a conflict between the Federal troops and the State. William A. Hall, David H. Armstrong, and J. Richard Barret accordingly persuaded Governor Jackson and General Price to ask for an interview with Lyon. The latter, upon the request of Mr. Hall and Colonel Thomas T. Gantt, consented to the interview upon condition that the Governor and General Price would come to St. Louis and hold it there, and he also stipulated in writing that if the Governor and the General, or either of them "should visit St. Louis on or before the 12th of June, in order to hold an interview with him for the purpose of effecting, if possible, a pacific solution of the troubles of Missouri, they should be free from molestation or arrest during their journey to St. Louis, and their return from St. Louis to Jefferson City."

With this safe conduct Governor Jackson and General Price left Jefferson City on the afternoon of the 10th, accompanied by one of the Governor's aides-de-camp, the writer of this narrative.

The Governor notified General Lyon the next morning that he was at the Planters' House, and would be pleased to confer with him there. Lyon replied that he would meet him and General Price at the arsenal instead. The Governor, rightly considering this reply as impertinent, informed General Lyon that he would confer with him at the Planters' House, and at no other place. Lyon accordingly came to the Planters' House, accompanied by Blair and Major Conant, his aide-de-camp, and the conference took place there.

Lyon opened it by saying that the discussion on the part of his Government " would be conducted by Colonel Blair, who enjoyed its confidence in the very highest degree, and was authorized to speak for it." Blair was, in fact, better fitted than any man in the Union to discuss with Jackson and Price the grave questions then at issue between the United States and the State of Missouri, and in all her borders there were no men better fitted than they to speak for Missouri on that momentous occasion.

But, despite the modesty of his opening, Lyon

was too much in earnest, too zealous, too well informed on the subject, too aggressive, and too fond of disputation to let Blair conduct the discussion on the part of his Government. In half an hour it was he that was conducting it, holding his own at every point against Jackson and Price, masters though they were of Missouri politics whose course they had been directing and controlling for years while he was only captain of an infantry regiment on the Plains. He had not, however, been a mere soldier in those days, but had been an earnest student of the very questions that he was now discussing, and he comprehended the matter as well as any man, and handled it in the soldierly way to which he had been bred, using the sword to cut knots that he could not untie.

It was to no purpose that they all sought, or pretended to seek, the basis of a new agreement for maintaining the peace of Missouri. If they really sought to find one, they did not. Finally, when the conference had lasted four or five hours, Lyon closed it, as he had opened it. "Rather," said he, (he was still seated, and spoke deliberately, slowly, and with a peculiar emphasis) "rather than concede to the State of Missouri the right to demand that my Government shall not enlist troops within her limits, or bring troops into the State whenever it pleases, or move its troops at its own will into, out of, or through the State; rather than concede to the State of Missouri for one single instant the right to dictate to my Government in any matter however unimportant, I would" (rising as he said this, and pointing in turn to every one in the room) "see you, and you, and you, and you, and you, and every man, woman, and child in the State, dead and buried." Then turning to the Governor, he said: "This means war. In an hour one of my officers will call for you and conduct you out of my lines." And then, without another word, without an inclination of the head, without even a look, he turned upon his heel and strode out of the room, rattling his spurs and clanking his sabre, while we, whom he left, and who had known each other for years, bade farewell to each other courteously and kindly, and separated—Blair and Conant to fight for the Union, we for the land of our birth.

On the way to Jefferson City it was decided that the Governor would forthwith issue a proclamation calling the people to arms; that General Price should take field at the head of whatever force he could muster, and make such resistance as he might to the advance of Lyon; and that the Confederate Government should be asked to send a co-operating army into the State as quickly as possible.

It was past two o'clock in the morning (June 12) when we reached Jefferson City. But there was no thought of sleep, for every one was sure that Lyon would hasten to follow. By daybreak the Governor's proclamation, which I had prepared in accordance with his instructions, was passing through the press; the State officers had packed the public records and papers, which they wished to take away; and everything betokened the speedy evacuation of the capital.

The Proclamation was published during the day (June 12), and was sent to all parts of the State. As it sets out fairly the matters which were then in dispute between the State and the United States, and the grounds upon which the Governor called the people to arms, it may be quoted in full:

"A series of unprovoked and unparalleled outrages have been inflicted upon the peace and dignity of this Commonwealth and upon the rights and liberties of its people by wicked and unprincipled men, professing to act under the authority of the United States Government. The solemn enactments of your Legislature have been nullified; your volunteer soldiers have been taken prisoners; your commerce with your sister States has been suspended; your trade with your own fellow-citizens has been, and is, subjected to the harassing control of an armed soldiery; peaceful citizens have been imprisoned without warrant of law; unoffending and defenceless men, women, and children have been ruthlessly shot down and murdered; and other unbearable indignities have been heaped upon your State and yourselves.

"To all these outrages and indignities you have submitted with a patriotic forbearance which has only encouraged the perpetrators of these grievous wrongs to attempt still bolder and more daring usurpations. It has been my earnest endeavor, under all these embarrassing circumstances, to maintain the peace of the State, and to avert, if possible, from our borders, the desolating effects of a civil war. With that object in view I authorized Major-General Price, several weeks ago, to arrange with General Harney commanding the Federal forces in this State, the terms of an agreement by which the peace of the State might be preserved. They came, on the 21st of May, to an understanding, which was made public. The State authorities have labored faithfully to carry out that agreement. The Federal Government, on the other hand, not only manifested its strong opposition to it by the instant dismissal of the distinguished officer who, on its part, entered into it, but it at once began, and has uninterruptedly carried out, a system of hostile operations in utter contempt of that agreement, and in reckless disregard of its own plighted faith. These acts latterly portended revolution and civil war so unmistakably, that I resolved to make one further effort to avert these dangers and sufferings from you. I therefore solicited an interview with Brigadier-General Lyon, commanding the Federal army in Missouri. It was granted on the 10th inst., and, waiving all questions personal and official, I went to St. Louis accompanied by Major-General Price.

"We had an interview on the 11th inst. with General Lyon and Colonel F. P. Blair, jr., at which I submitted to them this proposition: That I would disband the State Guard and break up its organization; that I would disarm all the companies which had been armed by the State; that I would pledge myself not to attempt to organize the militia under the Military Bill; that no arms or other munitions of war should be brought into the State; that I would protect all citizens equally in all their rights, regardless of their political opinions; that I would suppress all insurrectionary movements within the State; that I would repel all attempts to invade it from whatever quarter and by whomsoever made; and that I would thus maintain a strict neutrality in the present unhappy contest, and preserve the peace of the State. And I further proposed that I would, if necessary, invoke the assistance of the United States troops to carry out these pledges. All this I proposed to do upon condition that the Federal Government would undertake to disarm the Home Guards, which it has illegally organized and armed throughout the State, and pledge itself not to occupy with its troops any locality not occupied by them at this time.

"Nothing but the most earnest desire to avert the horrors of civil war from our State, could have tempted me to propose these humiliating terms. They were rejected by the Federal officers.

"They demanded not only the disorganization and disarming of the State militia and the nullification of the Military Bill; but they refused to disarm their own Home Guards, and insisted that the Federal Government should enjoy an unrestricted right to move and station its troops throughout the State, whenever and wherever that might, in the opinion of its officers, be necessary for the protection of the 'loyal subjects' of the Federal Government, or for the repelling of invasion; and they plainly announced that it was the intention of the Administration to take military occupation, under these pretexts, of the whole State, and to reduce it, as avowed by General Lyon himself, to 'the exact condition of Maryland.'

"The acceptance by me of these degrading terms would not only have sullied the honor of Missouri, but would have aroused the indignation of every brave citizen, and would have precipitated the very conflict which it has been my aim to prevent. We refused to accede to them and the conference was broken up.

"Fellow-citizens! all our efforts toward conciliation have failed. We can hope nothing from the moderation or justice of the agents of the Federal Government in this State. They are energetically hastening the execution of their bloody and revolutionary schemes for the inauguration of civil war in your midst; for the military occupation of your State by armed bands of lawless invaders; for the overthrow of your State Government, and the subversion of those liberties which that Government has always sought to protect; and they intend to exert their whole power to subjugate you, if possible, to the military despotism which has usurped the powers of the Federal Government.

"Now, therefore, I, Claiborne F. Jackson, Governor of the State of Missouri, do, in view of the foregoing facts and by virtue of the powers vested in me by the Constitution and laws of this Commonwealth, issue this my proclamation, calling the militia of the State to the number of fifty thousand into the active service of the State, for the purpose of repelling said invasion, and for the protection of the lives, liberties, and property of the citizens of this State. And I earnestly exhort all good citizens of Missouri to rally under the flag of their State, for the protection of their homes and firesides, and for the defence of their most sacred rights and dearest privileges.

"In issuing this proclamation I hold it to be my solemn duty to remind you that Missouri is still one of the United States; that the executive department of the State Government does not arrogate to itself the power to disturb that relation; that that power has been wisely vested in a convention, which will, at the proper time, express your sovereign will; and that meanwhile it is your duty to obey all constitutional requirements of the Federal Government.

"But it is equally my duty to advise you that your first allegiance is due to your own State, and that you are under no obligation whatever to obey the unconstitutional edicts of the military despotism which has enthroned itself at Washington, or to submit to the infamous and degrading sway of its minions in this State. No brave and true-hearted Missourian will obey the one or submit to the other. Rise then and drive out ignominiously the invaders, who have dared to desecrate the soil which your labors have made fruitful, and which is consecrated by your homes."

Immediately upon the removal of General Harney from the command of the Federal forces in Missouri, the Governor had, in anticipation of the speedy opening of hostilities, directed the quartermaster-general of the State to remove the armory and workshop, which had been established at Jefferson City, to the town of Booneville, as General

Price was of opinion that it was better to make a stand at the latter place, which was in the midst of a friendly population, and contiguous to the counties from which he expected the strongest support, than at the Capital, whose population, consisting largely of Germans, was unfriendly and hostile; and had decided that when the State forces should be compelled to retire from Jefferson City they would hold Booneville and the Missouri River above that point long enough to give the people of North Missouri an opportunity to come to his help. Both the Governor and General Price believed that, if this were done, they could within a week or two concentrate near Lexington an army strong enough to hold the western counties of Missouri until the Confederate States could send an army to their support, and arms and equipments for the State Guard.

Orders were accordingly issued on the 12th of June to the commanding officers of the several military districts to immediately assemble all of their available men, each (except General John B. Clark) at some convenient place within his own district, and to get them ready for instant service in the field. General Clark, whose district was north of the Missouri, was ordered to rendezvous his men at Booneville, and to organize them there as speedily as possible.

On Thursday the 13th the Governor learned that Lyon was embarking his troops at St. Louis, with the evident purpose to move against Jefferson City. General Price, who had already caused the railroad bridges across the Osage and the Gasconade to be destroyed so as to prevent Lyon's approach by rail, now ordered General Parsons, who had collected a small force at Jefferson City, to retire with it along the Pacific Railroad to a point south of Booneville, and there to await orders. He, together with the Governor, and their staff officers, and some of the State officials, and Captain Kelly's company, embarked the same afternoon on the steamer *White Cloud*, and reached Booneville during the night.

General John B. Clark was already there with several hundred men, who had eagerly answered the Governor's call. They continued to arrive during the next two days, Friday and Saturday, singly and in squads, bringing with them their shot guns and rifles. Most of them belonged to Colonel Marmaduke's regiment, which had been hastily organized at Jefferson City in May, but sent back to their homes before they could be taught either drill or discipline.

Rumors which greatly exaggerated the real facts reached Booneville on Saturday (June 15) that a skirmish had taken place on the 13th near Independence between some State troops under Colonel Edmunds B. Holloway, and a detachment of Federal dragoons from Fort Leavenworth; that Colonel Holloway had been killed; and that some State troops, which were rendezvousing at Lexington, were threatened by a large body of United States cavalry, and several regiments of Kansas volunteers. General Price determined, in consequence of these rumors, to proceed forthwith to Lexington and assume personal command of the State forces in that vicinity. He accordingly left the next morning (Sunday) for Lexington, after ordering General Clark, upon whom the command of the men at Booneville devolved, to hold that place as long as practicable, and then to effect a junction with General Parsons. He was already satisfied that, having no artillery with which to obstruct the navigation of the Missouri, he would have to abandon the line of that river, and to withdraw his force southward to some place where he could organize, arm and equip it.

CHAPTER XI.

BOONEVILLE AND CARTHAGE.

Lyon sends Sweeny and Sigel to the South-west—Pursues the Governor—Occupies Jefferson City—Advances on Booneville—The Engagement at Booneville—Important Consequences—General Price at Lexington—Orders Rains to retreat southward towards Lamar—Hastens to meet McCulloch—Governor Jackson retreats towards Warsaw—The Cole Camp Affair—Guibor and Barlow—Burbridge—The Governor reaches Lamar—Is joined by Rains and Slack—Temporary Organization of the State Guard—Lyon gets ready to pursue—Sturgis ordered to co-operate—Lyon and Sturgis move towards Clinton—Sigel tries to intercept the Governor—The Battle of Carthage—Defeat of Sigel.

HARDLY had Lyon left the Planters' House on the afternoon of the 11th of June when he telegraphed to the War Department for five thousand additional stand of arms, and for authority to enlist more troops in Missouri. His requests were instantly complied with.

He issued orders the same night for the movement of his troops.

Sigel, Salomon, and B. Gratz Brown were ordered towards Springfield with their regiments. They began moving on the 13th, and had all left St. Louis on the 15th, accompanied by two batteries (eight guns) under Major Backoff. The command of this expedition was given to Captain Thomas W. Sweeny acting as brigadier-general by election, and by assignment of General Harney. Its objects were to occupy the south-western part of the State; to oppose the apprehended advance of a Confederate army under Ben. McCulloch; and to cut off the retreat of Governor Jackson, General Price, and the State troops, all of whom Lyon proposed himself to drive in that direction.

In execution of this purpose he embarked on the 13th of June at St. Louis, with Totten's Light Battery, Company F, Second United States Artillery; Company B of the Second United States Infantry; two companies of United States Recruits; Blair's regiment of Missouri Volunteers; and nine companies of Boernstein's regiment; aggregating about two thousand men, and advanced by way of the Missouri River to Jefferson City. Arriving there on Saturday the 15th, about two P.M., he took quiet possession of the city, the State forces having evacuated it on Thursday.

Leaving Colonel Boernstein and three companies of his regiment at Jefferson City, Lyon himself proceeded the next day (Sunday, June 16), with the rest of his command—about seventeen hundred men—towards Booneville. When within fifteen miles of that city, the transports were ordered to lay by till daybreak; about which time they moved on to a point about eight miles below Booneville. There Lyon debarked all of his men, except one company of Blair's regiment, and a detachment of artillery with one howitzer. These he ordered to proceed up the river on the transports, in order to deceive the State troops and to create a diversion in favor of his real movement. Lyon himself advanced with his main body along the river road towards Booneville, moving very cautiously, as he had been led to believe that he would have to encounter at least "three or four thousand rebels."

Governor Jackson learned Sunday night that Lyon was approaching Booneville by way of the river. He at once ordered General Parsons who was at Tipton, some twenty miles to the south, to bring his whole command to Booneville forthwith. As soon as it was known on Monday morning that Lyon had debarked his force, and was advancing upon the city by land, the Governor ordered Marmaduke to take his own regiment, and all other armed men in the city, except Kelly's company, and to move out against Lyon, and impede his advance as much as possible. This was done in order to give Parsons time to come up, and also to give to such citizens as might want to escape, the opportunity to arrange their affairs and leave; and also to enable General Harding to destroy his ordnance shops, and the material which he had collected. Colonel Marmaduke, who had already protested against making any resistance at Booneville and had advised the Governor to concentrate his forces behind the Osage in the neighborhood of Warsaw, again represented to him that to meet Lyon now could only result in disaster to the State troops. The Governor, nevertheless repeated his order, and Marmaduke went out with between 400 and 500 men to confront the enemy.

Lyon had advanced about two miles when his skirmishers encountered Marmaduke, who at once opened such a brisk fire as to compel Lyon to bring up his artillery and deploy a part of his infantry. Having accomplished this, Marmaduke withdrew his men to a stronger position about a mile nearer to the city. There, under cover of some buildings and a dense wood, he made a stand, which appeared so formidable to Lyon, who greatly overestimated Marmaduke's strength, that he deployed his whole force in line of battle. A sharp engagement now took place, in the midst of which Colonel Marmaduke received orders from the Governor to fall back to the city, in order to form a junction with General Parsons, who was rapidly approaching.

It was no easy matter, however, to withdraw four or five hundred raw troops from a field, on which they were engaged with four times their own number of well armed and well disciplined soldiers commanded by a man like Lyon. They nevertheless fell back in some order at first, taking advantage of every good point to deliver their fire at the Federals; but they were in the end pretty thoroughly dispersed.

Such was the trifling engagement which has been called "the Battle of Booneville." The Federal loss was two men killed, and nine wounded. Of the State troops two were killed, and five or six were slightly wounded.

Insignificant as was this engagement in a military aspect, it was in fact a stunning blow to the Southern Rights' people of the State, and one which did incalculable and unending injury to the Confederates. It was indeed the consummation of Blair's statesmanlike scheme to make it impossible for Missouri to secede, or out of her great resources to contribute abundantly of men and material to the Southern cause as she would surely have done had her people been left free to do as they pleased.

It was also the crowning achievement of Lyon's well-conceived campaign. The capture of Camp Jackson had disarmed the State, and compelled the loyalty of St. Louis and all the adjacent counties. The advance upon Jefferson City had put the State Government to flight, and taken away from it that prestige which gives force to established authority.

The dispersion of the volunteers who had rushed to Booneville to fight under Price for Missouri and the South, extended Lyon's conquest over all the country lying between the Missouri and the State of Iowa; closed all the avenues by which the Southern men of that part of Missouri could make their way to Price; made the Missouri an unobstructed Federal highway from its source to its mouth; and rendered it impossible for Price to hold the rich, populous, and friendly counties in the vicinity of Lexington. Price had indeed no alternative now but to retreat in all haste to the south-western corner of the State, there to organize his army under the protection of the force which the Confederate Government was mustering in north-western Arkansas under General McCulloch, for the protection of that State and the Indian Territory.

When Price reached Lexington on the 18th of June, he found several thousand volunteers assembled there and in the adjoining county of Jackson under Brigadier-Generals Rains and Slack. His first care was to organize them. But hardly had he begun this work when news was brought of the disaster at Booneville, and of the retreat of the Governor, with Generals Parsons and Clark, towards Warsaw. Knowing that the unorganized force at Lexington was now threatened not only by the Federal troops at Fort Leavenworth and Kansas

City, 2,500 strong, but by Lyon and his army also, Price ordered Rains to assume command of all the State troops near Lexington and to move them as expeditiously as possible towards Lamar in Barton County. He, accompanied by his staff and a small mounted escort, made his way in all haste to Arkansas, in order to bring McCulloch to the rescue of both the Governor and Rains.

The Governor was, meanwhile, hurrying towards Warsaw, feeling that he would not be safe from Lyon's pursuit till he had gotten behind the Osage. He was met on the way by rumors that a well-armed regiment of Home Guards under Colonel Cook was at Cole Camp, on his line of march. On approaching the place, however, he learned, to his great relief, that the Home Guards had been surprised and badly whipped on the morning of the 19th by a battalion of State troops raised near Warsaw and led by two very dashing young soldiers, Lieutenant-Colonel Walter S. O'Kane and Major Thomas H. Murray. The news was quickly confirmed by the arrival of the battalion at the Governor's camp, with three hundred and sixty-two new muskets which they had taken from the Home Guards. Thus reinforced, the Governor continued his retreat to Warsaw, and across the Osage.

There he halted in order to ascertain the movements of General Price. During this time, two men, who had been arrested as spies, were brought before the Governor. They turned out to be Henry Guibor and William P. Barlow, lieutenants of the light battery which had been serving in the south-west under Bowen. They had been captured with the rest of the State troops at Camp Jackson and paroled. Holding that their capture was unlawful, and that their paroles were therefore not obligatory (as the courts subsequently decided), they had made their way to the army, and were eager to be placed on duty. They came very opportunely; for Parsons was still dragging along the four brass 6-pounders which had been captured at Liberty Arsenal, but he had no men that knew how to handle them. They were turned over to Guibor and Barlow. But having been brought along without equipments and without any fixed ammunition, they would still have been of very little present use but for the inventive genius and energy of the two young officers, who, surmounting every difficulty, enlisted a company, equipped the guns, prepared ammunition, and got the battery ready for instant service.

Another notable accession to the Governor's force at this time was John Q. Burbridge and ten other men from Pike County who came into camp, bringing with them from that remote county about one hundred and fifty muskets, which they had taken by guile from a company of State militia mostly loyal Germans, and had brought by force to the Governor. Within thirty-six hours Burbridge had enlisted and was in command of a well-armed company.

Having ascertained that General Price had gone to McCulloch's head-quarters, and that Rains was retreating southward, the Governor put his own column in motion, and a few days thereafter reached Montevallo, in Vernon County, and thence moved to Camp Lamar, on the right bank of Spring River, some three miles north of the village of Lamar.

There he was joined by Rains and Slack on the 3d of July. The march of their column had been greatly impeded and made laborious and fatiguing by the high waters of the streams across which they had to ferry their long-drawn, motley train of vehicles of every description laden not only with supplies for an army, but chiefly with household goods and utensils of every sort, conspicuous among which were feather-beds and frying-pans. The Governor, therefore, determined to halt at Camp Lamar for a few days in order to rest the men; and meanwhile to distribute them to the commands to which they properly belonged.

Rains was found to have nearly three thousand men, but many of them were unarmed. His effective strength was about twelve hundred infantry under Weightman, about six hundred mounted men under Cawthon, and a three-gun battery under Bledsoe. Parsons had about six hundred and fifty armed men. His infantry were commanded by Colonel Kelly, his mounted men by Colonel Brown, and his four-gun battery by Guibor. Clark had Burbridge's regiment of infantry, whose effective strength was three hundred and sixty-five officers and men. Slack's brigade consisted of about five hundred mounted men under Colonel Rives, and about seven hundred infantry under Colonel Hughes, and Major Thornton. Parsons, Clark, and Slack had also about eight hundred unarmed men.

Lyon was notified the day after the affair at Booneville (June 18th), that Missouri had been detached from the Department of the West, and attached to the Department of the Ohio, commanded by Major-General George B. McClellan. This had been done by the advice of General Scott, and through the solicitation of Attorney-General Bates, Judge Gamble and other St. Louisians, who did not like Blair, and had no great confidence in "Captain" Lyon. Fearing that this would interfere with their campaign, Blair hurried to Washington City to obtain a revocation of the order, and the assigment of Lyon to the command of military operations in Missouri. This he could not accomplish, but he finally persuaded the Administration on the 3d of July to organize Illinois together with Missouri and all the other States and Territories lying between the Mississippi River and the Rocky Mountains into a separate military command to be known as the *The Western Department*, under Major-General Fremont, with head-quarters at St. Louis.

McClellan did not interfere with Lyon during the short time that his command extended over Missouri, and the latter went on to execute the plans which Blair and he had devised for the conquest of the State, though he was severely crippled by the loss of Blair, whose presence and counsels were of inestimable importance to him. While procuring transportation and supplies, and reinforcing and reorganizing his army at Booneville, Lyon published a proclamation to the people of Missouri, promising not to molest any man who had taken up arms against the Government, if he would return to his home and remain there quietly. This wise measure had the effect which he anticipated, and kept thousands of men out of the ranks of the State Guard.

He next assigned Colonel John D. Stevenson to the command of the Missouri River from Kansas City to its mouth, and gave him a sufficient force to garrison Jefferson City, Booneville and Lexington, and ordered him also to protect the loyal inhabitants of the adjacent counties; to disperse all gatherings of men hostile to the Federal Government; and to prevent reinforcements from crossing the river to Price. All that part of the State north of the Missouri was entrusted temporarily to the command of Colonel Samuel R. Curtis, who had already occupied parts of it with the Second Iowa Infantry. South-eastern Missouri was left to the care of McClellan, who was for that purpose concentrating at Cairo an ample force, under Brigadier-General Prentiss. St. Louis and all the country within a hundred and fifty miles of it, had been thoroughly subjugated, and was occupied by sufficient garrisons.

Major Sturgis was already following Rains with about nine hundred regulars from Fort Leavenworth, and two regiments of Kansas Volunteers about sixteen hundred strong. Lyon himself moved from Booneville on the 3d of July with about two thousand three hundred and fifty men, of whom two hundred and fifty were regulars. The two columns had an effective strength of about four thousand eight hundred and fifty men. They were all well armed and equipped, and fully supplied with everything that an army in the field required. They were also officered by educated soldiers, many of whom afterwards rose to distinction. But Lyon had lost fifteen days of priceless time at Booneville, and the State troops were more than a week in advance of his own column, near Lamar.

In front of the Governor, though he did not himself know it, was the force which Lyon, before leaving St. Louis, had sent under Sweeney and Sigel to the south-west to cut off the retreat of the State troops, and to prevent McCulloch from succoring them. Sweeny, who reached Springfield on the 1st of July, found at and near that post and on the way thither from Rolla, about four thousand men, including one thousand Home Guards. Sigel, who had preceded him, had moved westward with his own regiment and Salomon's, and taken position at Neosho and Sarcoxie in order to intercept General Price. Finding that Price and his escort had already passed on to McCulloch's camp, he decided to throw himself in front of Governor Jackson, and to hold him north of Spring River till Lyon could come up with his own and Sturgis' columns and attack him in rear. In this determination he was confirmed by an order from Sweeny, who directed him to concentrate his force, and move toward Carthage, which was in the direct line of the Governor's retreat. Leaving one company of his own regiment and some detailed men at Neosho under command of Captain Conrad, he moved northward with the rest of his force, except Captain Indest's company, and encamped on the evening of the 4th of July on Spring River a little south-east of Carthage.

Just after the sun had gone down on the 4th of July, and while the State troops were still encamped near Lamar, resting from their fatigues, and getting themselves into some semblance of an army, a man rode hastily to General Parsons' quarters and told the general that Colonel Monroe (his quartermaster) who had gone to Carthage with a detachment of ninety-five men to collect forage and subsistence, was threatened there by a large force of the enemy, and wanted reinforcements. Parsons instantly ordered his whole command to get ready to march toward Carthage at ten o'clock that night, and then communicated the facts to the Governor.

This was the first intimation that the State troops had that an enemy was in their front with intent to cut off their retreat. But before the hour fixed by Parsons for the movement of his command had arrived, other couriers had come from Monroe saying that the Federals were approaching Carthage in great force. Governor Jackson thereupon assumed command in person of all his troops, and, countermanding Parsons' order for the movement of his own force, ordered the whole army to take up the march at day break (July 5), with Rains in front, and Captain Shelby's company in advance. The Governor, accompanied by General David R. Atchison and other volunteer aids and by some of his own staff, rode at the head of the column with General Rains. They had marched about five miles beyond Lamar when they were met by Colonel Monroe and informed by him that Sigel had already passed through Carthage, and was on the way to meet them and give battle. The column was quickly halted on the ridge of a prairie, which sloped gently down toward Cocn Creek, an affluent of Spring River. This creek, which was heavily bordered on both sides by "timber" and "brush," was about two miles in front of the State troops. Hardly had they been halted when the bayonets of the Federals were seen gleaming in the sunshine as they descended the opposite declivity in perfect order, before disappearing in "the timber" on that side of the creek.

The Governor at once deployed his men in line of battle, with Weightman's brigade on the right, and on its left Slack's Infantry. Between these two Bledsoe's three guns were thrown into battery. Guibor took position with his four guns on the left of Slack, and next to him came Parsons' Infantry, under Colonel Kelly. Clark's Infantry under Burbridge occupied the left. The right flank of the State troops was covered by Rains with the mounted men of his division, and their left flank by mounted men under Brown and Rives. The line thus formed consisted of twenty-six hundred infantry and artillery most of the former armed with shot guns and rifles, and about fifteen hundred mounted men similarly armed. The unarmed men, of whom there were about two thousand, all mounted, were sent to the rear with the wagons.

Every one, officers and men, now looked on with intense curiosity, as the Federals, with the precision of veterans which most of them were, emerged from "the brush" on the north side of the creek, and deployed into line on the prairie some twelve hundred yards away. They consisted of nine companies of Sigel's Regiment and seven companies of Salomon's, with an effective strength of nine hundred and fifty men, and seven pieces of artillery (one hundred and twenty-five men) under Major Backoff.

Sigel began the fight. Advancing his line about three hundred yards, he opened upon the State troops with all his guns, delivering a steady fire of round shot, shell and grape. Guibor replied with his four guns and was followed on the instant by Bledsoe. The ineffective artillery practice thus begun had been kept up nearly an hour, when the Governor ordered Rains to advance on the right with his mounted men, and Rives and Brown on the left. The unarmed men on horseback (about two thousand) were at the same time ordered to seek shelter in the heavy timber on the right of the State troops.

Sigel, seeing these movements, and that he was about to be attacked on both flanks, and fancying also that he was about to be taken in rear by the heavy mounted force which was taking shelter in the woods (for he did not know that they were not armed) withdrew his men in good order first to the timber, and then beyond the creek. Posting Essig's Battery, with a support of five companies of infantry on the high ground south of the creek in such way as to command the approach to the ford, he retired with the rest of his men to the defence of his train, then threatened by some mounted Missourians who had crossed the creek higher up.

The State troops following in some disorder were brought to a halt within four hundred yards of the ford by the well-directed fire of Essig's Battery. But Weightman rapidly reforming his line, opened fire with Bledsoe's guns, and under their cover and that of "the timber," advanced his own brigade along with Slack's toward the creek. It was now and here that the serious fighting of the day took place; for Essig continued to hold the ford with great obstinacy. But General Clark and General

Parsons managed at last to cross the creek at another ford and were endangering his retreat. Essig thereupon gave the order to retire, and fell back to the main body.

Sigel continued his retreat in good order, closely followed by a rabble of State troops and harassed on all sides by their mounted men, who did not, however, dare to attack his compact ranks. Crossing Spring River without opposition he held Carthage under cover of its houses and fences till his train was well on the road to Springfield. He then continued his retreat to Sarcoxie, fifteen miles away. Reaching that place at three o'clock in the morning, he rested his men there till daybreak, and then hastened along to Mount Vernon. Finding that he was no longer pursued, he halted there. As the engagement took place about nine miles north of Carthage, Sigel had on the 5th of July marched under a blazing sun more than ten miles, had met and fought on the same day an army four times as numerous as his own, and had then withdrawn his men in good order, first to Carthage nine miles from the field, and then to Sarcoxie fifteen miles further, without halting either to eat or to sleep.

The Federal loss in this "engagement near Carthage," generally called *The Battle of Carthage*, was thirteen killed and thirty-one wounded. The State troops lost ten killed and sixty-four wounded. The

Federal commander estimated Governor Jackson's losses at "not less than from three hundred and fifty to four hundred," and Confederate historians have estimated Sigel's loss "at from one hundred and fifty to two hundred killed, and from three hundred to four hundred wounded!"

The State troops occupied on the night of the battle the ground on which Sigel had camped the preceding night, and the next day (July 6) they marched leisurely and in great good spirits toward Granby.

CHAPTER XII.

THE CONFEDERATES ENTER MISSOURI.

Ben McCulloch assigned to defence of the Indian Territory—Concentrates his force, including Pearce's Brigade, near Fort Smith—Governor Jackson, before leaving Jefferson City, asks him to enter Missouri—McCulloch asks the President's consent—Advances to Maysville—Joins Price—Marches with him to rescue the Governor and the Missouri troops—Meets them—Price Assumes Command of the State Guard—Cowskin Prairie—Reorganization of the State Guard—Price's Difficulties—He surmounts them—Governor Jackson, Price, and McCulloch try to secure the co-operation of Polk and Hardee—Polk sends Pillow to New Madrid, but Hardee refuses to co-operate—Price, McCulloch, and Pearce move against Springfield—They concentrate their armies at Cassville.

BEN. MCCULLOCH, the well-known Texan ranger, had been appointed on the 13th of May, brigadier-general of the Provisional Army of the Confederate States, and assigned to the command of the Indian Territory with orders to guard it against invasion from Kansas or elsewhere. A regiment of infantry from Louisiana, a mounted regiment from Arkansas, and another from Texas were ordered to report to him, and he was also authorized to raise two regiments of Indians. On the 25th of May he reached Fort Smith and went a few days later into the Indian Territory to select a position for his command.

He found a suitable one in the Cherokee country, but discovered that John Ross, the Cherokee chief, and a majority of that nation were opposed to the occupation of their lands by any armed force. He, therefore, decided not to occupy the Territory, but to take a position at Fort Smith in western Arkansas instead. This change of plan led him to ask the Confederate Government to add north-western Arkansas to his command. This request was not granted. By the 12th of June he had, at and near Fort Smith, the Third Louisiana Infantry Colonel Louis Hébert, and seven companies of Churchill's Regiment of Mounted Riflemen (Arkansas). There was also in the same vicinity a brigade of Arkansas Militia, about one thousand five hundred strong, under command of Brigadier-General N. B. Pearce, a graduate of West Point.

This was the force which had excited the apprehensions of Blair and Lyon, and aroused the hopes of Governor Jackson and the Missouri Secessionists.

When the Governor, early in June, learned that McCulloch was at Fort Smith, he sent Captain Colton Greene to him with an urgent request that he would advance into the State with his army, in order to encourage the Southern Rights' people, and give General Price time to enlist and organize the State Guard. Greene reached Fort Smith on the 13th of June—the day that the Governor and General Price left Jefferson City—and at once laid the Governor's request before McCulloch, who listened attentively though with that cautious reserve which was one of his most noticeable characteristics. But the adjutant-general of his brigade Captain McIntosh, a very enterprising and intelligent young officer who had just resigned from the United States Army and been sent by Mr. Davis to Arkansas to help McCulloch organize and handle his troops, appreciated the importance of the movement which Governor Jackson suggested, and advocated it so earnestly that McCulloch promised to ask the President's permission to execute it. And he did, on the next day, the 14th of June, write to the Secretary of War as follows:

"I think the proposition made by the Governor is one of great importance to the Confederate Government, and I hope it may meet with your favorable consideration. I will briefly lay before you a plan of operations. The Chief of the Cherokees is not willing to have a force marched into his country, and he desires to remain neutral. The only way to force his country into the Confederacy is to throw a force into the north-western portion of this State, take possession of Fort Scott on the Missouri line, and subjugate that portion of Kansas. I am satisfied that Lane has no force yet of any importance, and the occupation of Fort Scott would not only place Kansas in my power, but would give heart and countenance to our friends in Missouri, and accomplish the very object for which I was sent here—preventing a force from the North invading the Indian Territory.

"All the border counties on the western line of Missouri are with us. We would therefore be able to draw our supplies from them. After strengthening myself at Fort Scott, I could, by co-operating with Missouri, take such a position on the Kansas River as I might desire. In order to carry out this plan I would again respectfully ask to have the Western Military Division of Arkansas put under my orders, with authority to muster the troops now in it (about sixteen hundred) into the provisional forces, and to accept such other regiments and battalions until my force is at least seven thousand strong."

He was opposed to employing Indians in Kansas, or elsewhere outside of their own territory.

This plan of campaign was both wise and feasible, and upon being outlined to the Governor of Arkansas, a few days later, was so heartily approved by him, that he telegraphed (June 21) to the Secretary of War that Arkansas had eight thousand armed men in the field, whom it would turn over to the Confederate Government for the proposed movement, and suggested that "an active campaign in Missouri would aid Virginia." But the policy of the Confederate Government, which, acting strictly on the defensive, did not then contemplate the invasion of any "loyal" State, and least of all Missouri, which it believed to be hopelessly subjugated! And this policy it observed so strictly that it would not now manifest any disposition to help the Governor array the State on the side of the South, or evince even a desire to utilize her great resources for the good of the Confederacy. But, on the contrary, under the influence of unwise counsellors and through its own unpardonable ignorance of the true condition of the State, it declined to make any effort to prevent the Federal Government from occupying her territory and using her power to crush the South.

To McCulloch's proposition to assist the Missourians the Secretary of War therefore replied coldly that he might, if he thought proper, take position at Fort Scott, and give such assistance to Missouri as would subserve the main purpose of his command, which was "to conciliate the Indian Nations, and to obtain *their* active co-operation in prosecuting the war."

Missouri, with her hundred thousand men and resources greater than those of all the Cotton States together, was worth nothing to the Confederacy in comparison with two or three regiments of semi-civilized Indians, who ought never to have been allowed to cross the frontiers of their own territory!

The Secretary did not even notice McCulloch's request for the addition of north-western Arkansas to his command. To have granted that request might have inflamed McCulloch's ambition, and would have given him the opportunity, and along with it the power, to make an active campaign in Missouri. Fearing that he might do this any way, the Secretary further admonished him, on the 4th of July, that "the position of Missouri, as a Southern State still in the Union, requires, as you will readily perceive, much prudence and circumspection, and it should only be when necessity and propriety unite that active and direct assistance should be afforded by crossing the boundary and entering the State."

Such was the military status in western Arkansas when McCulloch learned that Governor Jackson and General Price were retreating toward Arkansas, closely pursued by Lyon and Sturgis, with a large force of Federal troops. He "determined to march against this force, to hold it in check, and if an opportunity occurred, to strike it a blow in Missouri," and set out at once for Maysville, in the north-western corner of the State, ordering Hébert and Churchill to follow immediately with their regiments. Pearce had already moved thither with his brigade of Arkansas militia, for the protection of his own State. McCulloch had not yet learned that the Confederate Government did not approve his proposed invasion of Missouri.

General Price, as has been told, left Lexington with a small escort immediately after the affair at Booneville, and hastened toward Fort Smith, in order to persuade McCulloch to come to the rescue of Missouri. On the way he was joined by a fine mounted company, the Windsor Guards, from Henry County, and by other companies, and men in squads, until, when he reached Cowskin Prairie in the extreme south-western corner of the State, about twelve miles from Maysville, his force amounted to nearly twelve hundred men, though many of them had no arms at all. He there learned, July the 1st, that General Pearce was near Maysville with his Arkansas brigade. As soon, therefore, as he got his men into camp he pushed on to Pearce, who told him that McCulloch was on the march from Fort Smith, and would reach Maysville the next day.

Pearce also loaned him six hundred and fifteen muskets with which to arm his men. Returning to Cowskin Prairie Price hastily organized his force, placing such as were well mounted and well armed and fit for active service, under the immediate command of Alexander E. Steen, a promising young Missourian who had resigned his commission in the United States Army in order to serve his native State.

The next day, McCulloch, who had reached Maysville in advance of his men, rode over to General Price's head-quarters. While he was there they learned that the Governor and General Rains were trying to effect a junction of their forces north of Carthage, but were closely pressed by Lyon and Sturgis. McCulloch at once agreed to move to the assistance of the Missourians, and to persuade Pearce to unite in the movement. This Pearce gladly consented to do, and Churchill having reached Maysville the next morning by a forced march, McCulloch and Pearce entered Missouri the 4th of July, with Churchill's Regiment, Gratiot's Arkansas Infantry, Carroll's Mounted Régiment, and Woodruff's Battery. Reaching Price's camp the same day, they were there joined by him and continued their march northward. Hearing, the next day, that the Governor was not only pressed in rear by Lyon and Sturgis, but that Sigel had thrown himself in his front, McCulloch left his infantry behind, and he and Price then pushed forward with their mounted men.

On approaching Neosho (July 5), McCulloch sent forward two detachments of Churchill's Regiment—one under command of that officer, and the other under Captain McIntosh—to capture the company which Sigel had left there. Making a forced march they accomplished this without firing a shot, and found themselves in the unexpected possession of one hundred and thirty-seven prisoners, and, what they valued more highly, one hundred and fifty stand of arms and seven wagons laden with supplies.

During the night Price and McCulloch came up with the rest of their mounted force. Resuming the march at break of day on the 6th, they were well on their way to Carthage when the glad tidings came that the Governor, having effected a junction of all the State forces, had fallen upon Sigel and defeated him, and was marching toward them, his men rejoicing in their victory, and confident in their prowess.

Jackson and his troops did, indeed, have abundant cause to rejoice; for, though we had not won a great victory as we foolishly fancied, or established the independence of the Confederacy as some believed, we had escaped a very great danger. For Lyon had been close behind with an overwhelming force, and, had he overtaken, would have routed and dispersed, us. Now we were not only safe from pursuit and no enemy in our front, but we would, within an hour, be under the protecting folds of the Confederate flag, and side by side with that Confederate Army, for whose coming we had been so anxiously waiting. No wonder that we burst into loud huzzas when the redoubtable McCulloch came into sight, surrounded by his gaily-dressed staff, and when accompanied by Governor Jackson, General Price, and General Pearce, he rode down our dust-stained ranks to greet the men that had fought with Sigel and put him to flight.

We were all young then, and full of hope, and looked with delighted eyes on the first Confederate soldiers that we had ever seen, the men all dressed in sober gray, and their officers resplendent with gilded buttons, and golden braid and stars of gold. To look like these gallant soldiers; to be of them; to fight beside them for their homes and for our own, was the one desire of all the Missourians, who, on that summer day, stood on one of their own verdant prairies, gazing southward.

In all their motley array there was hardly a uniform to be seen, and then, and throughout all the brilliant campaign on which they were about to enter there was nothing to distinguish their officers, even a general, from the men in the ranks, save a bit of red flannel, or a piece of cotton cloth, fastened to the shoulder, or to the arm, of the former. But for all that they were the truest and best of soldiers. Many of them, when just emerging from boyhood, had fought under Price or Doniphan in Mexico; many had been across the great plains, and were enured to the dangers and privations of the wilderness; and many had engaged in the hot strife which had ensanguined the prairies of Kansas. Among them there was hardly a man who could not read and write, and who was not more intelligent than the great mass of American citizens; not one who had not voluntarily abandoned his home with all its tender ties, and thrown away all his possessions, and left father and mother, or wife and children, within the enemy's lines, that he might himself stand by the South in her hour of great peril, and help her to defend her fields and her firesides. And among them all there was not a man who had come forth to fight for slavery.

McCulloch and Pearce now returned with their troops to Maysville, and General Price, assuming command of the Missourians, led them by easy marches to Cowskin Prairie, which they reached on the 9th of July. Up to this time few of them had been formed into regiments, or even into companies. To organize, arm, and fit them somewhat for the field, was the first care of General Price. The difficulty of this task was greatly enhanced by the fact that he had no arms, no military supplies of any kind, and no money with which to procure any, even if any had been procurable. It mattered not at all that he had no money to pay the men. There was not one of them who expected or who wanted to be paid for his services, or who ever was paid. But men and horses must be fed; and on Cowskin Prairie there was for the men little but lean beef, and for their horses nothing but the grass of the prairie. To supply their more pressing wants Quarter-master General Harding, and Colonel John Reid, the chief commissary of the army, went first to Fort Smith, and thence to Little Rock, and afterwards to Memphis, but procured nothing in time for use in the impending campaign, though they obtained supplies which contributed greatly to the efficiency and comfort of the army during the ensuing fall and winter.

Another great difficulty which General Price had to overcome was the want of experienced soldiers, who could help him to organize his army aright and equip it for the field. He had, it is true, an abundance of officers fully competent to command a regiment or a brigade, and many excellent company officers, but for the important duties of the staff he had to rely upon men who had not been trained to a military life, and who had everything to learn. For instance, the chief of ordnance of his army was one of the Governor's aides who did not know the difference between a siege gun and a howitzer, and had never seen a musket cartridge in all the days of his life. Fortunately he had some administrative ability, and all around him were men who had from boyhood been handling shot guns and rifles, and were used to improvising just such ammunition as was most needed then, and who could act in an emergency. One of these, Major Thomas H. Price, a man admirably fitted for the work that had to be done, was put in charge of it. Lead, thanks to the proximity of the Granby mines, was abundant; powder, too, thanks to the wise foresight of Governor Jackson; and the neighboring forests were full of trees, which the major knew how to convert into monster moulds for making buckshot and bullets. He went zealously to work with a corps of assistants, and in a few days his ordnance shops were turning out heaps of bullets, and buck-and-ball cartridges—enough for the immediate wants of the State Guard. No educated soldier, no officer of the Ordnance Department, could have done what Major Price did. They are not educated for such emergencies, nor could they have found precedents or authority for anything that he did.

How the artillery was supplied with ammunition has been well told by Lieutenant Barlow of Guibor's Battery. "One of Sigel's captured wagons furnished a few loose, round shot. With these for a beginning, Guibor established an "arsenal of construction." A turning-lathe in Carthage supplied sabots; the owner of a tin-shop contributed straps and canisters; iron rods which a blacksmith gave and cut into small pieces made good slugs for the canisters; and a bolt of flannel, with needles and thread, freely donated by a dry-goods man, provided us with material for our cartridge bags. A bayonet made a good candle-stick; and at night, . . . the men went to work making cartridges; strapping shot to the sabots, and filling the bags from a barrel of powder placed some distance from the candle. . . . My first cartridge resembled a turnip, rather than the trim cylinders from the Federal arsenals, and would not take a gun on any terms. But we soon learned the trick and, at the close range at which our next battle was fought, our home-made ammunition proved as effective as the best."

General Price's perplexities were greatly augmented a few days later (July 19) by the departure for Richmond of his able and accomplished adjutant-general, Colonel Little; for it involved the necessity of assigning to that position an officer utterly without experience, his chief of ordnance, the writer of this book. In spite of all these embarrassments the work of organizing, equipping, and disciplining the State Guard progressed well, for never had man seen better material for an army, and every one did his best, under the wise guidance of the able soldier who, unconsciously to himself, was with a master's hand fashioning an army, which was destined to win many a victory and never to sustain a defeat.

Before the end of July it was ready to take the field with an effective strength of nearly five thouand, while two thousand unarmed men were waiting to pick up and use the arms of those who might sicken in camp or on the march, or who might fall in battle.

A few days after the troops had gone into camp on Cowskin Prairie, Governor Jackson left (July 12) for Memphis, in order to persuade General Polk, to whose command all the country west of the Mississippi was attached, to send into Missouri a sufficient force to repossess that State. For political, as well as for military reasons, this was a thing important to be done; for the State Convention had been summoned to meet at Jefferson City on the 22d of July, and it was known that one of its first acts would be to depose Governor Jackson, and that it would then organize a State Government which would wield the power of the State against the South. To prevent this great misfortune, Governor Jackson, General Price, and the State Guard were ready to risk their lives. If the Confederate Government had comprehended the situation it might, perhaps, have assisted them.

General Polk did appreciate the importance of the movement, and, on the 23d of July, ordered General Pillow to take six thousand men of various arms from the Western District of Tennessee and move with them into Missouri by way of New Madrid. There he was to be joined by a force of Missourians under Jeff. Thompson, and would be further reinforced till he should have an effective army of eleven thousand men. Taking these he would effect a junction with General Hardee, who was to meet him with seven thousand men, whom he was concentrating at Pocahontas in Arkansas. The combined forces would then either take Lyon in rear while Price and McCulloch were attacking him in front, or would march upon St. Louis, capture that city and thence sweep up the Missouri! "Having driven the enemy from the State, I will then enter Illinois," wrote the brave old soldier, "and take Cairo in rear on my return." The army which was to execute this magnificent plan of campaign was aptly called "The Army of Liberation." Its advance under General Pillow entered Missouri on the 28th of July, and occupied New Madrid. The Battle of Bull Run had just been fought, and the South believed itself to be invincible and irresistible.

Having learned that General Hardee had been assigned to the command of North Arkansas, and that he was concentrating an army at Pocahontas on the White River, McCulloch and Price sent special messengers to him, on the 19th of July, begging him to co-operate with them in a movement against Lyon, who was then at Springfield. These messengers found Hardee at Pittman's Ferry, within four hundred yards of the Missouri line, whence he might have easily co-operated in the movement against Lyon, either by advancing on Springfield, or by threatening to interrupt his communication with Rolla. But Hardee, who had not yet outgrown the "little learning" of the schools, nor emancipated himself from the tyranny of axioms which did not apply in the circumstances wherein he was called upon to act, replied: ". . . I have actually under my command less than 2,300 men. When all the forces in this part of the State are transferred, I shall have less than 5,000 men, badly organized, badly equipped, and wanting in discipline and instruction. One of my batteries has no harness and no horses, and not one of the regiments has transportation enough for active field service. . . . I am doing all in my power to remedy these deficiencies, but it takes time to get harness and transportation. I do not wish to march to your assistance with less than 5,000 men, well-appointed, and a full complement of artillery. With every desire to aid and co-operate with the forces in the West, I am compelled at this time to forego that gratification." There was then with these troops a man not bred to arms, but endowed with great good sense and enterprise, one who was quick to see and prompt to act, and who would have taken those men into Missouri, and, uniting with Price and McCulloch, would have utterly destroyed Lyon's army. But unfortunately for the Confederacy Hindman was not in command.

Before Hardee's letter reached Price, the latter, McCulloch and Pearce, were already on the march to Springfield. Price left Cowskin Prairie on the 25th of July, and reached Cassville on the 28th, Sunday. There he was joined by Brigadier-General McBride with two regiments of State troops and a company of mounted men. This, reinforcement, about 650 men, made Price's armed force over 5,000 men. McCulloch reached Cassville the next day with his brigade, "amounting to about 3,200 men, nearly all well armed." Pearce was within ten miles of Cassville with his brigade of 2,500 Arkansas troops. With these were two fine batteries, Woodruff's and Reid's. The entire force amounted to nearly eleven thousand men. Beside these there were nearly two thousand unarmed Missourians.

As Price, McCulloch, and Pearce had each an entirely independent command, they agreed upon an order of march, in conformity to which the combined forces began their movement towards Springfield, fifty-two miles distant, on the 31st of July. The advance guard consisting of ten companies of mounted Missourians under command of Brigadier-General Rains, and the First Division of the forces consisting of infantry and artillery under the immediate command of McCulloch, left Cassville that day. The other divisions, commanded by Pearce and Steen, left the two following days. General Price accompanied the Second Division without, however, taking immediate command of any force.

CHAPTER XIII.

LYON MOVES OUT TO ATTACK.

Junction of Lyon and Sturgis near Clinton—They pursue the Governor—Lyon learns of Sigel's Defeat—Hurries to Springfield—Begs for Reinforcements—Denounces General Scott—Fremont assumes Command of the Western Department—Fails to reinforce Lyon—Lyon marches out to prevent the Junction of Price and McCulloch—The Skirmish at Dug Springs—Lyon Retires to Springfield—Price induces McCulloch to Advance by relinquishing the Command to him—The Confederates Camp on Wilson's Creek—McCulloch hesitates to Advance—Price's Urgency—A Council of War—A Night March Ordered, and Countermanded—Lyon's Perplexity and Despair—He cannot Retreat—He orders an Attack—His Last Letter to his Government.

LYON leaving Booneville on the 3d of July marched rapidly toward Clinton, some eighty miles to the south-west. On the evening of the 7th he reached Grand River, at a point a few miles south of Clinton. There he was joined by Sturgis, who had been waiting for him three or four days. Crossing Grand River with some difficulty, for it was greatly swollen by constant rains, Lyon pushed forward with his entire force in pursuit of the State troops, not knowing that they had swept Sigel out of their path and effected a junction with Price and McCulloch.

These facts he learned on reaching the Osage at a crossing nine miles above Osceola, on the afternoon of the 9th. Fearing that Price and McCulloch were pursuing Sigel, he ferried his army and his trains across the river during the next day and night, and, early on the morning of the 11th, made in all haste for Springfield, which lay eighty miles to the south-east. After marching under a blazing July sun twenty-seven miles without a stop, he halted his column in the afternoon, that the men and horses might get much-needed rest, and something to eat. At sunset they were all again in motion, and before three o'clock in the morning of July the 12th were within thirty miles of Springfield. They had marched nearly fifty miles in one day! Here he learned that Price and McCulloch had gone toward Arkansas, and that Sigel was safe. Moving more leisurely now, he encamped that night within twelve miles of Springfield, and, early the next morning, went thither himself, leaving his army behind.

The chroniclers of the city still delight to tell of the brave appearance that he made that day, as he dashed through their streets " on his iron-gray horse, under escort of a body-guard of ten stalwart troopers enlisted from among the German butchers of St. Louis for that especial duty," and how " the fearless horsemanship and defiant bearing of these bearded warriors, mounted on powerful chargers and armed to the teeth with great revolvers and massive swords, their heroic size and ferocious aspect," gave lustre to the entry into the chief city of the South-west of the grim soldier who had captured the State troops at St. Louis, had driven the Governor from his capital, had dispersed the army that was gathering at Booneville, and had forced Jackson and Price and all their men to fly for safety into the uttermost corner of the State.

The force which Lyon now had at and near Springfield amounted to between 7,000 and 8,000 men. But the term of service of some 3,000 of them, who had been enlisted for ninety days, would expire before the middle of August. The force that was confronting him, was, as we know, about 11,000, but he estimated it at 30,000. Consequently, on the day that he reached Springfield, he telegraphed to Colonel Harding, whom he had left at St. Louis, in charge of matters at department head-quarters: "Governor Jackson will soon have in this vicinity not less than 30,000 men. I must have at once an additional force of 10,000 men, or abandon my position." Two days later Major Schofield, his adjutant-general, wrote to Harding, insisting that all the disposable troops at St. Louis should be sent to Springfield. The defence of St. Louis, he very justly observed, might be left to the Home Guards and to the troops which could in a few hours be brought from Illinois and Indiana, as there was no danger that any force would move up the Mississippi or through south-eastern Missouri so long as a Federal army held Cairo.

Instead of getting reinforcements, Lyon received an order (July 16) from General Scott, directing him to send eastward two of the companies of regular infantry which he had with him, and three companies that were at Fort Leavenworth. To this order he replied that the moral effect of the few regulars in his command was doubtless the main consideration which held the enemy in check; that to withdraw them would make his position imminently hazardous; and that therefore he would hold on to them until further instructed. In the same letter he complained that the volunteers with him had not been paid; that their clothing was dilapidated, and that they were "as a body, dispirited," and would not re-enlist.

To Harding he wrote: "If the Regulars leave me I can do nothing, and must retire, in the absence of other troops to supply their places. In fact, I am badly enough off at the best, and must utterly fail if my regulars all go. At Washington, troops from all the Northern, Middle, and Eastern States are available for the support of the Army of Virginia, and more are understood to be already there than are wanted. It seems strange to me that so many troops must go on from the West, and strip us of the means of defence. But *if it is the intention to give up the West, let it be so. It can only be the victim of imbecility or malice. Scott will cripple us if he can.* . . . Everything seems to combine against me at this point. Stir up Blair."

Blair laid Lyon's entreaties before Fremont who was at New York, and the latter feebly telegraphed to the War Department that "General Lyon calls for reinforcements." Blair then appealed to the Cabinet, whereupon General Scott ordered Fremont (July 18) to proceed straight to his command. On the 25th Fremont reached St. Louis, and assumed command of *The Western Department.*

Lyon had already sent Major Farrar, Captain Cavender, Colonel John S. Phelps, and others to meet him there and explain to him the state of affairs in the South-west, and to impress upon him the vital importance of forthwith reinforcing the army at Springfield. He assured them that five thousand men would be sent thither as soon as the orders could reach them. But an expedition to Cairo now occupied Fremont's attention to the exclusion of everything else, and it was not until the 4th of August that two regiments (Stevenson's, at Booneville, and Montgomery's at Leavenworth), were ordered to Springfield. Other messengers had meanwhile come from Lyon with yet more urgent entreaties "for soldiers, soldiers, soldiers," as Kelton telegraphed to Fremont, who was still at Cairo. One of these messengers told him, when he got back to St. Louis, that Lyon would fight at Springfield anyway. "If he fights," replied Fremont, "he will do it upon his own responsibility."

Lyon learned on the 1st of August that Price, McCulloch, and Pearce were advancing upon Springfield. As they had converged toward Cassville by three different roads, he was deceived into believing that they were marching upon Springfield by three different roads. He determined therefore to attack them in detail, and started the same day to meet the column which was advancing upon the road from Cassville. His force consisted of over five thousand men—infantry, cavalry, and artillery. That night he encamped on Tyrel's Creek about twelve miles from Springfield; and had moved some six miles further the next day, Friday, when being informed that the Confederates were strongly posted some four or five miles farther on, he went into camp for the night.

It was McCulloch's advance guard, under Rains, that was in front of Lyon. McCulloch was himself encamped with the rest of his division on Crane Creek, about twelve miles south of the spot where Lyon was going into camp.

When he learned, Friday morning August the 2d, that a Federal force was in his front he requested Price and Pearce to move up to his own position on Crane Creek. Pearce's divison came up during the forenoon. Rains had meanwhile become slightly engaged with the Federal advance consisting of Steele's battalion of regulars, Stanley's troop of cavalry and a section of Totten's Battery. As soon as McCulloch was informed of this, he sent Colonel McIntosh, with one hundred and fifty men to ascertain the position and strength of the enemy. McIntosh, after reconnoitring the ground with Rains, concluded that the Federals were not in force and started back to camp with his men, ordering Rains at the same time not to bring on an engagement. Hardly had he left, however, when Steele attacked Rains vigorously, opening upon him with two of Totten's guns, and put the Missourians to flight in the utmost confusion. The loss on either side was trifling, in this skirmish at Dug Springs, but the conduct of Rains' command on this occasion caused McCulloch and McIntosh to lose all confidence in the Missouri troops, and laid the foundation for that distrust and ill-feeling, which eventually separated the combined armies, and frustrated all their hopes.

The next day, August the 3d, Lyon advanced to McCulla's store, twenty-four miles from Springfield, and within six miles of the Confederate position; but being unable, after lying there twenty-four hours, to learn anything definite about the army in front of him, and fearful that the Confederates might with their superior force of mounted men flank him and cut off his communication with Springfield, he determined to return thither, and setting out on Sunday reached that place Monday evening.

Saturday the Confederates were all concentrated on Crane Creek, and were reinforced that night by Greer's South-Kansas-Texas Regiment.

While the two armies lay facing each other, General Price begged McCulloch to attack, but McCulloch, who had now made up his mind not to co-operate with the Missourians any longer unless Price would yield to him the command of the combined armies, refused to advance any further, alleging as an excuse that the Confederate Government had declined to give him leave to move into Missouri except for the defence of the Indian Territory; and that to advance further into the State might endanger the safety of that Territory and subject himself to the censure of his Government. While this was a very good excuse, it was not McCulloch's real reason for refusing to attack Lyon. He had in truth no confidence in the Missouri troops, and none in General Price, or in any of his officers, except Colonel Weightman. Rains he had disliked from the beginning, and now he was embittered against him by an open quarrel which had taken place between him and McIntosh, for whose opinions and soldierly accomplishments McCulloch had a veneration, which made him distrustful of his own capacity and which often hampered his action. Neither he nor McIntosh comprehended the serene wisdom of Price, his unerring common sense, his magnificent courage, and those great qualities which endeared him to his troops, nor could they believe that "the undisciplined mob" which Price commanded would under his eye fight as well as the veterans of Wellington or Napoleon ever fought. He had, therefore, determined not to advance another mile except in chief command of the entire force.

Price who saw this clearly enough did not hesitate, but went the next morning (Sunday) to McCulloch's quarters, taking the writer with him. After vainly trying once more to persuade McCulloch to attack Lyon, the general said: "I am an older man than you, General McCulloch, and I am not only your senior in rank now, but I was a brigadier-general in the Mexican War, with an independent command, when you were only a captain; I have fought and won more battles than you have ever witnessed; my force is twice as great as yours; and some of my officers rank, and have seen more service than you, and we are also upon the soil of our own State;

but, General McCulloch, if you will consent to help us to whip Lyon and to repossess Missouri, I will put myself and all my forces under your command, and we will obey you as faithfully as the humblest of your own men. We can whip Lyon, and we will whip him and drive the enemy out of Missouri, and all the honor and all the glory shall be yours. All that we want is to regain our homes and to establish the independence of Missouri and the South. If you refuse to accept this offer, I will move with the Missourians alone, against Lyon. For it is better that they and I should all perish than Missouri be abandoned without a struggle. You must either fight beside us, or look on at a safe distance, and see us fight all alone the army which you dare not attack even with our aid. I must have your answer before dark, for I intend to attack Lyon to-morrow."

McCulloch replied that he was expecting dispatches from the East, but would, in any event, make known his determination before sundown. Toward sunset, accompanied by McIntosh, he came to Price's quarters and informed him that he had just received dispatches from General Polk saying that General Pillow was advancing into Missouri from New Madrid with twelve thousand men, and that in consequence of this information he had concluded to accept command of the combined armies, and attack Lyon. General Price at once published an order announcing to his troops that he had turned over the command of the State Guard to General McCulloch, reserving to himself, however, the right to resume command at his own pleasure.

Believing that Lyon was still at McCulla's farm, McCulloch marched at midnight, expecting to surprise and attack him at daybreak. He was already some distance on the way when he learned that Lyon had left twenty hours previously and was retreating to Springfield. Pushing on in great haste, though the weather was intensely hot and the dust almost unendurable, McCulloch kept up the pursuit to Moody's Spring near Tyrel's Creek. Seeing then that Lyon had escaped, he halted there; but moved the next morning (August 6) some two miles nearer to Springfield, and took position on Wilson's Creek, so as to be within reach of some ripening fields of corn, which was to be the only subsistence of his army for the next day or two.

Wilson's Creek, rising in, and around, Springfield, flows westwardly some five miles and then, turning to the south, flows nine or ten miles in that direction before emptying into the James, an affluent of White River. A mile or so above its mouth it receives the waters of Tyrel's Creek, flowing into it from the west; and a mile and a half further north

Lyon Moves Out to Attack. 259

a smaller stream, Skegg's branch, flowing likewise from the west, empties into it. The road from Cassville, on which McCulloch was advancing toward Springfield (known also as the Fayetteville, or Telegraph Road) crosses both Tyrel's Creek and Skegg's Branch just above their mouths. After crossing the latter, it runs northward along the western bank of Wilson's Creek nearly a mile, and then, crossing the creek at a ford, turns north-eastward toward Springfield, which is nine or ten miles beyond.

Between Tyrel's Creek and Skegg's Branch there is a considerable valley, partly wooded, lying between the Fayetteville Road, and Wilson's Creek. In this valley the mounted regiments of Greer, and Churchill, and about seven hundred mounted Missourians, under Lieutenant Colonel Major and Colonel Brown, went into camp.

Between Skegg's Branch and the ford across Wilson's Creek, the valley through which the road passes is quite narrow, and the road runs within a few yards of the stream. Toward the west a hill, since known as *Bloody Hill*, rises gradually from the creek to the height of nearly a hundred feet, its sides deeply seamed with ravines, and dinted here and there with sink-holes. At this time it was densely covered with undergrowth through which was interspersed a species of scrub-oak (black-jacks), and near its summit the rock cropped out in many places. In the narrow valley between the base of this hill and the creek were bivouacked all the infantry of Price's command, except Weightman's Brigade. Price's quarters were on the road, and about five hundred yards south of the ford. McBride, Slack, Clark, and Parsons occupied the ground between his quarters and Skegg's Branch.

The hill on the eastern side of the creek rises abruptly to the height of about seventy-five feet. Upon this hill the infantry and artillery of Pearce's Arkansas Brigade were encamped—Woodruff's Battery on its northern face near the ford, and Reid's Battery on its southern declivity, opposite to Skegg's Branch, and the infantry between them. McCulloch's head-quarters were on the hill near Woodruff's Battery. The Third Louisiana and McRae's Battalion, both belonging to McCulloch's Brigade, were camped near by, and Weightman's Missouri Brigade was half a mile away to the south-east. McIntosh's Regiment (for McIntosh was colonel of a regiment, as well as adjutant-general of the brigade), pitched its tents on the east side of the creek just above the ford.

A mile further up the creek, on the northern slope of Bloody Hill, was Rains, with Cawthon's Brigade of mounted Missourians; his camps extending northward as far as Gibson's Mill. Rains' quarters were on the eastern side of the creek, and there a few of his men also bivouacked.

From Rains, on the extreme left of the Confederates, to Churchill and Greer, on their extreme right, the distance was just three miles up and down the creek.

While the army lay here waiting for its trains to come up, McCulloch would every day sling his Maynard rifle across his shoulder and reconnoitre towards Springfield, sometimes in force, and sometimes almost alone. But adventurous, daring, and skilful as he was, he could learn nothing positive as to either Lyon's strength, or as to the defences of Springfield. He could not even ascertain whether Lyon had fortified his position at all, or not. To all the entreaties of Price and the Missourians that he would advance he only replied that he "would not make a blind attack upon Springfield;" and, blaming them for his own want of success in reconnoitring, told them, at last, that he "would order the whole army back to Cassville rather than bring on an engagement with an unknown enemy."

On Thursday, the 8th, Price received information that Lyon was greatly perplexed; that he was in constant expectation of being attacked; that he kept his men under arms all the time; and that he was getting ready to abandon Springfield. Communicating this information to McCulloch, and vouching for the credibility of his informants, the general again urged him, with great earnestness, to move straightway upon Springfield. McCulloch having promised to consider the matter carefully, and to make known his decision that evening, rode once more to the front, rifle in hand, accompanied by McIntosh and a considerable force. It was late when he returned to camp, and he did not communicate his purpose to General Price that night, as he had promised to do.

The general, waking at daybreak, directed the writer to see McCulloch instantly, and to ask what he had decided to do. I hastened to his quarters, and was still talking with him when the general himself rode up, his impatience no longer controlable, and insisted with great vehemence that McCulloch should keep the promise which he had made at Crane Creek, and lead the army out against Lyon.

McCulloch finally consented to meet all the general officers of the command in council at Price's quarters at noon, and then to determine upon some plan of action. At this council McCulloch expressed great unwillingness to attack Lyon, or to enter upon any aggressive campaign. But Price declared emphatically that if orders were not forthwith issued for a forward movement, he would resume command of the Missouri troops, and himself give battle to Lyon, be the consequences what they might. He was warmly seconded by Generals Clark, Parsons, Rains, Slack, and McBride that

McCulloch yielded at last, and ordered the army to be in readiness to move that night (August 9), at nine o'clock. Before that time a slight rain began to fall, and the order to march was countermanded, the officers being instructed, however, to hold their men in readiness to move at any moment. This was wisely done, for most of the Missourians, having no cartridge-boxes, had to carry their ammunition in their pockets, and if a rain had fallen upon them during the march, it would have virtually disarmed three-fourths of them all.

The Confederates, therefore, lay upon their arms, waiting for the order to march. About dawn General Price sent me to ask McCulloch what he proposed to do. He and McIntosh returned with me to Price's quarters on the west side of the creek, at the foot of Bloody Hill which sloped down toward us from the north-west. As our breakfast of cornbread, lean beef, and coffee, was about to be served, McCulloch and McIntosh were invited to share it.

When Lyon got back to Springfield on Monday, the 5th of August, he was more embarrassed than ever. Not a man had come to him from Fremont; not even a word. Two regiments—the one in Kansas, and the other on the Missouri—had been ordered to him the day before, but they could not possibly reach him in less than a fortnight; and before that time the enlistments of one third of his men would have expired, and they would have returned to their homes.

Though he was convinced that he could not, with the force at his command, resist the armies which were gathering to attack him and whose strength he constantly overestimated, he was, nevertheless, loth to abandon Springfield and the South-west to the Confederates. For he fully realized the great advantage which Price would gain by occupying that region, which would not only feed and recruit his army, but open to him the rich counties on the Missouri, with their teeming resources and tens of thousands of volunteers. He knew too that it would encourage the Secessionists in every county, and dishearten all loyal men, and that it might lose to the Union every part of the State, except St. Louis.

But if it were difficult to advance, or to remain where he was, it was even more difficult to retreat; it was in fact impossible to retreat. The only road open to him was that which led to Rolla, from which place there was a railway to St. Louis. Between Springfield and Rolla, lay a rough country, through which the road ran for one hundred and fifteen miles over hills, and through ravines, and across a hundred streams. How could an army of six or seven thousand disheartened men, encumbered by four hundred army wagons, and impeded by crowds of refugees, fleeing with their families and household goods before the wrath of their own fellow-countrymen, hope to retreat over such a road, for such a distance, pursued by more than twice their own number of men under Price and McCulloch, and harassed and hindered at every step by an overwhelming force of mounted troops?

It were surely better to fight than to retreat.

Accordingly he called his principal officers together, on the evening of the 8th, explained the situation to them, and announced that it was his determination to move down the Fayetteville Road with his whole force at night, surprise the enemy in their camp on Wilson's Creek at daybreak, and trust everything to the hazard of a battle. The next day (Friday, August 9), after consultation with Colonel Sigel, he changed this plan, and, instead of advancing in a single column, and attacking the Confederates in front, ordered Sigel to take the Third and Fifth Regiments of Missouri Volunteers, six pieces of artillery, and two companies of regular cavalry, the whole aggregating about twelve hundred officers and men, and with them turn the right flank of the Confederates; while he, with the remainder of his force, about four thousand two hundred men in all, would move out and turn their left flank. Sigel was to make the attack as soon as he heard Lyon's guns. Both columns were to leave Springfield that afternoon about sunset. Before leaving, Lyon sent the following letter to General Fremont,—his last:

"I retired to this place, as I before informed you, reaching here on the 5th. The enemy followed to within ten miles of here. He has taken a strong position and is recruiting his supply of horses, mules, and provisions, by forays into the surrounding country; his large force of mounted men enabling him to do this without much annoyance from me. I find my position extremely embarrassing, and am at present unable to determine whether I shall be able to maintain my ground, or be forced to retire. I can resist any attack from the front, but, if the enemy were to surround me, I must retire. I shall hold my ground as long as possible, though I may, without knowing how far, endanger the safety of my entire force, with its valuable material, being induced, by the important considerations involved, to take this step. The enemy showed himself in considerable force yesterday five miles from here, and has doubtless a full purpose of attacking me."

Not one word about the desperate battle that he was to fight on the morrow; not one fault-finding utterance; not a breath of complaint!

But, true to his convictions; true to his flag; true to the Union men of Missouri who confided in and followed him; true to himself; and true to duty, he went out to battle against a force twice as great as his own, with a calmness that was as pathetic as his courage was sublime.

CHAPTER XIV.

THE BATTLE OF WILSON'S CREEK.

Lyon marches out by Night, and surprises the Confederates—The Fight in the Cornfield—The Rout of Sigel—The Battle on Bloody Hill—The Death of Lyon—His Army retreats—The Dead and the Wounded.

LEAVING Springfield about five o'clock Friday afternoon August the 9th, Lyon moved out about five miles on the road to Little York, and then turning southward across the prairie came, about one o'clock, in sight of Rains' camp-fires, which extended northward as far as Gibson's Mill. He had completely turned the Confederate left, and was in rear of them. Halting his column till dawn, he then resumed his march with Plummer's battalion of regulars in advance, followed by Osterhaus' battalion of Missouri volunteers and Totten's battery.

The Confederates were not yet aware of his approach, as they had withdrawn all their pickets at midnight. About this time, however, Colonel Cawthon, who was in immediate command of Rains' mounted brigade, sent out a picket in the direction from which Lyon was approaching.

This picket had not advanced more than a mile and a half beyond Gibson's Mill, when they discovered that an enemy was in their front. This fact being made known to Cawthon, he sent Colonel Hunter with "the effectives" of his regiment, some three hundred men, to ascertain whether this enemy was advancing in force or not. When Hunter reached the picket, about five A.M., the head of the Federal column was already in sight. His first intention was to attack. But Lyon, seeing that his approach was at last known to the Confederates and that his further advance would be contested, now deployed his men into line, sending Osterhaus' battalion to the right and Plummer's to the left as skirmishers, and bringing the First Missouri up to the support of Totten's battery. Hunter thereupon retreated, and Lyon moved forward as rapidly as the ground would permit.

Cawthon was meanwhile forming the rest of his brigade on the northern slope of Bloody Hill. He had about six hundred dismounted men in line. When Hunter, falling back before Lyon, reached this position, Cawthon ordered him to retire further down the creek and dismount his men, and then to return to the field and take position on his right.

But before this was done, Lyon appeared on the

brow of the opposite hill with the First Missouri, the First Kansas, and Totten's battery. A brisk skirmish took place, and Cawthon was driven back over the brow of Bloody Hill, to its southern slope, where he was safe for the time. Hunter and McCown, who had been separated from him, did not rejoin him again till late in the day.

While Lyon was thus getting into position, Sigel had perfectly executed his part of the plan. Leaving Springfield about sunset he moved down the Fayetteville road about four miles, and then making a *détour* to the left came, about daybreak, within a few hundred yards of Wilson's Creek, just below the point at which Tyrell's Creek empties into it. He had turned the Confederate right just as completely as Lyon had turned its left; and at dawn of Friday August the 10th the whole Confederate force lay between Lyon and Sigel, and utterly ignorant of their proximity.

Having discovered that Greer, Churchill, and other mounted Confederates were encamped just across the creek from his position, Sigel, in order to keep his presence from their knowledge, so disposed his men as to capture all stragglers from their camp and to arrest every one that was moving about. He then posted four of his guns on a hill east of the creek in such way as to command

Churchill's camp, which was hardly five hundred yards away. Leaving with these guns a small infantry support, he then crossed Wilson's Creek, with the rest of his command, just below the mouth of Tyrell's Creek; and facing northward waited for Lyon's signal gun.

Churchill and Greer had, like Rains, drawn in their pickets during the night.

Rains, whose quarters were near his mounted brigade (Cawthon's), but on the eastern side of the creek, and some distance south of Gibson's Mill, had learned, about the time that Hunter went to the front, that some sort of a force was coming toward him from the northwest. He accordingly directed Colonel Snyder, of his staff, to go and "see what was the matter." Snyder, on reaching the prairie, saw the Federals approaching. Hurrying back to Rains, he told him that the Federals were advancing in great force, "their soldiers and cannon covering the whole prairie." Rains ordered him to report the facts instantly to General Price.

It was now nearly six o'clock, and still neither Price nor McCulloch, who was then at Price's quarters, had any cause to suspect that Lyon had even left Springfield.

Snyder, coming up almost breathless with haste and excitement, said that Lyon was approaching with twenty thousand men and 100 pieces of artillery, and was then within less than a mile of Rains' camp. McCulloch, believing that this was "one of Rains' scares," told Snyder to say to that officer that he would himself come to the front directly. In two or three minutes another officer came dashing up and said that Rains was falling back before overwhelming numbers, and needed instant and heavy reinforcements.

Looking up, we could, ourselves, see a great crowd of men on horseback, some armed, and others unarmed, mixed in with wagons and teams and led horses, all in dreadful confusion, scampering over the hill, and rushing down toward us—a panic-stricken drove. In another instant, we saw the flash and heard the report of Totten's guns, which had gone into battery on the top of the hill, not more than a thousand yards away, and were throwing shot into the flying crowd. And then, in quick response, came the sound of Sigel's guns, as they opened upon Churchill, Greer, Major, and Brown, and drove them in confusion out of the valley in which they were encamped and into the thick woods that fringed the banks of Skeggs' Branch and covered the hills that rose on either side of that little stream.

In a moment McCulloch, followed by McIntosh, was in the saddle and on his way to take com-

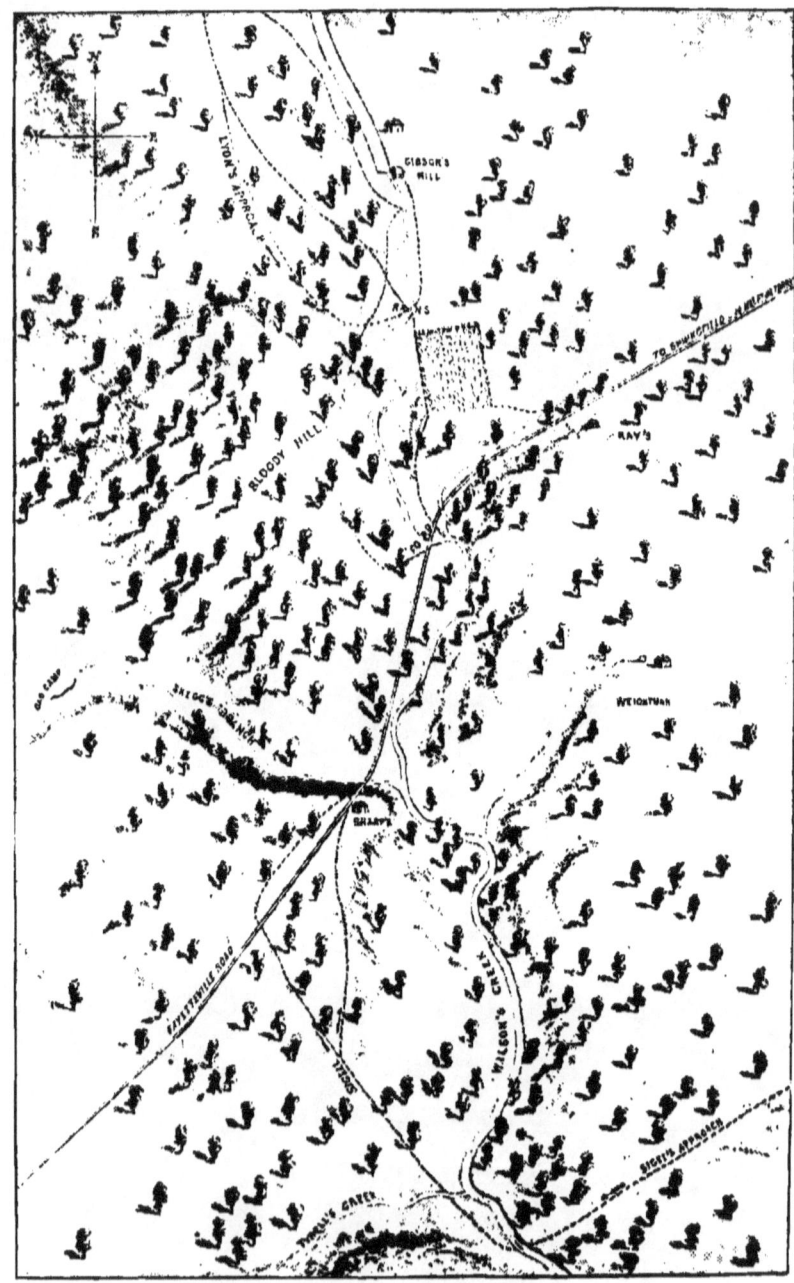

THE BATTLE FIELD OF WILSON'S CREEK.

NOTE.—Most of the ground was covered with a dense undergrowth which is not depicted in the sketch.

mand of the troops on the eastern side of the creek; and Price, having ordered his infantry and artillery to follow, was galloping up Bloody Hill to take command of Cawthon's brigade, which was still falling back before Lyon, resisting him all that it could. Price hoped with it to hold the Federals in check till the rest of his Missourians could come up.

These were already forming along the Fayetteville road, and were, within a few minutes, hastening up the hill at double-quick. Hardly had Price gotten Cawthon's men into line under the brow of the hill, where they were out of range of Totten's guns, and under cover of the trees and dense undergrowth which shade that part of the field, when Slack came up with Hughes' regiment and Thornton's battalion and formed on the left of Cawthon. Clark followed immediately with Burbridge's regiment, and took position on the left of Slack. Then came Parsons, with Kelly's regiment and Guibor's battery; while on the extreme left of Price's line McBride took position with his two regiments. Slack's command was soon reinforced by Colonel Rives, with about seventy dismounted men of his regiment; and half an hour later, Weightman, whose brigade had been encamped a mile or more from the rest of Price's infantry, came up with Clarkson's and Hurst's regiments, about seven hundred strong, and fell in between Slack and Cawthon.

The line thus formed by Price in front of Lyon aggregated, with Weightman's command, over thirty-one hundred men, with four pieces of artillery. He was greatly assisted from the beginning by Woodruff, who had with true soldierly instinct thrown his pieces into battery on the bluff east of the ford, at the first sound of Totten's guns, and opened upon Lyon a fire, which checked his advance and gave the Missourians time to reach Cawthon's position and form their line of battle there.

To Price's force Lyon opposed the First Missouri, the First Kansas, Osterhaus' battalion of Missouri volunteers, Totten's six-gun battery (regulars), and Dubois' four-gun battery (regulars), aggregating nearly nineteen hundred men. The rest of his force, except Plummer's battalion, he held in reserve.

The two lines were not more than three hundred yards apart, but they were entirely concealed from each other by the intervening foliage. As Price's men were armed almost exclusively with shot-guns and common rifles, it was imperatively necessary for him, near as the two forces already were to each other, either to advance more closely to the Union line, or to wait till it should approach his own. He chose the latter alternative, and awaited Lyon's advance.

He did not have to wait long, for in a few minutes the word "Forward!" was plainly heard, and was quickly followed by the tramp of men, and by the crackling of the brush through which they were coming. When Lyon's Missourians and their allies had come within easy range of Price's Missourians, out of the ranks of the latter there rang upon the air the sharp click of a thousand rifles, the report of a thousand shot-guns, and the roar of Guibor's guns; and the battle of Wilson's Creek had begun in earnest. Missourians now fought to the death against Missourians, on the leafy hill-side; while from opposing heights, Totten, who had but lately been stationed at Little Rock where his family still resided, fought furiously against Woodruff's Little Rock battery, which now turned against him the very guns which they had taken from him a few months before.

The battle thus joined upon the hill-side was now waged for hours with intense earnestness. The lines would approach again and again within less than fifty yards of each other, and then, after delivering a deadly fire, each would fall back a few paces to reform and reload, only to advance again, and again renew this strange battle in the woods. Peculiar in all its aspects, strange in all its surroundings, unique in every way, the most remarkable of all its characteristics was the deep silence which now and then fell upon the smoking field—fell upon it, and rested there undisturbed for many minutes, while the two armies, unseen of each other, lay but a few yards apart, gathering strength to grapple again in the death struggle for Missouri.

Meanwhile McCulloch, upon leaving Price, had gone with McIntosh to the eastern side of the creek, where the infantry of his own brigade, and the infantry and artillery of Pearce's were both encamped. His first object was to dispose these troops in such way as to meet Sigel's attack, the strength and meaning of which were not yet developed. In order to do this he posted Reid's battery on the bluff opposite to the mouth of Skegg's Branch, and ordered Walker's regiment to support it. He then placed Dockery's and Gratiot's regiments further north, along the bluff which forms the eastern bank of Wilson's Creek from Skegg's Branch northward, to the ford. These dispositions gave him command of the crossing of Skegg's Branch, over which Sigel would have to advance, if he should undertake to attack Price in rear. He then posted McRae's battalion, the Third Louisiana, and McIntosh's regiment, of his own brigade, north of Gratiot, and on the same bluff. It was upon the northern extremity of this bluff that Woodruff had taken position and gone into action.

While McCulloch was still making these dispositions Woodruff perceived that a part of Lyon's column, constituting the extreme left of his line, had crossed to the eastern side of the Creek, and was moving down its left bank towards the position occupied by his battery. As soon as this fact was made known to McCulloch he ordered Gratiot to the support of Woodruff, and sent McIntosh with his regiment dismounted, the Third Louisiana, and McRae's battalion to meet the advancing Federals.

McIntosh moved rapidly to the front, keeping on the eastern side of the creek. Though covered somewhat by Woodruff's guns he was greatly harrassed by Dubois, who hurled grape-shot and shell against him from the eastern brow of Bloody Hill. Crossing the Fayetteville road he led his men through a dense thicket to a large cornfield behind whose fence the Federals had taken position. They turned out to be Plummer's battalion of United States Infantry, supported at a safe distance by Captain Wright's Squadron of Home Guards. A fierce conflict ensued, the Confederates fighting under cover of "the brush," and the Federals behind the fence. McIntosh finding that the enemy's fire was playing havoc with his men ordered them to charge, and leading the way leaped the fence. The greater part of his own regiment, and of the Third Louisiana, followed him, and they quickly put

Plummer to flight, and drove him back to and across the creek to Lyon's main body. In the ardor of pursuit the Confederates came within close range of Dubois' battery, and Osterhaus' battalion, and were themselves driven back in some confusion. In this engagement, which began about seven o'clock and lasted nearly an hour, Plummer, who had about three hundred regulars, lost eighty officers and men, and was himself severely wounded. McIntosh took about one thousand men into action. His losses aggregated over one hundred.

While this fight was going on Sigel had advanced leisurely through the camps out of which he had driven the Confederates at sunrise, and had taken position with his entire force, some twelve hundred men, with six pieces of artillery, near Sharp's house on the bluff south of Skegg's Branch. His battery occupied a high plateau, and his infantry were drawn up on both sides of the Fayetteville road, with a company of United States cavalry on each flank. It was his purpose to hold this position so as to cut off the retreat of "the rebels" when they had been put to flight by Lyon.

McCulloch, after sending McIntosh to meet Plummer, had returned towards Skegg's Branch in order to look after Sigel. Finding that the further advance of the latter was effectually barred by

Pearce's Brigade and by a considerable force which was rallying under cover of the woods on the north side of the branch, he hurried back toward the point where McIntosh was engaged with Plummer. On getting there he found that the Confederates had won that engagement, and that there was no longer any danger in that direction.

Taking two companies of the Third Louisiana that were nearest to him, and ordering McIntosh to bring up the rest, McCulloch now hastened again towards Skegg's Branch, determined to attack Sigel. Lieutenant-Colonel Rosser had already taken position with his own men, O'Kane's battalion, and Bledsoe's battery, on the western side of the Fayetteville Road and north of the branch; Bledsoe's guns being so posted as to completely command Sigel's position.

Sigel and his men were in blissful ignorance of all that was happening in their front. For between them and the valley, in which their foes were gathering, stood a dense wood through whose luxuriant undergrowth no eye could pierce. Now and then a skirmisher, or an adventurous officer, would make his way to the bluff which overhung the little stream, and catch sight of the smoke that darkened Bloody Hill, and sometimes one more daring than the rest would venture far enough to see indistinctly what was going on in the upper part of the valley, towards the ford. At last one of these saw a gray-coated regiment hurrying down the road toward Skegg's Branch. Knowing that the First Iowa wore a gray uniform, he at once concluded that this must be the First Iowa, and such was the report that he bore back to Sigel. The latter communicated the glad news to his men, and warned them not to fire upon their approaching "friends." They waved their flags instead, in joyful welcome.

Just at this moment Reid on the east and Bledsoe on the west opened fire upon them at point-blank range. "It is impossible for me," says Sigel, "to describe the consternation and frightful confusion which were caused by this unfortunate event. 'They are firing against us,' spread like wild-fire through our ranks. The artillery men could hardly be brought forward to serve their pieces. The Infantry would not level their arms till too late." The consternation and confusion deepened into a panic when about four hundred of the gray-coated Third Louisiana dashing up the steep bluff with McCulloch and McIntosh at their head, and Rosser and O'Kane's battalion following, broke through the thick "brush," and charged right upon the Federal Battery. Sigel's whole force took to instant flight, abandoning five of their six guns, and throwing themselves for safety into the bushes which lined both sides of the Fayetteville road.

Here they got separated. Sigel and Salomon with about two hundred of their Germans and Carr's company of cavalry tried to make their way back to Springfield by the same route that they came, but they were set upon by Lieutenant-Colonel Major with some mounted Missourians and Texans, and the Germans, being abandoned by Captain Carr who made good his escape, were nearly all either killed, wounded, or made prisoners. Sigel himself got to Springfield with one man only. Another part of his column made its way to Little York and thence to Springfield.

It was now nearly nine o'clock. Churchill, who after being driven out of his camp in the early morning by Sigel had quickly rallied his men and taken them to the north side of Skegg's Branch and gone into the fight on Price's extreme left, was now moving to the centre of Price's line, where it was hardest pressed. After detailing enough men to hold the horses of those that were dismounted for the fight he had about five hundred "effectives." Forming these in line on the Fayetteville road, south of the ford, and within reach of the enemy's shot, he led them gallantly up the hill and went again into the fight on the left of Slack, and in the very front of Lyon's attack.

The Missourians, thus strengthened where they

most needed strengthening, advanced boldly, Guibor's guns keeping in line with the Infantry, and Woodruff throwing his shot high overhead into the midst of Lyon's reserves.

Lyon, finding that his men were giving way, brought forward a section of Totten's battery with a strong support to the right and front of his own line, and enfiladed the Confederates at two hundred yards, Totten and Gordon Granger both helping to work the guns.

McCulloch, who had gone with Churchill up Bloody Hill, diverted this fire by returning in all haste to the valley and sending Carroll's Arkansas cavalry and five companies of Greer's mounted Texans to turn Lyon's right and charge these guns in rear. The ground was ill-adapted to the operations of cavalry, and Greer and Carroll were finally driven back. But this movement relieved Price nevertheless, and at the same time so increased Lyon's anxiety that he ordered the First Iowa to the front and brought Steele's battalion of regulars to the further support of Totten.

Up to this time (ten o'clock) the infantry of Pearce's brigade, three fine regiments—Gratiot's, Dockery's, and Walker's—more than 1,700 strong, had not fired a shot, nor had Graves' Missouri regiment, about three hundred strong, that ought to have followed Weightman into battle. There they lay just across the creek, not half a mile away, with nothing to do and doing nothing.

Price, seeing the absolute necessity of instant and decisive action, for Lyon was now bringing every available man to the front and doing prodigies of valor, galloped over to Gratiot, during the pause of the fight which occurred in his own front while Greer and Carroll were attempting to flank Lyon's right, and begged him to bring his regiment to the help of the Missourians and Churchill. Gratiot, who had served under Price in Mexico and loved and honored him, did not hesitate an instant, but, ordered his regiment to follow Price who was already hastening back to his own men, and sent an officer to tell General Pearce what he had done. Pearce came forward at once and overtaking Price and Gratiot rode with them at the head of the regiment as it ran up Bloody Hill. When they drew near to the position which they were to occupy, Price said to the men: "You will soon be in a pretty hot place, men! but I will be near you, and I will take care of you; keep as cool as the inside of a cucumber and give them thunder." Turning to Gratiot he said: "That's your position, colonel; take it and hold it whatever you do. I will see that you are not too hard pressed. Don't yield an inch."

Gratiot moved, on the instant, towards the position which the general had indicated. As he did so his regiment came within range of Totten's guns. The men passed safely, but the rear of the regiment was swept of its field and staff. Gratiot's horse was killed and his orderly's too. The lieutenant-colonel was dismounted. The major's arm was broken. The quarter-master was killed and the regimental commissary severely wounded. But the regiment kept on and took the position that it had been ordered to take—took it, and held it under a fire so furious that in less than thirty minutes a hundred of its men were either dead or wounded— one hundred out of five hundred.

From the summit of Bloody Hill Lyon could see the entire field. It all lay before him, its outmost limits hardly a mile away. He knew now that Sigel had been defeated, and that the troops which had put him to flight would soon be coming, all flushed with victory, to join the force which Price was getting ready to hurl again against his own disheartened men. He could see Gratiot hurrying even now with more than five hundred fresh troops to give vigor to the assault that was about to be made upon his own weary men, broken down as these were by a long night-march, and by five hours of the very hardest fighting; could see him clambering up the hill-side now, himself and his men eager to fight under the eye of the brave soldier that was leading them to death or to victory. He could also see the rest of Pearce's brigade forming on the opposite hill and about to bring their bright muskets into the thickening fight, muskets that had not yet been tarnished by the smoke of battle. And all through the valley that lay beneath him he could see Missourians, and Texans, and Arkansians —men who had as yet taken no part in the desperate fight that had been raging since day-dawn, —thousands of men, taking heart again as they got used to the din of war, and clutching their shot-guns and rifles, resolved to be "in at the death." He saw all this and more; and there was no hope left within him but to dash upon Price with all his might and crush him to the ground before these gathering forces could come to his help.

He now brought every available battalion to the front. "The engagement at once became general, and almost inconceivably fierce along the entire line, the enemy" (these are the words of Schofield and Sturgis) "appearing in front, often in three or four ranks, lying down, kneeling, and standing, and the lines often approaching to within thirty or forty yards as the enemy would charge upon Totten's battery and be driven back."

Neither line of battle was more than a thousand yards in length. Price guarded carefully every part of his own. Wherever the danger was greatest and the battle most doubtful, thither would he hasten and there would he stay till the danger was all past. In the intervals of the fight he would ride far to the front among his skirmishers, and peer into the thick smoke which tangled itself among the trees and the bushes, and clung to the ground as though it wanted to hide the combatants from each other; would peer wistfully into it till through its rifts he could discern what the enemy was doing, and then his voice would ring down the whole length of his line, and officers and men would quickly spring forward to obey it: for long before the battle was over they had all learned that they were fighting under one of the best and truest of soldiers, under one who knew how to fight them to the greatest advantage, one who would expose them to no useless danger, nor to *any* danger which he would not himself share. Many a time did they cry out to him as with one voice: "Don't lead us, General; don't come with us; take care of yourself for the sake of us all; we will go without you." Several times his clothing was pierced by bullets, one of which inflicted a painful wound in his side. Turning with a smile to an officer that was near him he said: "That isn't fair; if I were as slim as Lyon that fellow would have missed me entirely." No one else knew till the battle was ended, that he had been struck. One of his aids, Colonel Allen of Saline, was killed while receiving an order; Weightman was borne to the rear dying; Cawthon and his adjutant were both mortally wounded; Slack was fearfully lacerated by a musket-ball, and Clark was shot in the leg. Colonel Ben Brown was killed, Churchill had two horses shot under him, Gratiot one. Colonels Burbridge, Foster and Kelly, and nearly every other field officer, were disabled. But in spite of all these losses Price grew stronger all the time, while Lyon's strength was fast wasting away.

Walking along his line from left to right encouraging his men by his own intrepid bearing and by a few well-spoken words; rallying them where they were beginning to give way; steadying them where they still stood to their duty; inspiring them with his own brave purpose to make one more effort to win the day, while yet there was time to try, Lyon had nearly reached the advanced section of Totten's battery when his horse, whose bridle he held in his hand, was killed, and himself was wounded in the leg and in the head. Stunned and dazed by the blow, and his brave soul cast down by the shock, he said in a confused sort of way to those that were nearest that he feared that the day was lost. But he came quickly to his senses, and ordering Sturgis to rally the First Iowa, which was beginning to break badly, he mounted a horse that was offered to him, and swinging his hat in the air, called out to his men to follow. A portion of Mitchell's Second Kansas, which Lieutenant Wherry had just brought again to the front, closed quickly around him and together they dashed into the fight. The next minute Mitchell was struck down severely wounded, and almost instantly thereafter a fatal ball pierced Lyon's breast. He fell from his horse into the arms of his faithful orderly, who had sprung forward to catch him, and in another minute he was dead.

The command devolved upon Major Sturgis. He called his chief officers together. Price had already been reinforced by Gratiot, and now Dockery's Arkansas regiment and a section of Reid's battery were getting into position, and with them was the Third Louisiana, which, for the first time since its encounter with Plummer in the early morning, had been gotten together under its colonel (Hébert), and was eager to add to the laurels which it had already gathered in the fields on which it had defeated Plummer, and routed Sigel.

Sturgis decided to retreat. The order was given, and was silently obeyed, Steele's battalion of regulars covering the retreat, and marching away from the field in perfect order.

It was now half past eleven. Silence had again fallen upon Bloody Hill, on whose rough surface the dead of both armies lay in great heaps. The

Confederates, stretched out among the bushes in which they had been fighting all day, were waiting for the enemy's next onset, or for Price's order to attack, and ready for either. Suddenly a cry rang along their ranks that the Federals were retreating; that they had already gotten away, and were ascending the hill from which they had begun the attack upon Rains at dawn of day; that they had *at last* abandoned the field for which they had fought so bravely and so well against unconquerable odds. Springing to their feet they gave utterance to their unspeakable relief and to their unbounded joy with that exultant cry which is never heard except upon a battle-field whereon its victors stand. It reached the ears of Weightman—true soldier and true gentleman—whose life was fast ebbing away in the midst of the men that loved him. "What is it?" he asked. "We have whipped them. They are gone." "Thank God!" he faintly whispered. In another instant he was dead. Of him General Price well said, in his report that:

"Among those who fell mortally wounded upon the battle-field none deserve a dearer place in the memory of Missourians than Richard Hanson Weightman, Colonel commanding the first brigade of the second division of this army. Taking up arms at the very beginning of this unhappy contest, he had already done distinguished service at the battle of Rock Creek, where he commanded the State forces after the death of the lamented Holloway, and at Carthage, where he won unfading laurels by the display of extraordinary coolness, courage and skill. He fell at the head of his brigade, wounded in three places, and died just as the victorious shouts of our army began to rise upon the air."

Nothing could better attest the constancy, the courage, and the devotion with which both armies fought that day on the wooded summit of the Ozark hills, than do the losses which each sustained.

In the engagement between McIntosh and Plummer, in the cornfield east of the creek, the Federals lost eighty of the three hundred men who took part in the fight; and the Confederates, who were over one thousand strong, lost one hundred and one.

In the final attack upon Sigel, which McCulloch and McIntosh led, the Confederate loss was trifling, but Sigel, whose panic-stricken men were pitilessly cut down by the Missourians and Texans who pursued, lost two hundred and ninety-three men. Of these, one hundred and sixty-seven were either killed or wounded, and one hundred and twenty-six were taken prisoners. These losses were confined exclusively to Sigel's Infantry and Artillery, which aggregated about one thousand and fifty men. Captain Carr's squadron of United States Cavalry which formed part of his column was not under fire and did not sustain any loss. This fact did not, however, prevent Captain Carr from being brevetted for gallant and meritorious conduct on the field.

But it was on Bloody Hill that the main battle was fought, and the heaviest losses were suffered. There Lyon and Price confronted each other, until, after four hours of desperate fighting, Lyon was killed; and still the battle raged for a time, till, overwhelmed by ever-increasing odds, Sturgis abandoned the unequal contest, and left the field. Here the Union Army lost not only its general, and so many of its field officers as to come out of the fight under command of a major, but of the 3500 men that went into action nearly nine hundred were either killed or wounded. The First Missouri alone lost 295 men out of less than eight hundred, the First Kansas 284, and Steele's Battalion of regulars sixty-one out of 275 officers and men.

The Confederates lost in almost the same proportion. Of the 4200 men who fought there under Price 988 were either killed or wounded. Nearly every one of his higher officers was disabled, and he was himself wounded. Churchill had two horses shot under him, and lost 197 of his 500 men.

The total losses of the Federals during the day

amounted to 1317 officers and men killed, wounded, and missing; that of the Confederates to 1230 killed and wounded.

Never before—considering the numbers engaged—had so bloody a battle been fought upon American soil; seldom has a bloodier one been fought on any modern field.

CHAPTER XV.

McCULLOCH, PRICE, AND LYON.

McCulloch lets the Union Army Escape—Its Flight to Rolla—The Confederate Government and McCulloch—His Mistaken Estimate of the Missouri Troops—Their Condition and their true Character—Sterling Price—Lyon wins the Fight for Missouri.

As soon as it was known that the Union Army was retreating General Price urged McCulloch to pursue; but urged him in vain, for McCulloch had made up his mind to advance no further into Missouri. It was a grave mistake that McCulloch made, for the Federals had barely three thousand weary and disheartened men, while the Confederates had nearly twice that number of fresh troops. Twenty-seven hundred of their mounted men, and two thousand of their infantry had hardly fired a shot, and Bledsoe's and Reid's batteries were both intact. Besides these there was the Third Louisiana, a splendid regiment, which could still muster five hundred men flushed with their victories over both Plummer and Sigel; and there were McRae's battalion, and O'Kane's, which, though they had been under fire, had not been scathed. And in addition to all these there were two thousand unarmed Missourians, who could have been equipped and sent in pursuit before sunset, for now there were arms for all, and to spare.

Price was still entreating McCulloch to advance when they were informed that Major Sturgis had sent an officer under a flag of truce to ask for the body of Lyon. They were still on that part of the field, where the two armies had come together again and again in the shock of battle, and where the dead and the wounded of both lay thick under the festering rays of an August sun. Even the fact— now first made known to them—that the enemy had lost their valiant leader did not shake McCulloch's fixed purpose. He would not pursue; but ordered the troops, instead, to care for the wounded and bury the dead.

General Price thereupon directed me to identify Lyon's body, and to deliver it to the bearer of the flag of truce. It had been borne to the rear of the Federal line of battle, and there under the shade of an oak it lay, still clad in the captain's uniform which he had worn just two months before, when, relying upon the strength of his manhood, on the might of his Government, and on the justice of his cause, he had boldly defied the Governor of the State and the Major-General of her forces, and in their presence had declared war against Missouri and against all who should dare to take up arms in her defence. Since that fateful day he had done many memorable deeds, and had well deserved the gratitude of all those who think that the union of these States is the chiefest of political blessings, and that they who gave their lives to perpetuate it ought to be forever held in honor by those who live under its flag. The body was delivered to the men who had come for it—delivered to them with all the respect and courtesy which were due to a brave soldier and the commander of an army, and they bore it away toward Springfield, whither the army which he had led out to battle was sadly and sullenly retreating.

The Confederates remained upon the field which they had won, and ministered to the wounded, and buried the dead of both armies. Before the unpitying sun had sunk behind the western hills, all those who had died for the Union, and all those who had died for the South, had been laid to rest, uncoffined, in the ground which their manhood had made memorable and which their blood had made sacred forever.

Sturgis, on reaching Springfield about five o'clock in the afternoon, turned over the command of the army to Colonel Sigel, who was believed to be the senior officer. Sigel assumed command at once, and, after consulting with his chief subordinates, decided to retreat instantly to Rolla, which was about one hundred and twenty-five miles distant. As there was a depot of supplies at that point, and a railway thence to St. Louis, the discomfited army would there be comparatively safe. The enormous army train, consisting of over four hundred heavily-laden wagons, among whose "spoils" were $250,000 in gold coin that had been "taken" from the State Bank at Springfield, took the road at once under a strong escort. The rest of the troops were ordered to march at two o'clock in the night, but did not begin to move till toward daybreak. They soon became so inextricably mixed up with the multitude of fugitives, who, with their wives and children, their horses and cattle, their wagons and carts and household goods, were flying before Ben McCulloch, whose very name was then a terror to the Union men of Missouri, that they "more nearly resembled a crowd of refugees than an army of organized troops." In this condition they scampered along toward Rolla, and arrived there during the evening of the 17th of August, seven days after the battle. Sturgis had meanwhile resumed command, it having been ascertained that Sigel's commission had expired.

All this time, during all this disorderly retreat of a defeated army over difficult roads and through a not friendly population, more than twice its number of well mounted, and willing, Southern soldiers lay absolutely idle at Springfield. They might have easily captured the entire force, and its richly loaded train, worth more than $1,500,000, and with the captured stores could have armed, equipped, and supplied ten thousand Confederates. But McCulloch sulked in his tent, and his army melted away.

Nothing excuses that brave soldier's conduct on this occasion except the fact that the Confederate Government was then opposed to an aggressive war, and therefore objected to the invasion of any State which had not seceded and joined the Confederacy. In entering Missouri at all he had violated both the orders under which he was acting, and the wishes of the Confederate Secretary of War, who had expressly cautioned him to remember that the main purpose of his command was to protect the Indian Territory, and had instructed him to assist the Missourians *only* when such assistance would subserve that "main purpose." But even these instructions hardly justify McCulloch's refusal to gather the fruits of a victory which had been won at the cost of so many lives and so much suffering, fruits which would have have been so valuable to the Confederacy, and which he could have gathered so easily and so abundantly.

He would, perhaps, have pursued even at the risk of displeasing his Government, had he not by this time become so prejudiced against the Missourians as to be wholly unable to recognize the skill with which they had been commanded, and the courage and constancy with which they had fought on Bloody Hill, from the beginning to the end of the battle. The distrust which he conceived the first moment that he saw their unorganized condition, and which had been increased by the behavior of a few of them at Dug Springs, had gone on increasing day by day ever since, and reached its height when, through his own fault, his army was completely surprised by Lyon and Sigel on the morning of the battle. "The fault was theirs;" he said to the Secretary of War, "the two extremes of the camp were composed of mounted men from Missouri, and it was their duty to have kept pickets upon the roads on which the enemy advanced." Though he ought to have known that one of these two extremes—the right—was composed of Texans and Arkansians of his own brigade, and that in any case it was his own duty to have kept his camp properly guarded, he unjustly attributed the blunder to the Missourians alone, and distrusted and disliked them more than ever. Nor could he keep contrasting their condition with that of his own well-organized, well-disciplined, well-equipped, and finely uniformed brigade, with its full complement of quarter-masters, commissaries and ordnance officers, unlimited supplies of all kinds, and an overflowing army-chest. Many of them had not even enlisted, but had only come out to fight; thousands of them had not been organized into regiments; many of them were unarmed; none of them were uniformed; very few of them had been drilled. Their arms were mostly shot-guns and rifles, and they had no other equipments of any kind; no tents at all; no supplies of any sort, and no depots from which to draw subsistence, or clothing, or ammunition, or anything. They had no muster-rolls and they made no morning reports. They bivouacked in the open air, they subsisted on the ripening corn, and they foraged their horses on the prairie-grass. McCulloch was not wise enough to see that they were, in despite of all these drawbacks, true soldiers, as brave as the bravest, and as good as the best, and he still distrusted them, even after they had unflinchingly borne the brunt of the battle for five hours, and with the aid of Churchill, Gratiot, and Woodruff, had won the main fight on Bloody Hill.

Both Schofield and Sturgis say in their reports of the battle that *after* the death of Lyon, "the fiercest and most bloody engagement of the day took place;" and that then "for the first time during the day, the Union line maintained its position with perfect firmness, till finally the enemy gave way and fled from the field;" that "The order to retreat was then given by Sturgis," and the whole column moved slowly to the high, open prairie, and thence to Springfield. Though these statements were doubtless believed at the time, the officers who made them would hardly repeat them now. If they had "driven the enemy precipitately from the field," they themselves would not have fled in such trepidation as to leave behind the dead body of their heroic commander.

The Union Army did leave in good order, but it left in a hurry; and Price, instead of being driven from the field, was still holding the line that he had taken at the beginning of the battle, nor had he been driven back one hundred yards from this line at any time during the entire day. But it is very easy to be mistaken as to what your enemy is doing on a battle-field, as any one can see who will take the trouble to study the reports of any hotly contested fight. Federals and Confederates alike made many such mistakes.

It is a noteworthy fact that the little army which fought under Lyon against Price and McCulloch furnished at least seven major-generals and thirteen brigadier-generals to the Union. Among the former were Schofield, Stanley, Steele, Sigel, Granger, Osterhaus, and Herron; and among the latter were Sturgis, Carr, Plummer, Mitchell, Sweeny, Totten, Gilbert, and Powell Clayton.

Among the Confederates who became General officers in their service were McCulloch, McIntosh, Churchill, Greer, Gratiot, Dockery, Hébert, and McRae. Among the Missourians who rose to that grade were Price, Parsons, Slack, Shelby, John B. Clark, Jr., Colton Greene, and Cockrell. Clark, who was one of the most gallant of soldiers, is now Clerk of the United States House of Representatives, and Cockrell is a Senator from Missouri.

Out of the dust and smoke and out of the din and carnage of the battle Sterling Price emerged the leader of his people. Never till now had they known him. That he was just and upright, that he had been a successful general in the war with Mexico, that he had governed Missouri wisely and well for four years, and was a man to be trusted at all times and in all circumstances they knew; but not till now had they seen him display that genius for war which fitted him for the command of great armies. Calm, quiet and unimpassioned in the affairs of every-day life, and somewhat slow of thought and of speech, the storm of battle aroused all the faculties of his soul, and made him " a hero in the strife." When friends and foes were falling fast around him, and Life and

Death waited upon his words, then it was that he saw as by intuition what was best to be done, and did it on the instant, with the calmness of conscious strength, and with all a soldier's might. Of danger he seemed to take no note, but he had none of that brilliant dash, of that fine frenzy of the fight, which men call gallantry, for he was great rather than brilliant. He was wise, too, and serenely brave, quick to see, prompt to act, and always right. From this time he was loved and trusted by his soldiers, as no Missourian had ever been; and never thereafter did he lose their trust and devotion, for throughout all the long years of war—years crowded with victories and with defeats—the virtues which he displayed that day grew more conspicuous all the time, while around them clustered others which increased the splendor of these—unselfish devotion to his native land, unending care for the men who fought under his flag, constancy under defeat, patience under wrongs that were grievous, justice toward all men, and kindness toward every one.

In its flight from Springfield the Union Army had again left the body of its General to the care of his foes. These caused it to be decently buried near the home of one of his friends.

Lyon had not fought and died in vain. Through him the rebellion which Blair had organized, and to which he had himself given force and strength, had succeeded at last. By capturing the State militia at Camp Jackson, and driving the Governor from the Capital, and all his troops into the uttermost corner of the State, and by holding Price and McCulloch at bay, he had given the Union men of Missouri time, opportunity, and courage to bring their State Convention together again; and had given the Convention an excuse and the power to depose Governor Jackson and Lieutenant-Governor Reynolds, to vacate the seats of the members of the General Assembly, and to establish a State Government, which was loyal to the Union, and which would use the whole organized power of the State, its Treasury, its Credit, its Militia, and all its great resources, to sustain the Union and crush the South. All this had been done while Lyon was boldly confronting the overwhelming strength of Price and McCulloch. Had he abandoned Springfield instead, and opened to Price a pathway to the Missouri; had he not been willing to die for the freedom of the negro, and for the preservation of the Union, none of these things would have then been done. By wisely planning, by boldly doing, and by bravely dying, he had won the fight for Missouri.

APPENDIX.

THE BATTLE OF WILSON'S CREEK.

THE FORCES ENGAGED.

CONFEDERATES.

No ONE will ever be able to state with absolute certainty the exact strength of the Confederate forces which were at Wilson's Creek on the 10th of August, 1861, inasmuch as the records of both McCulloch's and Pearce's Brigades have been lost, and as no trustworthy enumeration of the Missouri State Guard was ever made until after the battle.

The following tables may, however, be relied upon as stating with sufficient accuracy the number of officers and men who were "present for duty" on that day—that is to say the number that might have been put into the fight. The computation excludes, of course, all men without arms, all sick men, and all men detailed as teamsters or for extra duty of any kind.

McCulloch's Brigade.

McCulloch reported on the 30th of July to the War Department that his brigade aggregated about thirty-two hundred men. Whether this included Greer's Regiment, which did not join him till the 3d of August, I cannot discover; but it probably did, as the brigade reported only twenty-five hundred men "fit for duty" a few days after the battle. We know that Churchill's Regiment aggregated seven hundred and sixty-eight officers and men "present and absent." Of these, nearly two hundred were either absent, sick, or on extra duty, and more than seventy-five were detailed to hold the horses of those who were dismounted for the battle. This reduced its effective strength to about five hundred men, at the time that it went into action on Bloody Hill. Colonel Churchill (since then Brigadier-general and Governor), informs me that it was hardly as strong as that. The Third Louisiana aggregated eight hundred and sixty-eight officers and men, but there were not more than seven hundred "present for duty."

PEARCE'S BRIGADE.

The strength of this brigade was greatly weakened by the prevalence of a virulent form of measles. McCulloch said on the 30th of July that it numbered about twenty-five hundred men. This is the only trustworthy statement that I have seen about it, except that Gratiot's Regiment aggregated six hundred and twenty-nine officers and men. He tells me that his "effective strength" on the day of the battle was less than five hundred.

THE MISSOURI STATE GUARD.

Immediately after the battle, I took great pains to ascertain accurately how many officers and men of this command were "present for duty" when the battle was fought. The results are stated in General Price's report, and in other contemporaneous records, and therefore I am sure that the following Tables are essentially correct so far as they relate to the strength and casualties of the State Guard. They do not include the unarmed men of whom there were about two thousand, many of them with their commands.

It must be borne in mind that in the Confederate Records, this battle is known as the *Battle of the Oak Hills*, which was the name given to it by McCulloch. In Price's report it was called the *Battle of Springfield*.

Appendix.

THE UNION FORCES.

General Lyon, in a report made to Major-General Fremont on the 4th of August, estimated his own forces as follows:

The First Missouri	900
Osterhaus' Battalion	200
The First Iowa	900
The First Kansas	800
The Second Kansas	600
Steele's Battalion	300
Plummer's Battalion	350
Totten's Battery	84
Dubois' Battery	64
Four Companies United States Cavalry	250
Third Missouri	700
Fifth Missouri	600
Second Missouri Artillery (Sigel)	120
	5,868
And beside these there were of Home Guards about	1,250
	7,138

From other Official Records it appears that the force with which Lyon left Booneville consisted of

Brigadier-General and Staff	4
First Missouri Regiment	895
Osterhaus' Battalion	211
First Iowa Regiment	926
Regulars, Infantry	243
Regulars, Artillery	75
Aggregate	2,354

Aggregate brought forward............	2,354
And that Sturgis' Column consisted of Regulars................................	943
First and Second Kansas Regiments.........	1,600
Aggregate...........................	2,543
In addition to these there was Sigel's Brigade as above..	1,420
Making an aggregate of.........................	6,317
Home Guards	1,250
	7,567

Schofield, who was then Adjutant-General of Lyon's Army, says that the column which Lyon moved out to Wilson's Creek "amounted to about four thousand men, besides about two hundred and fifty Home Guards." Sturgis and others say that it consisted of thirty-seven hundred "men" exclusive of the Home Guards. Schofield knew better than any one else the force that Lyon led out to battle. The apparent discrepancy between him and Sturgis is reconciled by assuming that Schofield gives the "aggregate" of officers and men, while Sturgis, as the context shows, gives "the effective total" of the force, that is to say the men, exclusive of officers.

Sigel's column was generally estimated by the other Union officers at thirteen hundred men, but I have followed his own report in the main, and put his strength at twelve hundred officers and men. The "effective total" of his two infantry regiments was nine hundred and eighteen men. These, with their full complement of officers and his battalion of artillery, would aggregate about ten hundred and seventy-five officers and men. Carr's squadron of cavalry would raise the aggregate to twelve hundred.

UNION FORCES AT THE BATTLE OF WILSON'S CREEK.

I. Lyon's Column.

First Missouri Volunteers, Lieutenant-Colonel George L. Andrews.
Osterhaus' Battalion (two companies Second Missouri Volunteers), Major P. J. Osterhaus.
First Iowa Infantry, Lieutenant-Colonel William H. Merritt.
First Kansas Infantry, Colonel George W. Deitzler.
Second Kansas Infantry, Colonel Robert B. Mitchell.
Plummer's Battalion (Companies B, C, and D, First United States Infantry and one company Recruits).
Steele's Battalion (Companies B and E, Second United States Infantry, and two companies Recruits).
Company F, Second United States Artillery, six guns, Captain James Totten.
Light Battery, United States Artillery, four guns, Lieutenant John V. Dubois.
Company D, First United States Cavalry, Lieutenant Charles W. Canfield.
Captain Henry C. Wood's Company Kansas Mounted Rangers.
Captain Clark Wright's Squadron of Home Guards.

II. Sigel's Column.

Third Regiment Missouri Volunteers, Colonel Franz Sigel.
Fifth Regiment Missouri Volunteers, Colonel C. E. Salomon.
Light Battery, six guns, Lieutenants Schaefer and Schuetzenbach.
Company I, First United States Cavalry, Captain Eugene A. Carr.
Company C, Second United States Dragoons, Lieutenant Charles E. Farrand.

UNION FORCES AT WILSON'S CREEK—STRENGTH AND CASUALTIES OF EACH COMMAND.

LYON'S COLUMN.	Aggregate Present.	Killed.	Wounded.	Missing.	Total Casualties.
I. Main Body in fight on Bloody Hill.					
1 First Missouri...................	775	76	208	11	295
2 Osterhaus' Battalion.............	150	15	40		55
3 First Iowa Infantry..............	800	12	138	4	154
4 First Kansas Infantry............	800	77	187	20	284
5 Second Kansas Infantry..........	600	5	59	6	70
6 Steele's Battalion................	275	15	44	2	61
7 Totten's Battery, 6 guns.........	84	4	7		11
8 Dubois' Battery, 4 guns..........	66		2	1	3
Total on Bloody Hill.............	3,550	204	685	44	933
II. Left Wing, East of Creek.					
Plummer's Battalion................	300	19	52	9	80
III. Mounted Reserve.					
Comp'y D, 1st U. S. Cavalry ⎱ Kansas Rangers ⎰ Home Guards	350		4	3	7
Total—Lyon's Column............	4,200	223	741	56	1,020
SIGEL'S COLUMN.					
Infantry and Artillery (6 guns).......	1,075	35	132	126	293
Company I, First U. S. Cavalry.......	65			4	4
Company C, Second U. S. Dragoons....	60				
Total—Sigel's Column.............	1,200	35	132	130	297
Lyon's Column.....................	4,200	223	741	56	1,020
Sigel's Column.....................	1,200	35	132	130	297
Total...........................	5,400	258	873	186	1,317

Appendix. 311

CONFEDERATE FORCES AT THE BATTLE OF WILSON'S CREEK.

I. McCulloch's Confederate Brigade.

1. Third Louisiana Infantry, Colonel Louis Hébert.
2. Battalion Arkansas Infantry, Lieutenant-Colonel Dandridge McRae.
3. First Regiment Arkansas Mounted Riflemen, Colonel Thomas J. Churchill.
4. Second Regiment Arkansas Mounted Riflemen, Colonel James McIntosh.
5. South Kansas-Texas Regiment (Mounted), Colonel E. Greer.

II. Pearce's Brigade, Army of Arkansas.

1. Third Arkansas Infantry, Colonel John R. Gratiot.
2. Fourth Arkansas Infantry, Colonel J. D. Walker.
3. Fifth Arkansas Infantry, Colonel Tom P. Dockery.
4. First Arkansas Cavalry, Colonel DeRosey Carroll.
5. Company Arkansas Cavalry, Captain Charles A. Carroll.
6. Light Battery, Captain Wm. E. Woodruff, 4 guns.
7. Light Battery, Captain J. G. Reid, 4 guns.

III. The Missouri State Guard, Major-General Sterling Price.

1. Brigadier-General James S. Rains' command.
   Infantry Brigade, Colonel Richard H. Weightman.
   Mounted Brigade, Colonel Cawthon.
2. Brigadier-General Monroe M. Parsons' command.
3. Brigadier-General John B. Clark's command.
4. Brigadier-General William Y. Slack's command.
5. Brigadier-General James H. McBride's command.

NOTE.—The Missouri commands were territorial, each brigadier-general having command of the troops raised within his military district. Parsons, Clark, and McBride had respectively only 531, 552, and 649 officers and men on the field, and Slack only 940, but their commands were called *divisions*. Their regiments consisted of only eight companies of fifty men each, present and absent.

STRENGTH AND CASUALTIES OF THE CONFEDERATE FORCES AT WILSON'S CREEK.

	Aggregate Present for Duty.	Killed.	Wounded.	Total Casualties.
I. McCulloch's Brigade.				
Third Louisiana Infantry............	700	9	48	57
McRae's Battalion..................	220	3	6	9
Churchill's Regiment...............	600	42	155	197
McIntosh's Regiment...............	400	10	44	54
Greer's Regiment...................	800	4	23	27
	2,720	68	276	344
II. Pearce's Brigade.				
Gratiot's Regiment.................	500	25	84	109
Walker's Regiment.................	550			
Dockery's Regiment................	650	3	11	14
Carroll's Regiment.................	350	5	22	27
Carroll's Company.................	40			
Woodruff's Battery, 4 guns.........	71	3		3
Reid's Battery, 4 guns.............	73		1	1
	2,234	36	118	154
III. The Missouri State Guard.				
	12	1	2	3
Rains' Command...................	2,537	59	186	245
Parsons' Command	531	17	51	68
Clark's Command..................	552	23	86	109
Slack's Command..................	940	43	114	157
McBride's Command...............	649	32	118	150
	5,221	175	557	732
Resumé.				
I. McCulloch's Brigade...........	2,720	68	276	344
II. Pearce's Brigade	2,234	36	118	154
III. Missouri State Guard	5,221	175	557	732
Total	10,175	279	951	1,230

THE MISSOURI STATE GUARD AT WILSON'S CREEK.

		Aggregate Present for Duty.	Killed.	Wounded.	Total Casualties.
Major-General Price and Staff..		12	1	2	3
I. Rains' Command.........		11		1	1
1 Weightman's Brigade, 3 guns.	Infty. & Art'y	1,316	40	120	160
2 Cawthon's Brigade..........	Mounted	1,210	21	66	87
II. Parsons' Command......		8			
1 Kelly's Regiment (6 Cos.)...	Infantry	142	11	38	49
2 Brown's Regiment and 3 Companies	Mounted	320	3	2	5
3 Guibor's Battery, 4 guns....	Artillery	61	3	11	14
III. Clark's Command......		9		2	2
1 Burbidge's Regiment	Infantry	270	17	81	98
2 Major's Battalion...........	Mounted	273	6	5	11
IV. Slack's Command......		6	1	1	2
1 Hughes' Regiment..........	Infantry	650	36	106	142
2 Thornton's Battalion........	Infantry				
3 Rives' Regiment	Mounted	284	4	8	12
V. McBride's Command....		4			
1 Wingo's Regiment..........	Infantry	605	32	114	146
2 Foster's Regiment	Infantry				
3 Campbell's Company	Mounted	40			
		5,221	175	557	732

CONFEDERATE TROOPS ENGAGED ON BLOODY HILL.

	Aggregate Present.	Killed.	Wounded.	Total Casualties.
I. Missouri State Guard.				
General and Staff................	12	1	2	3
1 *Rains' Command*................	11		1	1
Weightman's Brigade (2 Regim'ts)..	720	38	97	135
Cawthon's Brigade, Dismounted....	600	19	60	79
2 *Parsons' Command*...............	8			
Kelly's Regiment..................	142	11	38	49
Guibor's Battery, 4 guns...........	61	3	11	14
3 *Clark's Command*................	9		2	2
Burbidge's Regiment..............	270	17	81	98
4 *Slack's Command*................	6	1	1	2
Hughes' Regiment and Thornton's Battalion }	650	36	106	142
Rives' Regiment, Dismounted......	70	3	6	9
5 *McBride's Command*..............	4			
Wingo's and Foster's Regiments....	605	32	114	146
	3,168	161	519	680
II. Arkansas Troops.				
Churchill's Regiment	500	42	155	197
Gratiot's Regiment } 4 guns....... Woodruff's Battery	571	26	85	111
Total......................	1,071	68	240	308
Missourians.......................	3,168	161	519	680
Arkansians.......................	1,071	68	240	308
Confederates on Bloody Hill........	4,239	229	759	988
Union Force on Bloody Hill........	3,550	204	685	892

Appendix.

FORCES WHICH FOUGHT EAST OF THE CREEK.

	Aggregate Present.	Killed.	Wounded.	Missing.	Total Casualties.
UNION FORCE.					
Plummer's Battalion...............	300	19	52	9	80
CONFEDERATE FORCE.					
Third Louisiana...................	700	9	48		57
McIntosh's Regiment..............	400	10	44		54
	1100	19	92		111

CONFEDERATE COMMANDS WHICH WERE ONLY SLIGHTLY ENGAGED.

	Aggregate Present.	Killed.	Wounded.	Total Casualties.
I. Infantry.				
Graves' Regiment, Missourians...........	271			
Rosser's Command, Missourians.........	300	2	23	25
McRae's Battalion, Arkansians..........	220	3	6	9
Dockery's Regiment, Arkansians........	650	3	11	14
Walker's Regiment, Arkansians.........	550			
II. Mounted Men.				
Missourians..........................	1,447	10	7	17
Texans..............................	800	4	23	27
Arkansians..........................	390	5	22	27
III. Artillery.				
Reid's Battery, 4 guns.................	73			
Bledsoe's Battery, 3 guns..............	35			*
	4,736	27	92	119

NOTE.—Rosser's Command, which formed part of Weightman's Brigade, consisted of fifty men of his own regiment, O'Kane's Battalion (Major Thomas H. Murray), and Bledsoe's 3-gun Battery. Bledsoe's losses are included in Rosser's.

INDEX.

Alabama, 35, 59, 73.
Allen, George W., 286.
Anderson, Robert, 8-11, 29, 141.
Andrews, George L., 166, 309.
Arkansas, 73, 144, 161, 194, 195, 229, 234. *See* Pearce's Brigade and McCulloch's Brigade.
Armstrong, David H., 197.
Arsenal, St. Louis, 100-118, 124-138, 147-157.
Arsenal, Liberty, 148, 152, 156, 185.
Atchison, David R., 53, 224.

Backoff, Major, 211, 225.
Barlow, Wm. P., 217, 241.
Barret, J. Richard, 197.
Barret, Overton W., 111.
Bast, G. Y., 81.
Bates, Edward, 57, 184, 189, 219.
Battles, etc.:
  Booneville, 211-15.
  Carthage, 222-228.
  Cole Camp, 216.
  Dug Spring, 254, 298.
  Rock Creek, 208, 209, 289.
  Wilson's Creek, 268-315.
Black, J. S., 8.
Blair, Jr., Francis P., 57, 58, 64-66, 68, 96, 104-106, 126, 129, 130, 131, 135-137, 154-157, 160, 164-169, 176, 183, 188-194, 198-200, 203, 214, 219, 220, 230, 252, 302.
Blair's Regiment, 165, 211, 269, 274, 291, 307, 309, 310.
Blair, Montgomery, 156, 189.
Blaine, James G., 89, 141, 142.
Bell, John, 12.

Bell, Wm. H., 100, 114-117.
Bernays, Dr., 189.
Beauregard, P. G. T., 73.
Benton, Thomas H., 17, 89.
Bledsoe, Hiram, 219, 224, 279, 280, 293, 313, 315.
Bledsoe's Battery. *See* Bledsoe.
Breckinridge, John C., 12, 31, 183.
Boernstein, Henry, 2.
Boernstein's Regiment, 211.
Border Slave States, 20, 42-44, 59, 70, 81, 92, 143.
Bowen John S., 149, 152, 171.
Booneville, 206-215.
Brown, Joseph E., 34.
Brown, B. Gratz, 210.
Brown's Regiment, 219, 225-6, 259, 272, 313, 314.
Brown, Benjamin, 287.
Brownlee, John A., 137, 147, 148, 155.
Broadhead, James O., 79, 81, 87, 88, 105, 165, 169, 190.
Buchanan, James, 4-11, 27-29, 35, 36, 70, 102, 116, 130.
Buckner, A. H., 61.
Bulletin, The, 54.
Burbridge John Q., 217, 219, 225, 273, 287, 313, 314.
Burbridge's Regiment. *See* Burbridge.

Cairo, 194, 221, 252.
Camp Jackson, 149, 152, 163-172, 178, 181, 214, 260, 262, 303.
Cameron, Simon, 142, 154, 156, 164, 190, 191.
Campbell, Robert, 44.

Index.

Carlisle, James H., 137, 155.
Carr, Eugene A., 221, 281, 291, 301, 308–310.
Carroll's Regiment (De Rosey), 236, 282, 283, 311, 312, 315.
Campbell's Company, 313.
Carroll's (Charles A.) Company.
Carthage. *See* Battles, etc.
Cass, Lewis, 8.
Cassville, 246.
Cawthon, Colonel, 219, 260, 268, 274, 287, 311, 313, 314.
Cawthon's Brigade. *See* Cawthon.
Champion, Rock, 110, 133.
Claiborne, N. C., 67, 75.
Clark, John B., 181, 184, 185, 207–9, 215, 219, 225–6, 260, 262, 273, 287, 311–14.
Clark, Jr., John B., 301
Clark, M. Lewis, 184.
Clayton, Powell, 301.
Clarkson's (J. J.) Regiment, 273.
Crane Creek, 253, 254.
Crittenden's Compromise, 5, 6, 45, 56, 81.
Coalter, John D., 60.
Cobb, Howell, 8.
Cockrell, Francis M., 301.
Coercion, 4, 7, 21, 26, 32, 33, 36, 37, 40, 42–46, 50, 51, 55, 63, 64, 70, 71, 74, 76, 81–88, 178.
Cotton States, 4, 6, 16, 20, 29, 143.
Cole Camp, 216.
Conant, Horace L., 198, 200.
Conditional Union Men, 53–56, 61–64, 83.
Confederate Government, 59, 72, 139–140, 161, 167, 168, 207, 231–5, 244, 297–8.
Congress, U. S., 4, 70, 73.
Conrad, Captain, 223, 237.
Conrow, A. H., 75.
Conventions. *See* Missouri, Nashville, Wheeling, and Peace Congress.
Cook, Colonel, 216.
Cooke, Wm. M., 147, 151.
Cowskin Prairie, 235, 239, 246.
Cunningham, J. F., 51.
Curtis, Samuel R., 195, 221.

Churchill, Samuel B., 67.
Churchill, Thomas J. *See* Churchill's Regiment.
Churchill's Regiment, 229, 230, 235–7, 259, 261, 270–2, 281–3, 291, 298, 299, 301, 305, 306, 311, 312, 314.

Davis, Jefferson, 72, 139–140, 150, 167–8.
Departments, Military, 99.
　of the Ohio, 219.
　of the West, 99, 156, 157, 180, 189–192, 219.
　Western, 220, 252.
Deitzler, Geo. W., 160, 195, 309.
Dick, Franklin A., 167, 188, 189.
Dockery's (Tom P.) Regiment, 276, 282, 288, 301, 311, 312, 315.
Doniphan, Alexander W., 54, 60, 81, 183, 184.
Douglas, Stephen A., 12, 31, 89, 143, 160, 182.
DuBois' (John V.) Battery, 274, 277, 278, 307, 309, 310.
Dug Spring, 254, 298.
Duke, Basil Wilson, 108, 111, 133, 136, 148, 150, 155, 167, 168.

Essig's (Christian) Battery, 226, 227.
Everett, Edward, 41.
Examiner, The, 54.

Freeman, Thomas W., 67.
Filley, Oliver D., 33, 34, 90, 105, 165, 169.
Fremont, John C., 220, 252, 253, 263, 266.
Forts, Leavenworth, 160, 194, 195, 209, 221.
　Smith, 229.
　Scott, 231, 232.
　Sumter, 9–11, 28, 38, 140, 141.
　Southern, 7–11, 27–29, 34, 35–38.
Foster, Colonel, 287.
Foster's Regiment, 313–314.

Index. 319

Florida, 35, 38, 59, 73.
Floyd, John B., 9, 10.
Frost, Daniel M., 111–116, 147–152, 163-4, 170, 171.
Frost's Brigade, 111–113, 134, 149, 154, 161, 166, 170, 171.
Fugitive Slave Law, 3, 62, 159.

Gamble, Hamilton R., 44, 54, 56, 79, 81, 183, 189, 219.
Gantt, Thomas T., 197.
Granger, Gordon, 222, 282, 301.
Gratiot, John R., 236, 283, 287, 301.
Gratiot's Regiment, 236, 276, 277, 282-4, 288, 299, 306, 311, 312, 314.
Graves' (John R.) Regiment, 282, 315.
Georgia, 34, 59, 69, 73.
Germans, 65, 105, 166, 171, 174, 175, 207, 249.
Glenn, Luther J., 69–72.
Greeley, Horace, 6.
Green, James S., 53, 88–90, 183.
Greene, Colton, 109, 133-135, 148, 150, 167, 168, 230, 301.
Greer's Regiment, 229, 255, 261, 270, 272, 281-3, 290, 298, 301, 305, 311, 312, 315.
Gibson's Mill, 260, 268, 269.
Gilbert, C. C., 301.
Glover, Samuel T., 105, 165, 169, 170.
Guibor, Henry, 217, 242.
Guibor's Battery, 217, 219, 224-5, 273, 275, 313, 314.

Hagner, Peter V., 117, 118, 124, 125, 127, 128, 130–132, 137, 154.
Hall, Wm. A., 54, 56, 62, 81, 82, 197.
Halliburton, Wesley D., 50.
Hardee, Wm. J., 73, 244-6.
Harding, Chester, 166, 167, 212, 250, 251.
Harding, James, 162, 206, 240.
Harney, Wm. S., 99–100, 125, 127, 129, 130, 135, 137, 152, 155–157, 167, 170, 175–180, 186–194, 196.

Harris, Thomas A., 51, 68, 70, 76, 77.
Hatcher, Robert A., 81.
Hazlitt, Dr., 156.
Hébert, Louis. *See* 3d Louisiana.
Henderson, John B., 79, 81, 83.
Herron Frank J., 301.
Hindman, Thomas C., 246.
Holt, Joseph, 10.
Holloway, Edmunds B., 209.
Home Guards, 68, 104-6, 126, 127, 133-7, 154-7, 165, 166, 174–176, 195, 204, 216, 222, 307-310.
How, John, 136, 165, 169, 170.
Hough, Harrison, 60, 81.
Hudgins, Prince L., 81, 84–86.
Hughes' Regiment (John T.), 219, 273, 313, 314.
Hunter's Regiment (D. W. C.), 269, 271.
Hursts' Regiment (Edgar V.), 273.

Illinois, 39, 160, 191, 194, 195.
Indian Territory, 194, 229, 231.
Iowa, 160, 180, 191, 194.
Iowa Infantry, First (Bates), 195, 280, 282, 287, 307, 309, 310.
Iowa Infantry, Second (Curtis), 195, 221.

Jackson, Claiborne F., 17–26, 31, 53, 66–70, 74, 94, 96, 106, 113, 147-153, 162, 163, 167, 168, 172, 173, 184, 186, 187, 191, 196–208, 212–19, 222-224, 230, 237, 238, 243, 244, 303.
Jefferson City, 185, 211.
Johnson, Waldo P., 60, 89.

Kansas, 160, 191, 194, 229, 231.
Kansas Infantry, First, 195, 209, 221, 270, 291, 307-10.
Kansas Infantry, Second, 195, 209, 221, 288, 307-10.
Kansas Rangers, 309, 310.
Kelly's Company, 163, 164, 185, 186, 188, 209, 212.
Kelly's Regiment, 219, 225, 273, 287, 313, 314.
Kentucky, 44, 144, 161
Kelton, John C., 254.

Lamar, 218.
Lane, James H., 231.
Lawson, L. M., 74, 75.
Lawton, Alex. R., 35.
Letcher, John, 42.
Lexington, 207, 209, 215.
Lincoln, Abraham, 3, 12, 74, 137, 141, 153, 154, 160, 165, 181, 188-195.
Little, Henry, 242.
Louisiana, 37, 59, 73.
Louisiana Infantry, Third, 229, 230, 234, 260, 276-80, 288, 293, 301, 306, 311, 312, 315.
Lyon, Nathaniel, 119-138, 151, 153-157, 160, 163-175, 183, 188-204, 210-15, 219-222, 236, 245, 248-258, 261-7, 268-78, 281-8, 291-5, 298-303, 307-310.

Macdonald, Emmet, 172.
McBride, James H., 184, 246, 260, 262, 273, 311-14.
McClellan, Geo. B., 219-221.
McCown, James, 270.
McCoy, Arthur, 133-135.
McCulla's Store, 254, 258.
McCulloch, Ben., 72, 194, 211, 215, 216, 222, 229-39, 245-7, 253-63, 271, 272, 276-80, 290, 293-303.
McCulloch's Brigade, 305, 306, 311-312, 314, 315.
McCulloch, Robert, 185, 186.
McGrath, M., 186.
McIntosh, James, 231, 237, 254, 255, 260-3, 272, 276-280, 290, 301, 311, 312, 315.
McIntyre, D. H., 185, 186.
McKinstry, Justus, 188.
McLaren, Charles, 137, 155.
McRae's Battalion (Dandridge), 260, 276, 277, 293, 301, 311, 312, 315.
Magoffin, Beriah, 44.
Major's Battalion, James P., 259, 272, 281, 290, 313.
Marmaduke, John S., 186, 208, 212, 213.
Maryland, 42, 161.
Massachusetts, 73.

Minute Men, 109-111, 133-135, 178.
Missouri, 13-16, 22, 29, 32, 44, 58, 62, 63, 69, 76, 79, 144, 206, 297, 303.
   Compromise, 3, 5, 46, 56, 57.
   Convention, 33, 46, 47, 53, 66, 69, 78-98, 126, 183, 196, 243, 302.
   General Assembly, 12, 46-52, 66-72, 74-77, 88-94, 103, 129, 151, 160-163, 172, 173, 180, 303.
   Governor. *See* Jackson.
   Military Bill, 33, 67, 74-77, 106, 173, 177, 179, 184, 188, 203.
   State Guard, 179, 184-188, 190, 195-7, 203, 207, 209, 238-243, 258, 298, 299, 305, 306, 311-315.
Missouri Volunteers (Union), 165, 166, 195.
Minnesota, 39, 180.
Mississippi, 38, 47, 59.
Mitchell, Robert, 195, 288, 301, 309.
Merritt, Wm. H., 309.
Monroe, Thomas, 223, 224.
Montgomery, James, 160, 212.
Morris, Walter B., 51.
Moss, James H., 81, 82, 83.
Murray, Thomas H., 216, 315.

Nashville Convention, 59.
Neosho, 222, 237.
New Madrid, 244, 257.
New York, 38, 39.
Neutrality, Armed, 16, 95.
North Carolina, 144, 161.
Northern Democrats, 6, 143, 158-160.

Ohio, 39.
O'Kane, Walter S., 216.
O'Kane's Battalion, 279, 280, 293, 315.
Osterhaus, P. J., 301.

Index. 321

Osterhaus' Battalion, 268, 274, 278, 397, 309, 310. *See* Boernstein's Regiment.

Parsons, M. M., 67, 68, 103, 184, 208, 209, 212, 215, 219, 223-7, 260, 262, 273, 301, 311-314.
Partridge, George, 51.
Paschall, Nathaniel, 44, 54, 56.
Planter's House Conference, 197-200.
Peace Congress, 60.
Pearce, N. B., 230, 235-9, 254, 284.
Pearce's Brigade, 230, 236, 246, 247, 253, 260, 276, 282-288, 305, 306, 311, 312, 314, 315.
Peckham, James, 51.
Pennsylvania, 39.
Phelps, John S., 54.
Prentiss, B. M., 221.
President. *See* Buchanan, Davis, Lincoln.
Price-Harney Agreement, 186-192, 196, 202.
Price, Sterling, 54, 78, 81, 92, 181-188, 196, 203, 207-9, 215-218, 222, 234-47, 252-7, 260-3.
Price, Thomas H., 241, 244, 257, 271-6, 281-91, 293-4.
Pillow, Gideon J., 300, 303, 306, 311-314.
Pritchard, Colonel, 154.
Polk, Leonidas, 243, 257.
Polk, Trusten, 53, 84.
Proclamations.
   Harney's, 177-179.
   Jackson's, 200-206.
   Lyon's, 220.
   Lincoln's, 141, 142.
Plummer's Battalion (Joseph B.), 268, 269, 277-9, 288, 290, 293, 301, 307, 309, 310.

Quinlan, James, 133, 135.

Rains, James S., 67, 184, 215, 216, 218, 224-7, 253-5, 260-262, 268, 271, 272, 289, 311-314.
Randolph, Beverly, 184.
Rector, Henry M., 232.

Redd, John T., 81, 86-7
Reid, John, 240.
Reid's Battery (John. G.), 246, 260, 276, 280, 288, 293, 311, 312, 315.
Republican, The, 45, 46, 54, 144, 147, 149, 161, 162, 179.
Reynolds, Thomas C., 30-33, 48, 49, 53, 303.
Rives' (B.A.) Regiment, 219, 225-6, 273, 313, 314.
Robertson, John, 60.
Robinson, Lt.
Rogers, Charles S., 287.
Rollins, James S., 61, 183.
Ross, John, 230.
Rosser, Thomas H., 279, 280, 315.
Russell, Dan. R., 47-50.
Rolla, 264, 296.

Salomon's Regiment, (C.E.), 210, 225, 265, 281, 307-310.
Shaler, James. R., 111, 168.
Slack, Wm. Y., 215, 218, 219, 224-6, 260, 262, 273, 281, 287, 301, 311-14.
Stanley, David S., 221, 301.
Stanton, Edwin M., 8, 28.
St. Louis, 44, 90, 94, 95, 174-6, 179, 195.
Star of the West, The, 28.
St. Louis Police, 90, 91, 136, 137.
Secessionists, 53, 55, 69, 90, 94, 95, 106, 129, 175, 181.
Shelby, Joseph O., 224, 301.
Steele's Battalion (Frederick), 160, 222, 254, 301-307, 309, 310.
Steen, Alexander E., 236, 247.
Stephens, A. H., 139, 140.
Stevenson, Jno. D., 48, 49, 66, 220, 252.
Stewart, Robert M., 12-17, 25, 26.
Sweeny, Thomas W., 166, 211, 222.
Sigel, Franz, 210, 222, 225-8, 236, 248, 249, 265, 266, 270-2, 276-81, 288, 290, 291, 293, 295, 296, 298, 301, 307-310.
Springfield, 210, 211, 249, 250, 264.

Switzler, Wm. F., 145, 146.
South Carolina, 4, 7-11, 21, 59, 60.
Schofield, John M., 166, 221, 250, 285, 299, 301, 308.
Scott, Winfield, 8, 28, 103, 117, 128, 130, 131, 152, 165, 177, 180, 219, 251, 252.
Sturgeon, Isaac H., 101-104, 107, 116, 117, 128.
Sturgis, S. D., 160, 221, 222, 236, 248, 285-288, 291, 294-6, 299-301, 308.
Submissionists, 64, 67, 68, 161.
Snyder, John F., 271, 272.

Taylor, Dan. G., 136, 155.
Thayer, James S., 40.
Tennessee, 43, 144, 161.
Texas, 59, 72.
Texas Regiment. *See* Greer's.
Twiggs, David E., 73.
Totten's Battery (James), 73, 164, 195, 211, 222 254, 268-70, 272-5, 282-4, 285, 287, 301, 307, 309, 310.
Thornton's Battalion (J. C. C.), 219, 273, 313, 314.
Thompson, M. Jeff, 244.
Tyler, John, 60.

Unconditional Union party, 53, 57, 58.

Union Safety Committee, 165, 169, 190.
Union Troops in Missouri, 195.

Van Dorn, Earl, 73.
Vest, George G., 50, 66-72, 92-94.
Virginia, 42, 60, 143, 161.
Walker, L. Pope, 231, 233, 297, 298.
Walker's Regiment (Jno. D.), 276, 282, 311, 312, 315.
Walworth, Chancellor, 41.
Watkins, N. W., 78, 81, 184.
Wheeling Convention, 59, 60.
Weightman, Richard H., 219, 224-6, 255, 260, 273, 282, 287-90, 311, 313, 314, 315.
Wherry, Wm. M., 288.
Wide Awakes, 33, 34, 65, 66.
Wilson's Creek, Description, 258.
Windsor Guards, 235.
Wisconsin, 39.
Witzig, Julius J., 105, 165, 169.
Wingo's Regiment, 313-14.
Wright, Clark, 309.
Woodruff's Battery (Wm. E.), 236, 246, 260, 274-7, 282, 299, 311, 312, 314.
Woods, Henry C., 309.
Yates, Richard, 106, 153.
Yeatman, James E., 44.

[From the CINCINNATI COMMERCIAL.]

"Scribner's 'Campaigns of the Civil War' are probably the ablest and most striking account of the late war that has yet been written. Choosing the flower of military authors, the publishers have assigned to each the task of writing the history of the events he knew most about. Thus, both accuracy and a life-like freshness have been secured."

THE CAMPAIGNS
OF
THE CIVIL WAR

13 VOLUMES, CLOTH. WITH MAPS AND PLANS.

Price per Volume, $1.00; per Set, $12.50.

A series of volumes, contributed by a number of leading actors in and students of the great conflict of 1861-'65, with a view to bringing together, for the first time, a full and authoritative military history of the suppression of the Rebellion.

The volumes are duodecimos of about 250 pages each, illustrated by maps and plans prepared under the direction of the authors.

1.—*The Outbreak of Rebellion.* By JOHN G. NICOLAY, Esq., Private Secretary to President Lincoln; late Consul-General to France, etc.

A preliminary volume, describing the opening of the war, and covering the period from the election of Lincoln to the end of the first battle of Bull Run.

II.—From Fort Henry to Corinth. By the Hon. M. F. FORCE, Justice of the Superior Court, Cincinnatti; late Brigadier-General and Bvt. Maj. Gen'l, U.S.V., commanding First Division, 17th Corps: in 1862, Lieut. Colonel of the 20th Ohio, commanding the regiment at Shiloh; Treasurer of the Society of the Army of the Tennessee.

The narrative of events in the West from the Summer of 1861 to May, 1862; covering the capture of Fts. Henry and Donelson, the Battle of Shiloh, etc., etc.

III.—The Peninsula. By ALEXANDER S. WEBB, LL.D., President of the College of the City of New York; Assistant Chief of Artillery, Army of the Potomac, 1861-'62; Inspector General Fifth Army Corps; General commanding 2d Div., 2d Corps; Major General Assigned, and Chief of Staff, Army of the Potomac.

The history of McClellan's Peninsula Campaign, from his appointment to the end of the Seven Days' Fight.

IV.—The Army under Pope. By JOHN C. ROPES, Esq., of the Military Historical Society of Massachusetts, the Massachusetts Historical Society, etc.

From the appointment of Pope to command the Army of Virginia, to the appointment of McClellan to the general command in September, 1862

V.—The Antietam and Fredericksburg. By FRANCIS WINTHROP PALFREY, Bvt. Brigadier Gen'l, U.S.V., and formerly Colonel 20th Mass. Infantry; Lieut. Col. of the 20th Massachusetts at the Battle of the Antietam; Member of the Military Historical Society of Massachusetts, of the Massachusetts Historical Society, etc.

From the appointment of McClellan to the general command, September, 1862, to the end of the battle of Fredericksburg.

VI.—Chancellorsville and Gettysburg. By ABNER DOUBLEDAY, Bvt. Maj. Gen'l, U.S.A., and Maj. Gen'l, U.S.V.; commanding the First Corps at Gettysburg, etc.

From the appointment of Hooker, through the campaigns of Chancellorsville and Gettysburg, to the retreat of Lee after the latter battle.

VII.—The Army of the Cumberland. By HENRY M. CIST, Brevet Brig. Gen'l U.S.V.; A.A.G. on the staff of Major Gen'l Rosecrans, and afterwards on that of Major Gen'l Thomas; Corresponding Secretary of the Society of the Army of the Cumberland.

From the formation of the Army of the Cumberland to the end of the battles at Chattanooga, November, 1863.

VIII.—*The Mississippi.* By Francis Vinton Greene, Lieut. of Engineers, U. S. Army; late Military Attaché to the U S. Legation in St. Petersburg; Author of "The Russian Army and its Campaigns in Turkey in 1877–78," and of "Army Life in Russia."

An account of the operations—especially at Vicksburg and Port Hudson—by which the Mississippi River and its shores were restored to the control of the Union.

IX.—*Atlanta.* By the Hon. Jacob D. Cox, Ex-Governor of Ohio; late Secretary of the Interior of the United States; Major General U. S. V., commanding Twenty-third Corps during the campaigns of Atlanta and the Carolinas, etc., etc.

From Sherman's first advance into Georgia in May, 1864, to the beginning of the March to the Sea.

X. -*The March to the Sea—Franklin and Nashville.* By the Hon. Jacob D. Cox.

From the beginning of the March to the Sea to the surrender of Johnston—Including also the operations of Thomas in Tennessee.

XI.—*The Shenandoah Valley in 1864. The Campaign of Sheridan.* By George E. Pond, Esq., Associate Editor of the *Army and Navy Journal.*

XII.—*The Virginia Campaign of '64 and '65. The Army of the Potomac and the Army of the James.* By Andrew A. Humphreys, Brigadier General and Bvt. Major General, U. S. A.; late Chief of Engineers; Chief of Staff, Army of the Potomac, 1863–64; commanding Second Corps, 1864–'65, etc., etc.

Statistical Record of the Armies of the United States. By Frederick Phisterer, late Captain U. S. A.

This Record includes the figures of the quotas and men actually furnished by all States; a list of all organizations mustered into the U. S. service; the strength of the army at various periods; its organization in armies, corps, etc.; the divisions of the country into departments, etc.; chronological list of all engagements, with the losses in each; tabulated statements of all losses in the war, with the causes of death, etc.; full lists of all general officers, and an immense amount of other valuable statistical matter relating to the War.

The complete Set, thirteen volumes, in a box. Price, $12.50
Single volumes, ... 1.00

⁎ *The above books for sale by all booksellers, or will be sent, post-paid, upon receipt of price, by*

CHARLES SCRIBNER'S SONS, Publishers,
743 and 745 Broadway, New York.

THE Navy in the Civil War

I.—THE BLOCKADE AND THE CRUISERS.

By Professor J. RUSSELL SOLEY, U. S. Navy.

"The book is well arranged, written clearly, without technical terms, and shows great familiarity with the subject. It is marked by thoroughness of preparation, sound judgment, and admirable impartiality. It is a promising beginning of the projected series; and if the other volumes prove worthy of this, they will make a valuable addition to the Army series, which has proved so useful and popular."—*The Nation.*

II.—THE ATLANTIC COAST.

By Real-Admiral DANIEL AMMEN, U. S. Navy.

Admiral Ammen's history of the naval operations on the Atlantic coast, from 1861 to the close of the war, describes the active work of the navy in attacking the defensive strongholds of the Confederacy from Hampton Roads to Florida Keys. It includes a full account of the long siege of Charleston, and the scarcely less arduous operations against Fort Fisher, the capture of Hatteras Inlet, Roanoke Island and Newbern, and other minor movements along the coast.

III.—THE GULF AND INLAND WATERS.

By Commander A. T. MAHAN, U. S. Navy.

The achievements of the Naval force on the Mississippi and its tributaries, and on the Gulf and the Red River, either independently or in co-operation with the Army, form one of the most thrilling chapters in the history of the Civil War. The exploits of Farragut, Foote and Porter, with their gallant crews and improvised vessels, teem with acts of daring, marvelous escapes, and terrific encounters. Commander Mahan has done full justice to this side of his narrative, but he has given at the same time a record of this part of the war that has greater claims to historic value than any which have preceded it.

Each One Volume, 12mo, with Maps and Plans.

Price per Volume, $1.00.

CHARLES SCRIBNER'S SONS, Publishers,
743 & 745 *Broadway, New York.*

ARMY LIFE IN RUSSIA.

By F. V. GREENE,

LIEUTENANT OF ENGINEERS, UNITED STATES ARMY,
Late Military Attaché to the U. S. Legation in St. Petersburg, and author of "*The Russian Army and its Campaigns in Turkey in 1877-78.*"

New Edition, One Volume, 12mo, . . $1.00.

Lieutenant Greene's opportunities for general as well as technical observation while with the Russian army in Turkey were such as have perhaps never fallen to any other student of the war. The story of this personal experience is embodied in this volume, which contains most vigorous and vivid descriptions of battle scenes, in the chapters on the Shipka Pass, Plevna, and in the very strong and excellent chapter on the winter campaign across the Balkans with Gourko. The chapters on the Tsar and the Russian generals, and the sections devoted to the Russian soldier, to St. Petersburg, and the army life of the Russian at home, are of absorbing interest.

"His sketches are excellently well done, graphic, evidently not exaggerated, and very readable. It is a book that will be read with pleasure, and one that contains a great deal of information."—*Hartford Courant.*

"This volume is in every way an admirable picture of army life in Russia. It is clear, concise, discriminating, and often very picturesque. The author, besides possessing an excellent style, is extremely modest, and there are very few books of travel in which the first person is kept so absolutely in the background."—*International Review.*

"Lieutenant Greene writes in a soldierly way, unaffected, straightforward, and graphic, and, though he has a keen eye for the picturesque, never sacrifices to rhetoric the absolute truthfulness so eminently to be desired in a narrative of this sort.—*New York World.*

"He was with the Russian army throughout the campaign, enjoying perfect freedom of movement, having every opportunity to visit the points of greatest activity, and to see the operations of greatest moment, in company with the officers who conducted them. His book is, therefore, for all the purposes of ordinary readers, a complete and satisfactory history of the war, founded upon intimate personal knowledge of its events, and of its spirit. It is a work of the rarest interest and of unusual merit."—*New York Evening Post.*

"It is most fortunate for the reputation of our country and our army that we had such an officer to send to the far-away land of Turkey in Europe, and most creditable to our War Department that it sent such a man. His book deseves to be universally read, and we are sure that no person whom these lines may lead to purchase it will fail to rejoice that they have been written."—*The Nation.*

⁎⁎* *For sale by all booksellers, or sent, post-paid, upon receipt of price, by*

CHARLES SCRIBNER'S SONS, PUBLISHERS,
743 AND 745 BROADWAY, NEW YORK.

LIFE OF
Lord Lawrence

BY

R. BOSWORTH SMITH, M.A.,

LATE FELLOW OF TRINITY COLLEGE; ASSISTANT MASTER AT HARROW SCHOOL.

With Maps and Portraits, 2 vols., 8vo, $5.00.

"As a biography, the work is an inthralling one, rich in anecdotes and incidents of Lord Lawrence's tempestuous nature and beneficent career that bring into bold relief his strongly-marked and almost colossal individuality, and rich also in instances of his courage, his fortitude, his perseverance, his self-control, his magnanimity, and in the details of the splendid results of his masterful and masterly policy. . . . We know of no work on India to which the reader can refer with so great certainty for full and dispassionate information relative to the government of the country, the characteristics of its people, and the fateful events of the forty eventful years of Lord Lawrence's Indian career."—*Harper's Magazine.*

"John Lawrence, the name by which the late Viceroy of India will always be best known, has been fortunate in his biographer, Mr. Bosworth Smith, who is an accomplished writer and a faithful, unflinching admirer of his hero. He has produced an entertaining as well as a valuable book; the general reader will certainly find it attractive; the student of recent history will discover in its pages matters of deep interest to him."—*London Daily Telegraph.*

⁎⁎⁎ For sale by all booksellers, or sent, post-paid, upon receipt of price, by

CHARLES SCRIBNER'S SONS, PUBLISHERS,

743 AND 745 BROADWAY, NEW YORK

www.ingramcontent.com/pod-product-compliance
Lightning Source LLC
Chambersburg PA
CBHW031859220426
43663CB00006B/685